Energy in Packaging and Waste

Related titles from VNR

A.V. Bridgwater & K. Lidgren
Household Waste Management in Europe: economics and techniques

J. Butlin & K. Lidgren
Container Costs

Energy in Packaging and Waste

Edited by

A.V. Bridgwater
Department of Chemical Engineering
University of Aston in Birmingham, UK

K. Lidgren
The TEM Group
University of Lund, Sweden

 Van Nostrand Reinhold (UK) Co. Ltd.

Published by Van Nostrand Reinhold (UK) Co. Ltd.
Molly Millars Lane, Wokingham, Berkshire, England

Library of Congress Cataloging in Publication Data

Main entry under title:

Energy in packaging and waste.

Includes index.
1. Package goods industry—Energy conservation.
2. Package goods industry—Energy consumption.
3. Factory and trade waste.   4. Recycling (Waste, etc.)
I. Bridgwater, A.V.   II. Lidgren, Karl, 1947-
TJ163.5.P33E53   1983   688.8   83-6897
ISBN 0-442-30570-2

Printed in Great Britain at the University Press, Cambridge

Preface

This book has evolved from a meeting which addressed questions relating energy to production of packaging and other materials which are discarded. Successive oil crises have focussed attention on energy as a vital but depleting resource, and caused many studies to be performed on aspects of energy inputs and outputs in various sectors of industry. One of the objectives of the meeting was to appraise the status of research and development in these areas and examine the consequences and values of the results for industry and governments both now and in the future. As in the associated book *Household Waste Management in Europe*, one further objective was to identify key questions and attempt to provide topical and useful answers to give either new directions or reassurance to those involved in this subject area.

One of the more interesting and valuable aspects of the meeting and this book is the diversity of interests and disciplines. While most of the contributors are academically based, all have demonstrable close ties with industry and government which permit balanced and sensible views to be propounded. It is also encouraging to see such good harmony and collaboration not only between the wide range of disciplines represented, but also in the international approaches fostered by the meeting. This can only result in improved benefits to all institutions and countries involved, with a better understanding of each other's problems, heuristics and solutions. Our appreciation to Karl Lidgren must be recorded for his initiative in arranging the meeting in Boppard, West Germany, from which this book has emerged.

Tony Bridgwater
July 1983

Contents

1 Energy Resources and Analysis

A.V. Bridgwater

INTRODUCTION

In order to exploit a natural resource, manpower (labour) is needed, together with equipment to aid the manpower, and energy to use the equipment. At its simplest this describes ancient man, his pickaxe and his food. In our conventional world, the resource might be an ore body or oilfield; with the manpower as an integrated team of managers, engineers and labourers; using drilling, excavating and mining machinery; with electricity, fuel oil and diesel as energy.

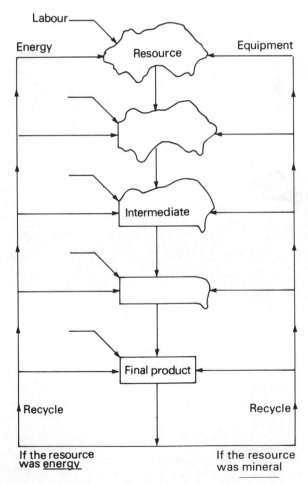

Fig. 1.1 Resource development.

The recovered resource is then utilized and converted in a series of operations as depicted in Fig. 1.1. Every piece of equipment or product has a multiplicity of such sequences for each component material such as steel, copper and plastics.

Thus there are two basic resources available — labour and natural resources. The latter can be usefully divided into two — energy resources, which are consumed in many processes and products, and mineral resources, which are not usually consumed, but remain in the product in a converted or refined form. This is depicted in Fig. 1.2.

The production requirements of anything can, therefore, be related to these three resources. For example, with capital goods for the process industries, the relationship in cost terms is approximately 70% labour, 20% energy (as oil equivalent) and 10% minerals (iron ore). This book is concerned with energy, and therefore only energy resources are further considered, particularly with regard to waste materials.

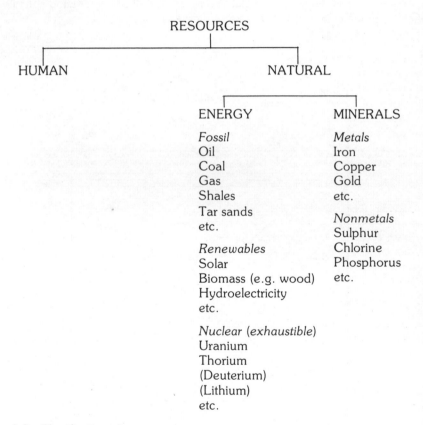

Fig. 1.2 Classification of resources.

ENERGY FORMS

A variety of energy inputs is required to produce any material or product. A variety of energy outputs also results. These energies can be simplistically classified as either *chemical* energy or *thermal* energy.

Chemical energy can be converted to heat .(thermal energy) or power: for example, oil and paper may be burned to release heat which can be used for a variety of purposes, directly or indirectly; and gas can be converted to power in an engine. This energy content is usually expressed as heat of combustion, heat of oxidation, higher heating value (HHV) or lower heating value (LHV) according to the physical state of any water produced from combustion. Chemical energy thus provides a method of storing energy in physical form for utilization when required.

While such combustion processes are exothermic, in that heat is released, not all exothermic processes are useful in this way: oxidation of iron to rust, for example, is an exothermic process but is difficult to utilize — indeed considerable energy is spent in trying to prevent it. Oxidation of aluminium is also highly exothermic, and this is employed in thermic welding, but it cannot, for example, be compared to combustion of coal in terms of controllability and overall efficiency among a wide range of other factors. The usefulness of chemical energy thus needs careful assessment. In all processes where heat is released (or power produced) there are inefficiencies in both conversion and utilization which also affect such assessment.

Thermal or sensible energy, i.e. heat of which 'quality' is probably the most important factor, in addition to form, quantity, source, location, reliability, etc., also includes other transient energy forms, such as power and electricity. The importance of quality is summarized below and constantly referred to in the book. Thermal energy can be converted to chemical energy only by enabling chemical reactions to occur that would otherwise not happen, i.e. absorb energy. This is the most usual way of storing thermal energy by converting it into a physical material, i.e. a chemical material with a heating value. Inefficiencies arise in any conversion process and these must also be considered.

The energy introduced during processing or manufacture is either transposed into chemical energy that appears in the product, by-product, or waste material (which may or may not be realizable as explained above); or is recovered/recycled internally as material or energy or is lost as heat. Energy is recoverable from the product, the by-product and waste stream in chemical or thermal form as long as these are still geographically and chronologically related to the manufacturing process. However, for consumer products destined for disposal, the only energy recoverable is usually the chemical energy associated with the product. This is usually recoverable by combustion or conversion to give thermal energy or power which may be further converted into a more useful energy form.

ENERGY INPUTS SYSTEM

Energy inputs to a system or manufacturing process are conventionally described by the process engineer as the inherent chemical energy of the raw materials together with energy resource-derived utilities or services such as fuel oil, natural gas, coal, electricity, water, air, vacuum and refrigeration. These utilities or services are either chemicals with stored energy in their own right (oil, gas, coal, etc.) or are derived from such chemicals (electricity, steam, compressed air) or from some other source such as electricity from solar power or hydro schemes. The process engineer can readily measure all these direct inputs to the process; and similarly energy outputs may be measured. This information is usually regularly collated for process optimization and cost minimization.

There are in addition, however, many other energy inputs necessary for production of any product. Some are historic, some are concurrent with the manufacturing process, and some will arise in the future.

Historic energy inputs Each item of equipment required to manufacture the product in the process was itself a product of a manufacturing process which required energy for production. And that manufacturing process itself required equipment which needed energy and so on. There is thus an extensive chain of historic energy inputs into all previous materials back to the natural resource in the ground. This is depicted in Fig. 1.3. There is no way of affecting historic energy inputs — only present or future energy considerations can be influenced, by recovering the stored energy — either directly, for example by combustion, or indirectly, for example by reducing the total energy requirement for secondary materials production by recycling materials such as metals which reduces process energy requirements.

Current energy inputs The energy and other resource inputs required for a process may come from primary energy sources — oil, coal, gas, etc. — and/or from secondary/recycled energy sources. These energy expenditures in the present can be controlled and reduced by analysis and subsequent technical and financial investment. In addition to the direct and indirect process energy inputs, there is a range of associated ancillary requirements such as transportation of materials and product; heating, lighting and food provisions for labour; and supply of energy. A significant value of energy analysis thus lies in identifying major energy requirements to enable the most effective actions to be taken. There are, however, limitations to what can be achieved which are determined by current technical, economic, social and political constraints.

Future energy inputs This is the most important consideration, since the widest range of options is available, and hence the greatest opportunity to optimize the effective use of resources. This is countered, however, by the uncertainty that affects all aspects of the future — technology, economics and politics — and a general inability to determine outcomes or exercise practical controls in any of these areas. Technological progress is the least uncertain in that it is reasonable to assume that only positive progress will be made, and therefore the uncertainty lies in the rate and/or extent of progress. However, both economics and particularly politics can move in a positive or adverse direction without warning and usually without the possibility of exercising any influence on the outcomes. For both aspects there are significant effects of time and location which can sometimes be quantified and used to advantage.

The value of this book thus lies both in identifying current problems and possibilities, and in proposing strategies for the future to reduce the range of options and provide indicators for policy-makers.

ENERGY BALANCE

The energy balance over a process can be specified in more detail by relation to

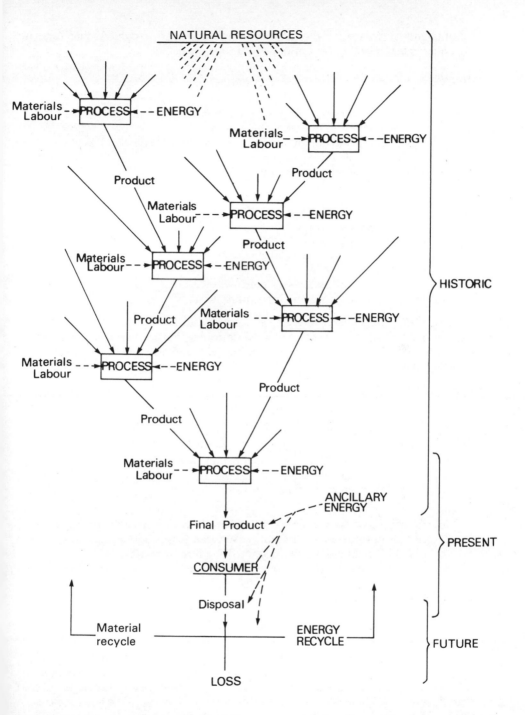

Fig. 1.3   Cumulative energy input system.

inputs and outputs using the methodology developed above. At this stage no account is taken of the form or quality of the energy.

Inputs

Direct:
  (a) Energy content of the primary feed material.
  (b) Energy content of the other reagent inputs.
  (c) Essential process energy for conversion (theoretical).
  (d) Inefficiencies or losses associated with conversion.
  (e) Ancillary energy requirements.

Indirect:
  (f) Energy investment in equipment in the process.
  (g) Energy investment in pre-process equipment.
  (h) Essential (theoretical) process energy investment in providing feed material (NB: This may be included in (a), the energy content of the primary feed material).
  (i) Inefficiencies or losses associated with feed material production.
  (j) Pre-process ancillary energy requirements.

For analysis, the indirect energies should be further subdivided into different stages of production from raw materials/natural resources extraction to provision of primary feed material, as indicated in Fig. 1.3; and also into each resource and intermediate product.

Outputs

Direct:
  (k) Energy content of the primary product.
  (l) Energy content of secondary or by-products.
  (m) Energy content of waste streams from process.
  (n) Losses from conversion, (d).
  (o) Losses from ancillary energy inputs, (e).

Indirect:
  (p) Energy content of process equipment, (f). Inclusion of the energy content of the pre-process equipment, associated losses and other energy losses could be included but this does not seem reasonable.

ENERGY QUALITY

Energy is measured in various ways and occurs in several forms as described above.

Chemical energy is represented by the heating value — LHV or HHV. This is a fundamental and widely used property, but is only one aspect to be considered as the energy realized on combustion should be in a useful and useable form, and produced at the highest possible efficiency and, generally, the lowest possible cost. The method of realization will also influence the quality of the resultant energy. Refuse, for example, can be burned to heat, which can be converted to steam, thence electricity; it may also be converted to low-grade fuel gas or medium-grade fuel gas, or converted to methane, methanol and a range of fuels/chemicals. All these products have different uses, different values, and are produced at different yields in technical, energetic and economic terms. The composition of the refuse in terms of constituents and water, i.e. its quality, will affect the yield of any product and the quality of the primary products. There are a wide range of factors for assessing quality of feed material or product relating to usefulness and usability in technical and economic terms.

It is, however, in relation to thermal and other transient energy forms, such as electricity and power, that quality becomes important.

Units

Thermal energy measurement is usually in GJ or analogous units, and power measurement is typically in kW. While there are scientific relationships between such units they cannot be directly added since conversion necessarily involves substantial losses due to inefficiencies from thermodynamic considerations. Typically, for example, heat from coal is converted to electricity at about 30% efficiency, which is further reduced by losses in transmission to the user. The problem is sometimes compounded by quoting electrical units in thermal terms by direct conversion which should be expressed as kW_{th} as opposed to kW_e for electrical energy. kW_e is typically $0.25-0.3$ kW_{th} for a thermal power station, but nearer $0.8-0.9$ kW_{th} for hydro production.

Grade

Generally the higher the temperature of thermal energy, the more useful it is. 1 GJ steam at 20 bars and 250 °C is much more useful than 1 GJ warm water at 75 °C. Similar considerations apply to any energy form, whether thermal, electrical or chemical, and again great care is necessary in presenting results of energy analysis to avoid oversimplification with regard to grade of energy.

Efficiency

The final aspect of quality considered here — although there are many other factors to be considered, which are described in individual contributions — is the efficiency of conversion of one energy form to another. Electricity conversion has already been mentioned in both thermal and hydro terms, but all conversion processes have some inefficiency and hence loss associated with them. A boiler or furnace, for example, is unlikely to achieve better than 80% conversion efficiency, i.e. 80% of the energy value of the fuel is absorbed by the material being processed and the rest is lost to the environment. The more times an energy form or quality is changed, therefore, the more energy is lost. A primary consideration of the energy analyst is therefore the minimization of loss and maximization of utilization of energy.

CONCLUSIONS

This introductory chapter has attempted to put energy into perspective as an essential and significant resource which is needed for all stages of production from natural resources in the ground to consumer products which are discarded at the end of their useful life. The rest of the book is concerned with solid wastes with a high energy content — particularly packaging, which has both a significant energy input and content and a substantial energy value when discarded.

Four main aspects of energy in packaging and waste are covered:

(i)   establishing the energy content of packaging,
(ii) assessing the significance of this energy,
(iii) considering the needs and methods of controlling the energy requirements,
(iv) identifying the methods and potential for realizing the energy value of packaging and related solid wastes.

Most goods are protected by packaging that is discarded and thus becomes waste. The needs, functions and alternatives to packaging are discussed in Chapters 2 and 3. The growth of interest in energy as a declining resource has caused much interest to be paid to the energy content of packaging, and this forms the theme of the next three chapters — Chapters 4, 5 and 6 — particularly with regard to energy analysis. After identifying energy flows, methodologies for controlling and/or reducing the energy flows are considered in Chapters 7, 8 and 9, followed by consideration of their intervention measures to implement controls in Chapters 10 and 11. Finally, realization of the energy value of wastes is discussed in Chapters 12, 13 and 14, with some conclusions being presented in Chapter 15.

In the consideration of the energy inputs and outputs of the production of packaging and the disposal of the resultant waste, many questions arise. These were discussed throughout the meeting, and the closing session attempted to formulate answers. The more important questions are listed below, and the 'answers' form the conclusion to this book in Chapter 15.

QUESTIONS

1. Can a common method be derived for energy analyses and modelling?
2. In energy analyses what figures should be employed: a mean, a maximum, the best technology currently available, or a range?
3. Should historic energy investments be written off, and only new energy investment in machinery and equipment be considered?
4. Should the energetic value of waste be conserved by downgrading it as little as possible?
5. Should direct and/or indirect energy inputs be minimized? Is it necessary to distinguish between the various forms and grades of energy?
6. Should utilization of the energy content of packaging and waste be maximized; and/or its dissipation minimized?
7. Should low energy-consuming materials be substituted for high energy-consuming materials?
8. Can energy be saved in the packaging sector? What are the consequences?
9. Should public decisions be made using the criteria of minimizing and/or conserving energetic value?
10. Should there be concern with conserving energy; recovering energy; conserving mineral resources; recovering/recycling mineral resources; or various combinations of these alternatives?
11. Is there too much preoccupation with energy? Is it exerting too great an influence on our lives?
12. What is the best way to use the energy value of household waste up to 1990?
13. How important is energy cost in different packaging systems?
14. What is the role of the consumer in management of packaging systems?
15. What intervention should there be in controlling energy usage and recovery?

2 Ecological Profile of Packages

P. Fink

INTRODUCTION

Again and again it is claimed that packaging expenditure is too high, not only for the consumer, but also in terms of raw materials and energy resources. The proportion of packaging in waste is already considerable, and growing. Packaging materials also dominate the litter problem. One-way packages are a symbol of our throw-away society. Does this give a realistic picture of the packaging world? The interactions are much too complex to be answered by such simple statements, but the derivation of an ecological profile of packaging may clarify this problem.

Packaging — a Service for Goods

Goods are made ready for the market and sale by packing them to ensure safe delivery to the final consignee and to maintain their quality — all at the lowest possible cost. Therefore this is considered a sub-system and its complexity is depicted in Fig. 2.1. Today various highly developed techniques and materials are employed to satisfy the requirements set by the product, the market, the consumer and also by the environment. Optimal solutions may be found by con-

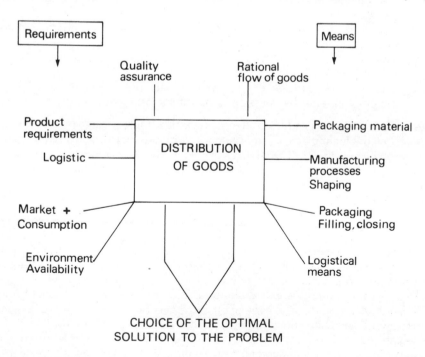

Fig. 2.1 Packaging: a basic system for the distribution of goods.

sideration of quality assurance and a rationalized understanding of the flow of goods.

Environmental Requirements of the Packaging Industry

There is a growing trend towards preservation of our quality of life and control of our environment. The first environmental requirement of the packaging industry was in handling the waste. Individual packaging products were classified according to their suitability for composting, burning or disposal. Waste balances were established and the proportion of packaging determined. A special problem was caused by litter. In this connection it was also requested that packaging made of plastics be biologically or photochemically degradable. Finally, the recycling of waste was also studied in this phase. It was determined that individual methods of disposal and recycling procedures require different expenditures and that they can also cause ecological problems.

Establishing integral ecological balances was therefore suggested and, as the most important criterion, the flow of energy was examined as it occurs in nearly every activity. In this sense, Spreng[1] made his energy-ethical requirement: 'all human activities for a given economic value have to be made in such a way that a minimal energy flow is connected to it'. Such considerations become meaningful only if alternatives to be compared are as complete as possible. It is necessary therefore to consider whole systems in terms of expenditure of energy and material as well as the emission of harmful substances. By including the ecological requirements, a heavily interdisciplinary field of study results for the packaging economy:

(i) The technician examines the criteria at the production, packaging and handling stages.

(ii) The consumer is interested in quality and makes demands as regards hygiene, comfort and information.

(iii) The economist is involved in the necessary investments and business expenditures and the market.

(iv) The ecologist considers the scarcity of the raw materials, the energy expenditure and the emission of harmful substances.

These individual activities have different priorities. Only packaging alternatives satisfying all the technological requirements of the product and acceptable to the market can be considered. Calculations of costs made by economist and ecologist must, therefore, be limited to variations that are technically feasible.

The Ecological Profile

The ecological profile of a package is the projection of both expenditure and return of the packaging-relevant measures of each step in the distribution of goods, from the ecological viewpoint, to a cost standard relating to the environment. This relates to a specified distribution system using appropriate packaging.

Ecological profiles cannot just be made for any packaging material or empty package, as the requirements for manufacturing must also be calculated for a given material: comparison or evaluation of the gain or performance in ecological terms cannot be made independently of the application. Ecological data for packaging materials or empty packages can be stated, for example in terms of energy requirements or pollution when manufacturing 1 kg of packaging material or 1000 empty packages of a defined size. Such information, which often also includes preliminary steps of manufacture, is often useful for establishing ecological profiles for packages, but does not relate to the performance of the package and is therefore not suitable for comparative evaluations of distribution methods. An ecological profile can emphasize any point of view, depending on the chosen projection. Therefore a very flexible system is needed for consideration and evaluation of packaging performance.

Much information is lost if a projection is made in such a way that only one point is considered and the interactions between individual points are ignored. Information can also get lost in formulating ecological indexes by scaling and adding all charges that maybe ecologically relevant. Such a general index would be not only very inaccurate but also completely inappropriate for answering most questions, and could lead to wrong conclusions.

The ecological profile becomes more accurate as the system being examined is better defined. The most precise decision-making documents are therefore obtained by analysing specific production and distribution systems. A main distributor, for example, may establish the ecological profile on the basis of his infrastructure and include and evaluate the activities of his subcontractors, and possibly also of further potential suppliers. A real conflict can arise between the environmentally minded packaging-planner and the active all round environmentalist. The packaging planner is interested in real situations. The general environmentalist, on the other hand, is interested in all aspects of human activity, at least on a regional basis. At this level, however, it is inevitable that information becomes diffuse and less accurate. Global considerations are based on a steadily changing system and necessitate consideration of many assumptions in order that, to a certain degree, the entire system can be quantitatively understood. However, it is important for the packaging sector to examine real ecological consequences. This necessitates mostly an examination of relatively narrow, well defined systems that provide relatively reliable and specific information. Generalities should be avoided if at all possible. It is important that an objective is clearly set, so that the analysis and procedures can best satisfy that objective.

There is a tendency to include all expenditure, starting from the procurement of raw materials through to the investment: the administrative expenses, the production costs and financial return and finally waste disposal by destruction or recycling. This can easily extend to a consideration of the entire economy with feedback control systems. To answer the question we are interested in, it is generally sufficient to consider only one section. It is important to specify clearly the size and position of this section, so that all relevant activities are included for a comparison of different systems. External systems or sections, usually a major part of the infrastructure, may often be omitted.

It is only sensible to establish ecological profiles for real packaging examples. Real packaging is defined by the packaging requirements of the product. The technical requirements and the market-related aspects are relatively easy to achieve within defined but narrow limits. This permits establishment of a framework for study, but it must not be forgotten that the problem of satisfying the product requirements can often be met by different variations. These variations may not only be different as regards the application of the chosen package, but also as regards transportation, storage, etc. A specific methodology may be chosen for establishing the ecological profile, or a variety of methods may be assessed on a regional or worldwide basis for the product concerned.

The ecological profile identifies a number of points, all of which must be considered:

(i) Formulation of the problem to be examined identifies the system to be considered and supplies the framework of the method of assessment to be applied. A clear answer may be expected only if the formulation is clear. The methodology for establishing the ecological profile has to be flexible.

(ii) Numerical data are necessary for expressing both expenditure and return, and the figures should be independent of each other. If different dimensions are to be converted into common units, the relationship between these units has to be clear, and the individual figures have to be compatible.

(iii) The strategic targets of the packaging ecology form the basis for the evaluation criteria. Their relevance to the field considered has to be constantly checked.

(iv) The collection of data follows the formulation of questions. Part of the data can be collected by direct measurement when examining specific procedures. There is also considerable information on procedures in the literature, together with relevant data. Collation and comparison of this published material provides a sound basis for assessing reliability of various data, as well as setting maxima and minima. Furthermore, it is a useful starting point for collaboration with industry. It is sometimes possible to obtain only global values — for example when considering the performance of motors and such devices, or if energy consumption is known only overall and not divided into individual processes.

In summary, it is clear that the following conditions have to be met when establishing the ecological profile:

(i) The problem of packaging and distribution has to be clearly described.

(ii) A number of decisions have to be made based on the formulation of the problem, involving not only yes/no decisions but often also either/or decisions.

(iii) An extensive data bank and a flexible model are required.

If all these conditions are met, the ecological profile is useful for finding optimal packaging solutions.

The procedure of establishing an ecological balance is shown in Table 2.1. This shows that, first of all, the packaging performance to be examined is determined in the first phase. In the second step the materials, the energy requirements and pollution problems are covered in the form of a balance; and in many cases the costs of the different solutions to problems are also included as a third phase.

ESTABLISHING DATA BANKS AND BALANCES

The highly adaptive approach suggested in formulating questions for production of the ecological profile requires a corresponding flexibility and objectivity when establishing data banks and balances. To derive a useful ecological profile, it is necessary that each point and assumption made for such an examination is made clear. The degree of quantification aimed for requires that the appropriate figures are available and that a specific subject is to be examined. The accuracy and reliability of the conclusions are essentially influenced by the corresponding quality of the data employed in the balance and how well defined is the subject of the study.

Table 2.1   Procedure for Establishing Ecological Profiles

Phase 1: Assessment of Packaging Performance

determine the applied packaging performance and the kind of distribution

profile of the packaging requirements for goods:

technological
market
logistic
consumer

choice of packaging alternatives to be examined

packaging material and form — possibly as a matrix showing all variants corresponding to the profile of requirements

system delineation to be derived from formulation of the task

flow diagram for:

distribution of goods
materials
energy
processes
emission of harmful products/pollution

Phase 2: Balancing

balance of materials:

availability
recycling

balance of energy:

energy of feedstock
process energy
energy required for distribution and elimination of waste balance of harmful products

required types of energy:

heat
electricity
work

Phase 3: Cost Analyses

Choice and Definition of System

As already mentioned, considerable importance is given to the delineation of the system to be examined. The possible wide range of such examinations is illustrated by packages for foodstuff in Fig. 2.2. There are even studies covering the entire foodstuff system and including the package as one step within this substantial complex. Such documentation is certainly valuable for the generally interested ecologist and may also indicate to the politician the importance of a specific item, the package in this case, in a total system. This wide framework, however, is inappropriate for the optimal choice of a distribution system for goods. It is sufficient to cover only the section that leads to answers relevant to packaging.

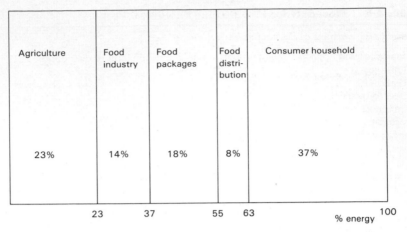

Fig. 2.2   The relative use of energy within the entire food production system.[2]

In such examinations, limitations — such as to one factory or organization — are often set in the formulation of questions. The geographic zone also has to be carefully chosen. Distinct regional differences may occur so that a worldwide evaluation very often gives an average of limited use and validity. Regional influences especially affect data such as the kind of energy available.

It also has to be decided whether only materials and energy are considered or whether administrative costs (which include information) and the infrastructure have also to be included. Generally, just material and energy is sufficient. However, the inclusion of equipment installation is necessary where alternatives may be effected only with additional and considerable investment. In these cases the expected service life of the installation and the age of the equipment actually in use have to be correctly considered in the calculations. The administrative costs are generally significantly affected by labour costs and have relatively little effect on energy consumption, although they may have an influence on the social structure.

Producing products or granting services can usually be achieved by various technical processes which can vary in efficiency. Increasing ecological requirements have caused technical processes constantly to improve; for example, efficiency has increased in terms of the consumption of both energy and material, and processes result in reducing levels of pollution, or even elimination of pollution in some cases. A process manufacturing paper or aluminium may show significant differences as regards the need for energy and materials, and in emissions of wastes, according to the technology of the equipment. It then has to be decided, whether to apply a regionally or globally determined average technology, or a modern environment-conscious technology. Least problems arise when very precisely defined systems are examined, as the technology is then fixed to a large extent and there is only the question of performance to consider.

Another aspect to bear in mind when considering regional or global technology is that it is constantly adapting toward an ecologically beneficial technology, and the speed of the adaptation depends on both legislation and financial economics. This development process will probably move faster in the highly industrialized countries than in the developing countries. Applying data from the most

14

Table 2.2   Flow of Goods

Steps:

    manufacture
    finishing
    portioning
    packaging
    transportation
    storage
    marketing
    selling
    use
    elimination

Each step has a defined expenditure to achieve the specified requirements

The formulation of a step determines the interactions with the other steps

Requirements of each step are determined by the nature of the goods

Each step requires raw materials and energy, and emits waste heat and harmful products to the environment

Consequence: Packaging expenditure is dependent on the formulation of the other steps

Optimal flow of goods = Minimal total expenditure

---

advanced technology identifies what can be achieved and provides motivation for less advanced producers. It also identifies where weak points are, so that improvements may be made as regards ecological circumstances or energy requirements. In this sense, different technical installations should be repeatedly compared with the mean of the ecological profile.

A multi-stage flow of goods requires not only that every individual process is considered by itself, but also that the sum of all the steps is evaluated. Table 2.2 shows, for example, that packaging expenditure depends essentially on the formulation of the other steps in the flow of goods — e.g. good protection by the package may result in a smaller expenditure in the transportation and storage steps. Take the case of the milk package for pasteurized milk and UHT milk: a higher degree of conservation is achieved by the high-temperature process, and the product has to be better protected against degradation by packaging in cardboard coated with aluminium foil. The pasteurized milk can be put into a less demanding package, but it has to be stored cool and has a shorter shelf life. One of these variations of pretreatment and packing of milk will be more economical, depending on consumption habits.

Packaging is a service for goods and a balance must therefore also consider disposal or return of the packaging. If different packaging alternatives are compared for their effect on the environment, it is relevant that the packaging disposal or return is stated and included, for example in the sense of minimum requirements to the package. The ecological profile can then make comparisons between variations of packaging and distribution of goods, all achieving basically the same performance. Whether any of the alternatives provides desirable, however not essential, additional performance may well be interesting to the trade but it is not directly evaluated by the ecological profile.

In global economic terms, as for example foodstuff production (see Fig. 2.3), it

15

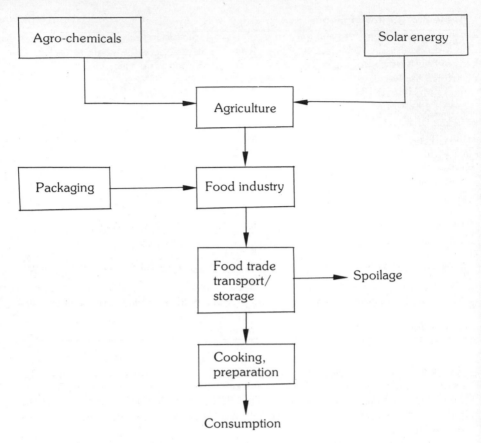

Fig. 2.3 Overall foodstuff production system.

is necessary not only that the ecological balance cover individual expenditure but also that a return is made. Difficulties can arise in ensuring that expenditures and returns are expressed in the same terms.

As packaging performance depends essentially on the other steps in the entire system, generalized assessment is rather difficult. It becomes somewhat easier when considering well defined products; for example, it is of importance in what state the product is packed, i.e. as basic foodstuff or as convenience food. Considering packaging recycling is very difficult without extensive analysis, and therefore this is often left out. This can, however, easily cause misunderstandings, as only the expenditure side of the package is considered and it is quickly forgotten what would happen if the performance resulting from the package were non-existent. In this connection it becomes clear that an ecological profile which includes an assessment of packaging performance gives a much clearer and more useful basis for decision-making than ecological calculations which omit any aspect of performance, i.e. which consider only calculations of expenditure.

Establishing an Ecological Balance

Theoretical Considerations

Although, according to the first law of thermodynamics, energy is neither pro-

16

duced nor destroyed in a closed system, only converted from one form into another, the flow of energy plays a very important role in technical processes. A high-grade energy form (energy that is able to perform a mechanical operation) is often converted into a lower-grade energy form (energy that is no longer able to perform any work and which has come close to the energy level of the surroundings). More economical use of energy reserves will force the realization that energy flow must be minimized.

Energy flows occur in chemical conversions as well as in processes treating materials. The transmission of energy may be made in the form of heat and/or work. The internal energy of the material may, however (but not necessarily), be altered by that energy flow. The energy requirement for transportation and storage has to be considered in addition for the energy balance. Historic energy flows and process energy are considered equally. Energy occurs in different forms which may be converted into each another. Depending upon the applied process of conversion, a loss of energy can occur, which may or may not be significant. The most important forms of energy transfer are heat and work. In the frame of energy transfer, however, a body can perform work or produce heat. Transmitting work is, in general, reversible and the transfer of heat is irreversible. Heat flows from the body with a high temperature to the body having a lower temperature.) The energy is not consumed but it becomes unusable by dilution as temperatures approach those of the surroundings.

Energy of different grades is needed to carry out individual technical processes. The balance should consider that fact, possibly by examining the flow of energy. This is appropriate for energy transfer in the form of work; however, it is questionable for pure thermal processes. There is furthermore a problem of the exact definition of the energy (e.g. determination of an ambient temperature to relate to) and the practical measuring method. Also linked processes, such as heat-power coupling or using waste heat with a heat pump, could not be integrated completely into such a calculation.

It has been demonstrated practicable to group individual types of useful energy when constructing balances using the following classification:

(i)   high-grade useful energy such as electricity and mechanical performance/work,
(ii) heat at a high temperature level,
(iii) heat at a low temperature level,
(iv) energy content of the products (enthalpy).

It is also important whether a process is reversible or irreversible. For general considerations the second law of thermodynamics and entropy, describing the thermodynamic state of a system, play an important role. In a closed system, irreversible processes are related to an increase in entropy. With the aid of entropy it is possible to calculate the part of the heat energy that cannot be converted into mechanical energy because of its equal distribution throughout the system. This suggests that the entropy of a system could be used as a quantitative measure for environmentally related energy flow. An open, unsteady system is usually examined over a defined period when establishing an ecological profile, with energy transfer in the form of heat and work taking place. The complete energy chain has to be considered for the balance.

All these factors contribute to a view that changes in thermodynamic entropy may well be considered as a criterion for evaluation for individual processes, but it is not a practical proposition for an ecological profile. For a closed system such as a chemical reaction, the entropy consideration may be justified and it can also lead to a meaningful evaluation of such a process.

Energy Chains and Grading of Energy Forms

Well defined energies are required for both technical processes and many other activities. These useful energies, such as light, power or heat, are obtained from a so-called primary energy source over different steps through an energy chain to secondary energy such as coke or gasoline. The last link in the chain of secondary energy is called final energy and represents the form of energy to be applied in the respective process which often requires a well defined final energy, for example electric power. For the specified process, it is not relevant how this final energy is obtained from any primary energy source over different steps having different efficiencies. However, it is necessary to produce an energy balance based on primary energy.

The starting point of ecological energy balances is the primary or raw energy, i.e. energy as provided by nature, such as coal or oil. Only transforming the primary energy into useful energy makes it usable for a process. After processing or use, this energy is either stored in the products or it is given up to the environment as waste heat. The penultimate link in the chain of energy transformation is the final energy, i.e. the energy that the user employs to produce the desired useful energy. The allocation of that final energy is either known or can be collected. However, it is often less clear by what chain of transformation that final energy was obtained from the primary energy, or its dependence on regional conditions. The overall degree of efficiency can also vary according to the energy transformation chain. Levels of pollution discharged to the environment (see also balance of harmful products) are also different, depending on the form of energy transformation. If the energy chain involves a thermal step with transformation of heat into mechanical work, only about one third of the energy present in the form of heat can be transformed, even under ideal conditions based on the Carnot cycle. Energy chains without thermal steps are unusual for producing electricity except for hydroelectric power stations.

Therefore it is important when establishing energy balances to state in what form the useful energy is used, and over what steps it has been procured. Heat, for example for drying purposes or to produce higher temperatures, may be obtained with a relatively high degree of efficiency by a combustion process. However, if electric energy were required it would have to be obtained from a nuclear power plant, for example. The final energies required for individual processes may have been obtained from widely different energy chains and have different primary energy requirements, depending on the energy transformation chain employed. Pollution emissions by the energy transformation processes can also vary. It has therefore to be decided whether to consider average energy transformation chains for the individual final energies on a regional or even a worldwide basis, or whether to consider only the energy transformation chain actually employed for the problem studied. In most cases it will be advantageous to at least consider a regional energy split.

Individual final energies will not be of the same grade or quality. Nevertheless, comparison should be made possible. Foremost is the relationship between thermal energy and electrical energy. In all energy balances it is important first to determine whether a unit is electrical or thermal, and then, if relevant, the conversion factor from thermal to electrical energy and vice versa has to be clearly defined. Most ecological calculations are carried out in thermal energy units.

However, there are also some that use electrical energy units on the basis that high-grade electrical energy is the most intensive and valuable form and it is desirable to know how much of that high-grade energy is devoted to a given activity. Determination of the conversion factor for transforming electrical into thermal energy is made according to different principals. One is to take the average of individual energy transformation steps on a regional basis. The factor then becomes lower as more hydroelectric power plants are in use compared to thermal power plants in the region considered. Switzerland, for example, has a relatively favourable factor which, however, becomes worse with every new nuclear power plant.

Other calculations start from calculations based on the degree of efficiency of a thermal power plant, i.e. that a factor of about 3 has to be applied. While consideration of regional energy conditions requires adjustment, the so-called incremental consideration avoids this problem by simply assuming that additional energy needs are met by balancing which can be met only by thermal power plants. This gives a simpler basis for calculation, but discriminates against the process under examination: in the present case of packaging, for example, additional unfavourable energy chains would have to be provided. It should be considered whether a conversion factor appropriate to the problem can be applied. Introducing a general conversion factor would, however, limit the flexibility required in ecological profiles. Table 2.3 gives some basic values for the calculation of energy balances.

Establishing Balances of Harmful Products and Pollution

Quantification and Weighting of the Harmful Products

Harmful products from processes are often emitted to the atmosphere, watercourses and ground. Evaluation of these emissions must consider their toxicity, the time of impact and speed of degradation. The toxicity of harmful products is often described by critical limit concentrations, exceeding which indicates a hazard. Attempts have been made to define the extent of discharges to air, land or water from specific processes in terms of critical concentrations. On the other hand, legislative requirements are becoming more stringent, thus requiring pollution control procedures which consume more energy.

Pollution can therefore be reduced only at the expense of energy consumption. A realistic evaluation of the harmful product emissions seems, therefore, to be possible by considering that, in industrial regions, pollution of air, water or land is severely limited by law. Only procedures that satisfy these controls are considered, i.e. procedures which have waste treatment steps provided in such a way that no inadmissible emissions are permitted. This expenditure then appears in the energy balance. It is also advisable to identify, in addition, the most important and most critical harmful products for individual processes. Quantitative assessment of harmful products is made more difficult by the fact that there are usually several ways of manufacturing a certain product, each causing a different level of pollution.

Source of Pollution

There must be differentiation between process-derived pollution and pollution originating from the production of energy — e.g. waste heat, carbon dioxide, radiation or aesthetic considerations. These cannot be effectively eliminated and care has to be taken to minimize such problems. It is clear that balancing such

Table 2.3   Energy in Packaging Materials

(a) Average energy requirement values for packaging materials (kWh$_{th}$/kg)

Material	Energy content of feedstock	Process energy	Total
Aluminium			
raw	—	—	35.6
foil	—	—	41.7
Paper	4.4	8	12.4
Glass			3.0
Polystyrene			
suspension			
polymerization	16	19	35
bulk			
polymerization	16	7	23
Polypropylene	17.2	8.8	26
Polyethylene	17.2	9.8	27

(b) Energy inputs for plastic materials

Three types of calculation are in the literature:
    process energy only
    process energy and energy content
    energy content of crude oil needed for the production of 1 unit of plastic

Representative figures, tonnes oil equivalent per tonne plastic						
	PS	XPS	PP	LDPE	MDPE	PVC
Process	1.7	1.7	1.2	0.7	0.9	1.2
Process + feedstock	2.8	2.9	2.3	1.8	1.9	1.7
Quantity of oil resource (toe/tonne plastics produced: 1 toe/tonne = 12.32 kWh$_{th}$/kg)	65	65	35	17	17	9

PS = polystyrene, XPS = expanded polystyrene, PP = polypropylene,
LDPE = low-density polyethylene, MDPE = medium-density polyethylene,
PVC = polyvinyl chloride.

debits and credits is extremely difficult and complex. A main target of ecology must be to eliminate harmful products as far as possible, and not permit their release to the environment. Such control will have an impact on technical processes, and occasionally it will also lead to new processes.

Raw Material Balances

Assessment of resource depletion plays an essential role in evaluating raw material requirements. It is relatively easy to determine the material requirements, for example to produce 1 kg of packaging material (see Table 2.4). However, this material expenditure should be evaluated in relation to its scarcity. Crude oil is an example of a scarce resource, however only about 3% of the total crude oil production is used for manufacturing plastic materials, while 25% goes to transport fuels. A similar situation exists for other raw materials of the packaging industry, such as wood, only 4% of which produces paper.

Table 2.4 Raw Material Requirements

	Material input for 1 kg
Aluminium	4–5 kg bauxite (crude alumina)
	150 g sodium hydroxide
	50 g calcium carbonate
	10 l water
	0.45 kg carbon anode
	25–35 g fluorine as F^- (fluoride)
Glass	592–726 g silica (quartz)
	153–210 g dolomite
	70 g feldspar
	45 g sodium carbonate
	180 g cullet
Paper (1 kg cellulose pulp)	2.7 kg wood
	130 g calcium carbonate
	85 g sulphur
	40–70 g chlorine
	500 l water
Polystyrene	1.1 kg crude oil
Polypropylene	1.05 kg natural gas
Polyethylene	1.06 kg natural gas, or 1.5 kg oil

However, the raw material situation can be ameliorated by recycling waste materials. There are two possibilities: either to recycle back to raw materials, or to use waste material for new applications. The recycling possibilities are now well established for paper and cardboard, as well as glass, in the packaging sector, and rapidly developing for other packaging material, such as aluminium, tinplate and plastics. Waste may be used to produce energy in an incineration plant, for example, and thus supply an energy credit to the total balance.

However, it will always be important that recycling possibilities, as well as waste elimination, are subject to a thorough analysis to determine the precise contribution to the ecological balance, particularly as recycling also involves a distinct energy requirement. Energy-intensive products are therefore generally more profitably recycled as materials rather than energy.

The Problem of One-Way or Multi-way Packages

The re-usable package is widely discussed, particularly for beverages, where the re-usable bottle competes with the one-way bottle, the one-way can or a one-way soft package, such as a sachet. A re-usable package has, in principle, to be designed to be longer lasting, and therefore involves a higher expenditure. The more often such a package is re-used, the more economical it becomes compared to the one-way package for which a new expenditure is involved each time.

The problem of one-way/multi-way is best explained in graphical terms. In Fig. 2.4, expenditure in terms of energy or cost is stated as a function of the number of refils or cycles. The intersection of the two functions shows the crossover point at which a re-usable package becomes energy-saving or more economical.

It is not difficult to see that goods distribution systems exist for which a multi-way system is advantageous at a determined number of cycles. On the other hand, there are distribution systems for which the number of cycles necessary for multi-way packages to be preferred cannot be attained in practice. The level of returns

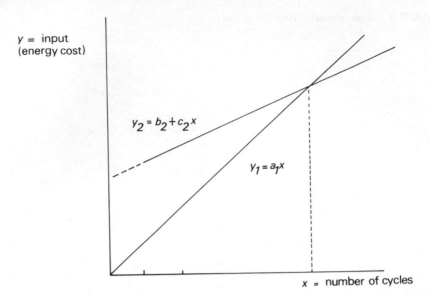

$y =$ input
(energy cost)

$y_2 = b_2 + c_2 x$

$y_1 = a_1 x$

$x =$ number of cycles

Fig. 2.4   One-way and multi-way (returnable) packages. $y_1 = a_1 x$: one way ($a_1 =$ input for 1 package). $y_2 = b_2 + c_2 x$: returnable ($b_2 =$ input for the empty returnable package, c_2 = input for one recycle). $x_n = b_2/(a_1 - c_1)$: break even point.

or cycles of a re-usable package will, in many cases, be very decisive and must often be encouraged by requiring a deposit on the container.

Accuracy of Balances

The accuracy of many ecological balances is fairly limited. The more specific an examination, the more accurate the results will be. However, if it is intended to make the results as widely applicable as possible, for example for an entire region or globally, the accuracy will be only about ±20-25% because of uncertainties and different practices. In a developing technology, data have to be constantly checked, updated and adjusted to the new conditions. In such situations, a transient or dynamic system has to be evolved from instantaneous facts. For such reasons, it is often more appropriate to consider ranges than to operate with precise numbers. For ecological balances to be useful, it is furthermore essential that the assumptions on which the calculations are based are clearly stated.

PRACTICAL ASPECTS OF ESTABLISHING ECOLOGICAL PROFILES

In the last few years, various evaluations have been carried out according to the schemes described above for ecological profiles, all concerned with comparing alternatives for providing the same packaging performance. The most detailed study involved packages for individual portions of yoghurt, and the results are summarized below.

Swiss Yoghurt Study

What is the best way to distribute yoghurt in respect of:

technological aspects,
economics,
convenience,
ecological viewpoint?

The alternatives are a glass or plastic cup, and a paperboard cup in times of shortage of plastic.

The market for yoghurt in 180-g portions was studied in Switzerland for the Swiss dairy industry, the main distributors, the packaging industry and the consumers. The basic problem and results illustrate how to do a comparison of packaging systems. The problem is set out as follows.

Case Study: Yoghurt Packaging

Yoghurt   420 Million 180-g portions are consumed each year. They have the following characteristics: semi-solid or stirred, in more than 50 varieties, has its own biology requiring prevention of outside infection, needs cold storage (for, on average, 5 days), requires a durability of 3-4 weeks, ready to eat (package = dish), sale by distribution chains and dairies.

  Technical requirements
  Protection of the contents against:
    spoilage
    outside infection
    loss
  Package needs:
    impermeable packaging material
    a tight cover
    unbreakable
    no interaction between contents and packaging
    no transfer of odour or taste
    no migration of substances in the product
    resistance down to pH 4
  Manufacturing:
    efficient mass production
  Processing:
    automatic filling, marking and printing
    incubation (temperature resistant)
  Consumption:
    easy to open
    disposal without problems (one-way or returnable packaging)

  Packaging components
  Package = Yoghurt + Container + Cover(lid)
            (provided)
                        Packaging material + Form
                            (variable)   (variable)

  Packaging material selection
  Criteria:
    suitable for product
    available
    manufacturing and engineering of materials:

23

    plastics
    glass
    paper/board/coated
    metal (aluminium)

Form (shape) requirements
    suitable for storage and transport
    meets requirements for consumption
    minimum material requirements
    attractive
Cover/lid considerations
    hot sealing
    flanging

Results   An energy balance was constructed for each alternative, derived from all combinations of the options described above. Included were the energy content of the packaging materials, process energy, energy for transport and storage/cooling, and net energy for disposal/recycling/recovery. The results in energy consumption terms are shown in Table 2.5, indicating that there is little significant difference in overall figures for different combinations.

Knowledge resulting from the study   Constant technical development concerning ecology has affected the following:

    reduction in the materials required
    availability of raw materials
    energetically advantageous processes
    recycling

Type of energy applied and contribution to environment affects:

    classification of the type of energy
    evaluation of environmental effects from energy generation

Conclusions
    (i) Include ecological evaluation of packaging systems into overall energy assessment.
    (ii) Rising energy costs confirm the view that optimal economic solutions are also ecologically correct.
    (iii) Ensure sufficient provision is made for flexibility in technology and economics for further development of ecological balances.

Overall aspects of packaging requirements
    Technical
    Economic   Expenditure corresponding to the utility
    Ecological   of the packaging

    The environmentalist wants to maintain viable conditions in nature
        with a minimum involvement of technology in nature.
    Industry wants viable and rational production and distribution of
        goods, with maximum use of technical processes, energy and
        materials.
    The consumer wants good products and a high standard of living.

Within certain limits, all these requirements can be met.

Table 2.5 Energy Balance for 1000 Yoghurt Cups (kWh$_{th}$)

Type of packaging	Package: cup, foil	Transport			Storage (cooling)	Disposal	Total kWh$_{th}$
		New material	Delivery	Return			
Plastic cup:							
Polystyrene 8 g	337.300[a]	0.990	12.733	2.338	5.875	− 50.400	309
	241.300[b]	0.990	12.733	2.338	5.875	− 50.400	213
Polystyrene 7 g	217.800	0.880	12.678	2.338	5.875	− 44.100	195
Polypropylene	241.900	0.880	12.678	2.338	5.875	− 47.460	216
Brown glass 112 g (one-way)	416.600	5.439	18.728	2.613	7.638	+ 11.760	463
Combi-glass (50% return)	238.200	5.439	18.728	5.693	7.638	+ 3.528	279
Paper 9 g	229.200	0.990	12.733	2.338	5.875	− 16.700	234

(a) Polystyrene produced by suspension polymerisation.
(b) Polystyrene produced by bulk polymerisation.

Covering Packages

Packing for despatch of bottles was also examined. One package was of pure corrugated board, while the others consisted of a combination of polystyrene foam and cardboard. The required criterion was that this packaging satisfy the requirements of the Swiss Postal Authority. Here also, it became evident that the energy expenditure for performing the same requirement was about equal in spite of the different construction and materials of these two package types.

CONCLUSIONS

The waste mountain to which packaging makes a contribution, and the expenditure for its disposal, have led to the question of whether this packaging expenditure is necessary at all. The ecological profile tries to provide an answer. First of all, it is able to show that a minimal package is necessary for a defined distribution of goods. It can also be shown that the choice of packaging should be made on ecological as well as economical grounds. If packaging systems are identified that are not acceptable ecologically, they can be eliminated. Such considerations may also, of course, induce authorities and environment protectors to introduce guidelines for better environmental protection.

Greater value, however, is attributed to balances that affect medium-range planning, for which an optimal packaging system is required. For the long term, it may be assumed that the ecologically relevant criteria of availability of energy and raw materials will be the ones that have to be considered from a technical and economic viewpoint. By using the ecological profile, it is therefore possible to make prognoses for packaging systems. The future belongs to those packages having a favourable ecological profile, and it is believed that establishing ecological profiles represents an important task of modern packaging research and is a reliable aid for decision-making in the packaging sector.

REFERENCES

1. SPRENG, D., Energetische Betrachtungen zum Verpackungsproblem. *Neue Zürcher Zeitung* 14.1.1974, technical annex.
2. JÖNSON, G., International Packaging Congress, 18-19 November 1980, Paris.
3. FINK, P., Proceeding of the Second International Symposium on Commodity Science and Technology, State University of Gent, 1979. EMPA/FAH, *Analyse der Verpackung v. Yoghurt*, 1979.

Professor Dr. Fink is Director of the Swiss Federal Laboratories for Materials Testing in St. Gallen.

3   The Food-Producing System

M. Backman

INTRODUCTION

Following rapid energy price increases, the energy economy measures taken by society have become the subject of wide-ranging debate in the media, as well as among the general public and politicians. Particular attention has been devoted to the packaging industry as a prolific waster of energy. This criticism is, however, in many respects unfounded, in that packaging does not in general constitute an unnecessary evil which merely contributes to an increase in society's energy usage. By taking an overall view, it is possible to demonstrate the direct opposite: for example, by facilitating transport and handling, evening out seasonal variations and reducing loss, packaging can contribute to a considerable reduction in society's total energy usage.

From a narrow viewpoint, it can be ascertained that different packages intended for, in principle, the same product can require different amounts of energy in their manufacture. It will be shown below, for example, that plastic bags for frozen peas require considerably less energy in manufacture than metal cans for preserved peas. If this observation is broadened to relate to the entire production and consumption chain, it is notable that frozen peas are just as energy-demanding as preserved peas. Thus there is a clear risk of suboptimization if only the energy usage of the package itself is taken into consideration. Since the package constitutes an integral part of the entire production and distribution process of goods, the energy content of packaging is considered in this larger context in this study. A brief introduction to the problems involved in energy analysis methods is presented first.

ENERGY ANALYSIS CONSIDERATIONS

The aim of energy analysis is to identify the energy usage in the manufacture of goods (a product) and/or in the execution of a function (a service). If the aim is to produce a complete picture of energy usage, the analysis must be given very broad scope. To restrict the analysis to only certain links in the production chain of a product involves conscious disregard of some energy contributions which could have considerable importance. Depending on the scope selected, the following energy inputs can be included:

I   Direct energy supply to the system under observation.

II   Corresponding energy inputs in raw materials or semi-finished goods manufacture which lie outside the system under observation, in which materials are traced back to the natural raw materials. No energy quantities other than the specified inputs are included. Natural raw materials other than fuels are imputed to have no energy value.

III   The actual recoverable energy of the natural raw material is also included, for example the heating value of wood for the forestry industry. (Wood may clearly be used as a fuel instead of as an industrial raw material.)

IV   Finally, there are the energy inputs for production equipment and industrial plant.

Opinions vary as regards the most suitable calculation routine in totalling different energy forms to a common measurement unit. It is obvious that fossil fuels and electric power cannot be directly added together without taking into account in some way, for example, the losses in electric power production and distribution. But how large are the losses in hydroelectricity and uranium-based electricity production? In certain energy balances, the energy supplied to the hydroelectric plant is presented as the potential energy in the water reservoir, and the 'input side' of a nuclear power station is shown as the amount of heat released on nuclear fission (the thermal burn-up). In a hydroelectric power station, about 85% of the potential energy is typically converted into electric power; and in a nuclear power station, the degree of efficiency is calculated in accordance with the above at about 30%. Other research workers assert that in energy analysis both nuclear and hydroelectric power plants should be set at 100% efficiency, on the grounds that it is not desirable to consider the losses, or that the losses are unavoidable. While the warm coolant water from a nuclear power station could be used for heating, for example, private dwellings, this is not current practice, for which reason the uranium supplied can be claimed as being effectively utilized at 100%.

Electric energy and fossil fuels cannot, however, be added together, even after agreement has been reached on the above questions. Since electricity, as such, cannot be stored, production at any time must be adapted to needs. The requirement varies constantly, but there is always a certain base load, summer or winter, day or night. The power needs of this base load are preset, and are met in power stations which have both the correct production conditions and cost characteristics which make them suitable for continuous basic power production. Temporary peak loads are met by means of power plants operating at low fixed and high variable costs. As a supplement to basic production in hydroelectric and nuclear power plants, as well as peak and stand-by power from gas turbines, etc., intermediate power plants also have their place in the production system in order to minimize costs. Using this brief description of the general structure of electric power supply as a starting point, several calculation models can be produced. The example of electricity generation is used to illustrate a number of problems.

Advocates of so-called *marginal reasoning* assert that if, for example, all production of packaging were suddenly to cease, this would result in a power excess, and thus electricity production from oil-fired power stations could be reduced. Thus, all nuclear power and hydroelectric power-based electricity production should, according to this model, be evaluated in accordance with the amount of oil which would need to be supplied to oil-fired power stations to produce the equivalent amount of electricity. This model has among its advocates those countries dependent, to a great extent, on oil and coal for their electric power production, whose primary aim is to illustrate the import situation and the value of domestically produced electric energy. When this model is used, an efficiency of 33% is often assumed, and the final use of electricity (net energy) can thus quite simply be multiplied by a factor of 3 to obtain the gross energy.

The basic consumption model can also be derived from the earlier description of the general structure of electricity production. It was postulated that the needs of basic power consumers are covered by energy produced in hydroelectric and nuclear power plants. The packaging industry in this approach is considered to be such a basic power consumer, and can therefore assert that the electric power used is theoretically produced with a 100% degree of efficiency. Hence, all supplied electric power and the energy content in the fossil fuel used can be added directly together.

A commonly occurring calculation model is *the mean degree of efficiency model*. Here, the weighted mean degree of efficiency (*n*) in prevailing power stations is calculated, from which the gross energy is obtained if the net energy is multiplied by a factor of $1/n$. In this context, it should be observed that the percentage distribution between different power plants, and thereby also the so-called mean degree of efficiency, varies from year to year and from country to country. The energy consumption presented for a certain package is thus changed if, for example, foreign raw materials or semi-finished goods for which the energy consumed abroad is included in the calculation. It also changes each year when new statistics for electric power production are available.

Apart from the actual energy consumption rates, it is also preferable to include the type of energy resource consumed, for example renewable such as wood, or finite such as oil.

Even if the scope, efficiency and calculation routes can be successfully established, a great number of practical problems remain in energy analysis work. These are described and discussed in later chapters.

ENERGY FLOWS WITHIN THE FOOD-PRODUCING SYSTEM

General

The total energy usage within the Swedish food-producing system is presented in Table 3.1. The calculations include energy inputs up to and including scope level

Table 3.1   Energy Usage within the Swedish Food-Producing System, 1975

Reproduced from P. Olsson, *System Studies for the Food Sector*, STU-report 77-6552, June 1979, by permission of the Swedish Food Institute.

Sectors	Fossil fuel/TWh	Electricity/TWh
Fertilizer industry	3.0	0.5
Imported fertilizers	1.5	0.5
Feedstuffs industry	0.2	0.1
Farming	3.2	0.8
plant cultivation	(2.9)	(0.2)
animal products	(0.3)	(0.6)
Food industry	5.0	1.0
Food packaging	2.6	4.6
Paper	(0.2)	(2.3)
Plastic	(2.1)	(0.1)
Metal	(0.2)	(1.6)
Glass	(0.1)	(0.6)
Food transport	1.9	0.1
Wholesalers (internal handling)	—	0.2
Food trade	0.2	1.0
Large households	—	0.7
Transport between retailer and households	1.5	—
Households	7.9	5.3
Total	27.0	14.8

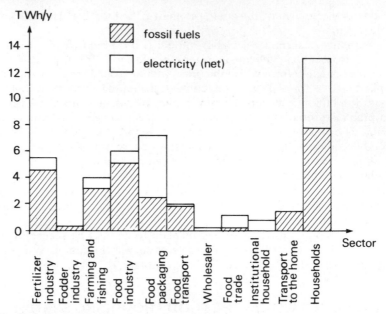

Fig. 3.1 Energy usage within the food-producing system.

III described earlier. This includes all energy except that for production equipment and industrial plant, i.e.:

(i) direct energy supply,
(ii) corresponding energy inputs in raw materials and semi-finished goods manufacture,
(iii) auxiliary energy for lighting and heating of factory premises, etc. (permits production),
(iv) energy to refrigerators, dishwashers, freezers and cookers (allows consumption),
(v) recoverable energy in the raw materials supplied.

Summation of the two energy forms, in order to compare this with the total energy usage of the country, presupposes that a decision has been reached concerning questions on conversion and distribution losses in electric power production as previously discussed. Depending upon which method is preferred, energy usage within the food-producing system can vary between about 9 and 12% of Sweden's total energy consumption. Table 3.1 is illustrated graphically in Fig. 3.1. Concerning electric energy usage, net values are presented, as in the table (the final usage).

Specific Food Groups

A compilation of energy consumption by different sub-processes in the production and distribution of nine different food groups is shown in Table 3.2. The scope level is the same as that described earlier, including energy consumed in the home in the storage, preparation and dishwashing operations. Dishwashing has a notably high energy requirement, which gives high energy consumption figures for all products.

30

Table 3.2   The Energy Flow, Nine Food Groups in MJ/kg

Reproduced from P. Olsson, *System Studies for the Food Sector*, STU-report 77-6552, June 1979, by permission of the Swedish Food Institute

| Product group | Farming, fishing | Industry | Distribution | | Packaging | Consumption | | Total including the home, approximately |
			Transport	Retailer + fridge + freezer		Large household	Home	
Peas (vegetables)								
Frozen	2	2.7	0.6	2.6	4.2	(6.5)	10.5	22.6
Sterilized	2	2.1	0.7	0.5	10.7	(4.2)	6.6	22.6
Potatoes								
Frozen	2	2.9	0.6	2.6	4.2	(6.5)	10.5	22.8
Sterilized	2	3.1	0.7	0.5	9.0	(4.2)	6.6	21.9
Bread	4	5	0.9	0.5	1.4	(1.2)	5.4	17.2
Sugar	2.2	10.6	0.4	0.5	0.9	(1.2)	5.4	20.0
Margarine	12.9	4.1	0.6	1.1	4.6	(3.5)	9.3	32.6
Milk	4.4	2.7	0.9	1.1	1.9-2.0	(3.5)	9.3	20.3-20.4
Meat, fresh								
Beef	45.2	5.4	0.6	1.1	1.4	(6.5)	10.5	64.2
Pork	36.4							
Chicken	34.4							
Meat, preserved beef								
Cooled	45.2	9.1*	1.7	1.1	2.3	(6.5)	10.5	69.9
Frozen	45.2	10.3	3.1	2.6	4.2	(6.5)	10.5	75.9
Sterilized	45.2	13.0	1.2	0.5	10.7	(4.2)	6.6	77.2
Fish (Cod)								
Frozen	47	3.7	1.6-4.6	2.6	4.2	(6.5)	10.5	69.6-72.6
Sterilized	50	5.6	1.7-4.7	0.5	10.7	(4.2)	6.6	75.1-78.1

* Including slaughter: 5.4 MJ/kg.

Table 3.3   **Energy Consumption in kWh/tonne in the Preservation of Corn and Green Peas**

Freezing	Canning	Source reference
3000	2800	2
2470–2910	4560–6920	3
2910	5110	4
2797	4139	5
8400 (corn)	7400 (corn)	6
8667	9608	7
	8445	8
6278	6278	1

The fact that the energy consumption figures in Table 3.2 are given to an accuracy of one decimal place should in no way be interpreted as a measure of exactitude. In order to show the effect which the selection of system limits and calculation routines has, Table 3.3 shows the final results from several investigations which considered the energy requirements for the preservation, treatment and distribution of green peas and corn. The total value of 22.6 MJ/kg given for these vegetables corresponds to 6278 kWh/tonne. The reason for the substantial variations in Table 3.3 is basically the selection of different system limits. A compilation which includes only the energy usage within the narrow system limits of food industry-retailer gives the more closely agreeing results of Table 3.4.

Table 3.4   **Energy Consumption in the Processing, Distribution and Storage of Frozen Peas in kWh/tonne**

Source reference	Process				
	Processing (including packing)	Packaging	Transport	Storage (not the) home)	Total
1	750	1167	167	722	2806
2	559	1500	105	440	2604
3	555	1360	160	580	2655
4	570	1360	160	580	2670
5	342	944	—	692	1978
6	1810	1140	700		3650
7	2000	1027	500	1889	5416

One example of the effect of the extent of processing on energy needs is given in Table 3.5. Considerably more energy is consumed in the various methods of industrial preparation of potatoes compared to domestic preparation. This would be expected in view of the additional treatment stages, greater packaging demands, and several temperature changes, etc.

CONCLUSIONS

From the above discussion, a few general conclusions concerning energy usage within the food-producing system can be drawn:

Table 3.5   The Effect of Degree of Processing of Potatoes on Energy Consumption

Energy usage is expressed in MJ/kg, and is calculated on the basis of 1 kg of finished product, i.e. corrected at various stages for peeling losses, etc. (Reproduced from P. Olsson, *System Studies for the Food Sector*, STU-report 77-6552, June 1979, by permission of the Swedish Food Institute.)

	Peeled after boiling	Peeled before boiling	Industrial peeling	Canned potatoes	Ready frozen potatoes	Chipped potatoes (frozen) Potatoes	Oil plant (incl. refining)
Cultivation	2.23	2.53	2.64	2.64	2.23	4.42 + 2.6	
Transport	0.55	0.63	0.65	0.65	0.55	1.09 + 0.07	
Peeling	—	—	0.69	0.69	—	1.32	
Industrial preparation	—	—	—	2.2	1.1	1.8	
Freezing	—	—	—	—	0.35	0.32	
Packaging	1.76	2.2	3.2	10.4	6.60	6.0	
Cold storage	—	—	—	—	2.30	2.09	
Transport	—	—	—	—	0.75	0.68	
Cold storage in home	—	—	—	—	0.95	0.86	
Preparation	2.2	2.0	2.0	1.0	1.1	3	
Energy usage/kg of product	6.7	7.4	9.2	17.6	15.9	24.3	

(i)   Energy usage in the home is surprisingly high. Above all, the dishwashing step contributes most.

(ii)   Preservation by freezing is not, viewed overall, more energy-demanding than canning. This can be ascribed, to a great extent, to the differences concerning packaging requirements.

(iii)   Much energy is consumed in non-process-linked energy, such as heating, lighting and ventilation.

(iv)   Fish is about as energy-demanding to process as meat from farming.

(v)   The energy requirement for production of meat and dairy products is two to three times as great as for the production of vegetables. The differences occurs primarily in the agricultural sector.

(vi)   The total energy costs in food production and distribution (agriculture /fish retailer) are responsible for about 5% of the sales price.

(vii)   Food packaging is responsible for almost 20% of the energy usage within the Swedish food-producing system, which is equivalent to about 2% of Sweden's total energy usage.

DISCUSSION

Energy analyses are associated with a series of considerations, standpoints and fundamental assumptions which, to a great extent, direct the result. It has not been possible to achieve any degree of unification concerning these questions despite several investigations, and despite the fact that energy analysis calculations have been carried out ever since the Second World War. All energy analyses other than one's own can therefore be claimed to be incorrect. However, the analyses can, nevertheless, fulfil a certain function in identifying the significant energy-consuming operations and their relationship to other activities. For comparisons between individual products, the energy analysis result must, however, be used with extreme caution.

Energy analyses dealing with the food-producing system, as described above, show that packaging, viewed individually, is responsible for an appreciable proportion of the total energy usage within the system. However, as previously emphasized, it is essential to consider the packaging as an integral part of the whole production and distribution system. By facilitating transport and handling, evening out seasonal variations and reducing loss, packaging contributes to a reduction in energy usage within all the other sectors in the system, Nevertheless, this does not exclude the concept that measures to reduce energy usage within the packaging sector can be desirable. There should, however, be an awareness that economic, food hygiene, administrative, practical, technical and marketing aspects greatly restrict opportunities to make any drastic changes in packaging within most food areas.

There are, however, certain areas within the food-producing sector in which different types of packages are used for identical products. One well known example of this is the beverage sector, and other examples include spices, coffee, jams and preserves. It may seem attractive to politicians to attempt to control consumption in such sectors in favour of the packaging alternative which is the least energy-consuming. It must then be assumed that the control which results in increased energy prices must be considered insufficient.

Control in the use of packaging in this direction would seem, however, to run contrary to society's mode of operation within other product areas. The design of a product is directly related most often to its capacity to meet different functional requirements. Thus, glass packages for spices are considered better for retaining the aroma of the spices, are easier to use, more attractive in appearance, and easier to store than different types of bag which, nevertheless, are less energy-demanding. In the same way, many consumers are prepared to pay the extra cost of disposable packages for beer and soft drinks, as compared with 'inconvenient' returnable bottles regardless of energy consumption. Similar linkages between the properties of a product and its energy usage can be assumed to prevail within all areas where there is freedom of choice. For example, a hardback book is more energy-demanding than a paperback; a Mercedes requires more energy than a Volkswagen, both in manufacture and in running; a ten-geared bicycle requires considerably more energy to make than a minibike, etc. Moreover, there are no guarantees that the total energy usage would be reduced simply by steering consumption in a direction towards less energy-demanding products within a small number of areas. It is obvious that if many people prefer to spend their monetary savings made as a result of being forced to buy an energy-minimum package on, for example, increased use of the sauna, the total energy consumption becomes much more complex.

Thus, it is highly improbable that a transition towards less energy-demanding packaging alternatives within the few food areas where this is at all possible could lead to any perceptible changes in society's usage of energy. Since single-use packaging has become a symbol of the so-called 'energy waste, paper cup mentality', measures which are perceived as being intended to reduce 'waste' can nevertheless be politically viable and possibly have a positive psychological effect, to enhance the tendency of people to cooperate in other forms of savings activities.

REFERENCES

1. OLSSON, P., *System Studies for the Food Sector*, STU-report 77-6552, June 1979.
2. SANDSTRÖM, B., *Energy Consumption in the Preservation and Storage of Foods*, SIK report No. 352, 1974.
3. MATTISSON, L., *Energy Consumption in Food Preservation*, 1975.
4. LÖNDAHL, G., Freeze Conservation — comparison from the point of view of energy with other methods of preservation. 10th Nordic Cooling Congress, 1977.
5. DOE, P.E., Energy Wastage in Food Processing, *Food Technology in Australia*, April 1977.
6. HENIG, Y.S. and SCHOEN, H.M., Energy requirements: freezing vs. canning, *Food Engineering*, September 1976.
7. ROE, M.A., *A Comparative Study of Energy Consumption for Refrigerated, Canned and Frozen Peas*, Dept. of Food Science and Technology, Cornell University, New York, 1977.
8. LEACH, G., *Energy and Food Production*, International Institute for Environment and Development, 1976.

Mikael Backman is a university lecturer at the Transportation and Materials Handling Engineering Department, Lund Institute of Technology. He is also working as a researcher in an independent research group called TEM (Transportation, Environment and Management). During the last five years he has been working with education and research mainly within the fields: transportation engineering, packaging engineering, recycling, energy usage and energy savings. This work has, so far, resulted in about 15 reports and publications.

4 Fundamentals and Methodology of Investigating the Total Energy Consumption for Industrial Products

H. Schaefer and D.R. Hartmann

INTRODUCTION

National energy requirements have grown over the decades at the same rate as both population and the demands of that population. Per capita consumption of energy has not only to satisfy basic needs such as heating or lighting in a home and the preparation of food, but also to meet the advances of technology, for example in transport, production of consumer and capital goods, and provision of services. It is only on rare occasions that many individuals appreciate that energy is actually required in various activities — for instance, when the petrol tank of a car or the fuel tank of a home heating system is filled up, or when a fire is lit or a gas stove is used. Bills which have to be paid for electricity, gas and fuel oil are also a reminder of how much energy is consumed.

However, very often little is known about the energy required to produce goods which meet a need. For example, in the case of food or clothing, a whole chain of processes is necessary to produce the finished item. Each process consumes energy which enters into the balance of an economy. In order to analyse this kind of hidden energy consumption, data are required on the cumulative energy consumption involved in producing and consuming capital and consumer goods and services. This cumulative energy consumption is the total energy required to produce one unit of a given product, including the energy used in winning and processing raw materials and auxiliary materials, manufacturing the product itself and the energy needed for removing waste or for recycling after the product has been used. Other authors use the terms 'grey energy', 'hidden energy' or 'vergegenständlichte Energie', in this connection

To follow this approach further, exact data are required on the total energy consumption involved in the purchase and consumption of capital goods, consumer goods and services. An illustration of the importance of such investigations is given in Fig. 4.1, which represents the mean specific primary energy consumption in the production of natural yoghurt.[1] The study covers such varied aspects as the provision of fertilizers, fodder production, dairy cow husbandry, and transport and processing of milk in the dairy up to the transport of the finished yoghurt to the trade; and also includes aspects of packaging material production, the share of energy used in constructing buildings, plants and machinery as well as materials and supplies.

An assessment of the orders of magnitude involved will reveal that the energy used for producing the packaging material accounts for 41%, which is the highest share of the total energy consumption for yoghurt as a product. This is followed by

36

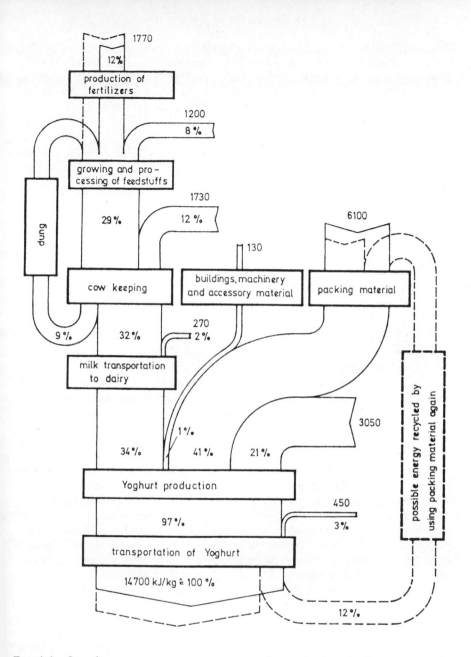

Fig. 4.1 Specific primary energy consumption for yoghurt production in the Federal Republic of Germany (1975/76). Data are given in kJ/kg and %.

the energy required for agricultural production up to the raw milk stage, with 32%. Only third in line comes the energy requirement of the dairy itself, with 21%, and the energy used in transport which makes up a total of 5% of the overall consumption. The use of dung and its importance in energy terms is also shown in Fig. 4.1, as is the significance of packaging material which is burnt in the incinerator after use.

The energy that goes into making 1 kg of yoghurt is five times as high, at 14 700 kJ/kg, as the nutritional value of the yoghurt (nutritional value 3100 kJ/kg). Fig 4.1 shows figures which are valid in the period under review and under the specific conditions of the technology used. If these conditions change and/or if the specific energy consumption changes in any production process, the figure will need to be revised.

METHODOLOGY

The basic conditions that need to be fulfilled to analyse energy consumption are:

definition of the system,
type of energy sources used,
energy supply structure within the system,
selection of representative technologies,
plant utilization,
indirect energy consumption,
energy consumed for the production of machinery and buildings,
evaluation of related products,
evaluation of recycled material.

These are discussed below. In addition, the two most important methods for determining the cumulated energy consumption are presented.

The maximum scope of the system or energy balance circle, as it is referred to, is determined by the objectives of the analysis. However, precise quantification of energies and materials considered is not possible because of the great expense involved, and, further, the contribution of many individual items is often negligible compared with the total energy consumption. Therefore, to reduce costs, a complex production scheme should be analysed only to the point at which all the major contributions can be determined. The circle of the analysis is defined according to criteria based on materials, time, location and technology. The choice of the appropriate balance circle must be based on a thorough knowledge of production processes and their role in the respective energy context. Individual subsystems to be analysed need to be determined in relation to the entire balance circle. It also has to be established whether the cumulative energy required in each step of the production process is to be analysed at plant level, or on a regional, national or international basis.

As for the time scope, it is important to appreciate that the manufacturing process of a product usually covers a significant period of time. Raw materials and semi-finished goods need to be acquired and/or produced at an earlier point in time than the finished product, and the same applies to machinery, materials and supplies. Apart from the fact that it would be practically impossible to determine the exact point in time at which all major feed materials need to be made available for production, the product flow would hardly be representative at any given moment because of short-term fluctuations in parameters and input variables. For determining the cumulative energy consumption, therefore, mean values should be used which cover a representative period of time.

Specific Energy Consumption Analysis

Basically, specific energy consumption values can be derived for the consumption of useful energy, final energy and/or primary energy.

The final energy consumption needed to produce an item does not reflect the energy requirement at primary source level, since all types of final energy are produced at varying conversion factors; nor does the final energy consumption include the non-energy consumption. For this reason, the primary energy consumption should be calculated in addition to the final energy consumption. Whenever international comparisons are carried out on the basis of primary energy consumption, such comparisons should account for the energy situation of the countries concerned, and in particular the energy conversion structure, which explains why the cumulated primary energy consumption is not an absolute yardstick. To be able to relate final energy consumption to primary energy consumption, it is imperative to distinguish between the energy demand met by electricity and that met by fuel. It is important to have a detailed knowledge of the type of fuel used and the structure of energy supply at micro- and macro-economic level.

The conversion of final users' electric energy consumption into primary energy consumption, for instance, in the Federal Republic of Germany, is based on the principle of substitution, taking into account a mean utilization of conventional thermal power plant of 34%, which includes electricity distribution losses. The efficiency of converting fossil fuels into secondary energy and the provision of either is currently based on an average of 93% in the Federal Republic of Germany. Approximately 7% of the energy content of fossil fuel is used for making available different types of secondary energy, the percentage being a mean value that covers all fossil fuels, such as coke, coal, fuel oil and gas.

Analysis of Energy Consumption

Two different levels of analysis are distinguished for determining the total specific energy consumption:

(i) Micro-analysis covers all investigations at plant level or at a series of defined plants; with the data collected being mostly unaggregated.

(ii) Macro-analysis denotes the processing of recorded energy consumption data at a higher level of aggregation; that is, including, as a minimum, whole groups of plants.

In the simplest case, and ignoring extended interconnections, the summation of specific energy consumptions is determined by the energy load of material flows. The only comprehensive listing of economic interdependence appears in the form of input/output tables listing flows of goods (excluding capital investment) in terms of money between the sectors of a national economy. Both these and the statistics of final energy consumption by industrial sectors permit a computation of the specific energy consumption per unit of output in monetary terms. However, this input/output method (2) is not suitable for the determination of the total energy consumption (1) because:

(i)   in the case of heterogeneous production, the mean values obtained cannot be used to determine the value of single products, since the price of a product is only very rarely proportional to its energy consumption;

(ii) an expression in monetary terms is not appropriate for all those goods which are sold at a discount or rebate;

(iii) it is difficult to compare the specific energy consumption of one year with that of another in view of the current inflation rate, variations in the pur-

39

chasing power of individual countries and a constantly changing product range.

Input/output analysis does not, therefore, really lend itself to a detailed and meaningful determination of the amount of energy consumed per product unit, mass or volume. It does, however, provide a useful tool for revealing the major centres of energy consumption in a process chain to be further analysed by means of micro-analysis. Micro-analysis produces results which are very close to the actual energy consumption. The production process is broken down into single production steps which are investigated in the context of production machinery and equipment. For each link in the production chain, energy and material balances are determined. Since considerable time and money goes into carrying out such analyses, only the links in the process chain that are relevant in energy consumption terms are investigated. This also explains why the share of total energy consumption hidden in working materials, machinery and buildings can often be neglected in the first approach. As indicated in various studies[1], the energy required to manufacture and construct working equipment is usually negligible compared with the energy needed to run it.

The analysis of the production process covers only the direct consumption of energy and material and, although indirect consumption is in many cases low compared with direct consumption, it cannot be completely neglected. Indirect energy consumption here means the energy needed for light, heat and air-condition plants, workshops and canteens; in other words, the requirement not directly related to the production process itself.

To obtain results which are representative of a type of product, suitable processes need to be identified. This constitutes the main problem involved in a process chain analysis. An exact approach would require research and measurements to be taken at a great number of plants and a sufficiently large sample size would be needed in order to determine energy characteristics and/or mean values of specific energy consumption. Such an approach will in most cases be discarded because of the great expense. Therefore, only a limited number of plants is analysed. In case the results obtained are to be generalized, the type and sequence of production steps and production flow, the type and size of plant and their technical features, mode of operation, and parameters of working conditions should be as representative as possible.

An important aid in determining a specific energy consumption is the energy characteristics of the plant being analysed. As an example, Fig. 4.2 shows the energy consumption of a dry mansard as a function of utilization. As in all processes of energy technology, a considerable part of energy consumption is not a function of the load but of the type or size of the system. Hence, the specific consumption decreases with rising throughput. The efficiency of a plant can therefore be greatly enhanced[3], if full use is made of existing capacities and downtimes are reduced or avoided. However, the relationship between specific energy consumption and utilization is only one parameter. Other factors influencing the specific energy consumption are, for instance, ambient temperature, varying conditions of production and the structure of energy supply.

Coupled Products

No clear line can be drawn in the case of energy demand for coupled products, since individual shares cannot be identified or attributed to physical or chemical processes. Therefore, arbitrary rules need to be established for the purpose of

40

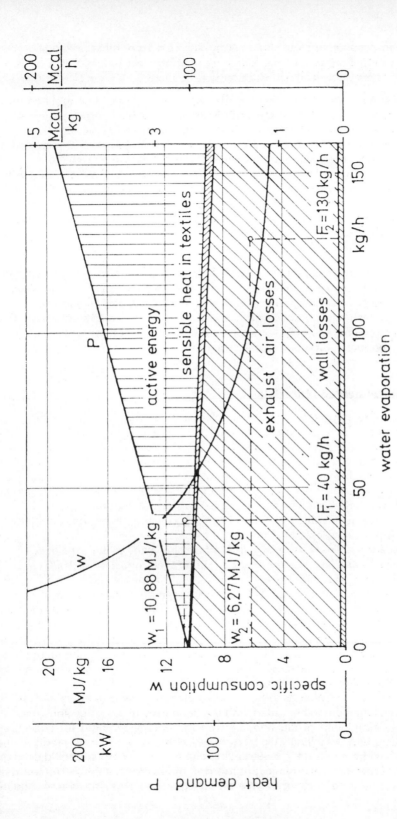

Fig. 4.2 Specific heat consumption and heat consumption per hour in a drying mansard.

energy consumption analysis. By analogy with cost accounting methods used in coupled production, any of the following methods can be used as a basis for allocating energy consumption shares:

(i) distribute the total energy consumed in the process among all coupled products according to physical parameters, such as mass and enthalpy;
(ii) analyse products in financial terms, such as price or revenue;
(iii) concentrate the entire energy consumption on the product regarded as the main product, leaving all other products as energy-free;
(iv) allocate according to the residual value method; i.e. attribute a specific energy consumption to those products for which data are available from other technological processes. The difference between these derived consumption data and the energy actually consumed in the coupled production is then allocated to the other, residual, coupled products, using one of the above methods.

Since the energy consumption derived for a coupled product varies with the mode of allocation, it is absolutely necessary that the mode of allocation is stated with the analysis. Generally, allocation based on physical parameters best reflects the energy consumed in physical processes; however, it is worth emphasising that there can be no absolutely right or wrong method for allocating shares of energy to coupled products, although some methods are more suited to particular situations.

Value of Recovered Materials

There is another important problem in determining the total energy consumption of industrial products, and that is the valuation of recycled material.

Losses of material occur at many stages of production. In the light of the present work it appears sensible to relate the total energy consumption of one production stage to the usable output of that particular production stage only. Since lost material is very often recovered and internally recycled, this material should be regarded as energy-free when re-used, except for the energy consumed for its reprocessing. The advantage in terms of energy consumption is thus attributed to all those products which contain recycled material.

This situation is illustrated in Fig. 4.3, which shows the material balance of the aluminium can and lid[5]. All figures are based on the production of 1000 cans. At the stage where aluminium sheet is produced, trimmings and other scrap are introduced as recycled material. This reduces the amount of aluminium to be produced from primary material from 32 kg to 25.8 kg per 1000 cans. In the can production phase another 20% of the feed material becomes production waste. Due to oil and paint contamination, this material cannot be used in the production of sheet aluminium, but is recast. More than 90% of this secondary aluminium is re-used to make cast products. Secondary aluminium is substantially less energy-intensive than aluminium from primary sources.

This raises the question as to how such a material flow is to be valued. Is the secondary aluminium to be loaded with the previously high energy consumption of primary aluminium production, or with the energy required for collecting, reprocessing and remelting only? There will either be an energy credit to the process chain from which the material flow comes, with a corresponding debit on the secondary aluminium energy requirement, or this credit/debit can be ignored, in addition, there is a range of intermediate assignations. As in the case of coupled

42

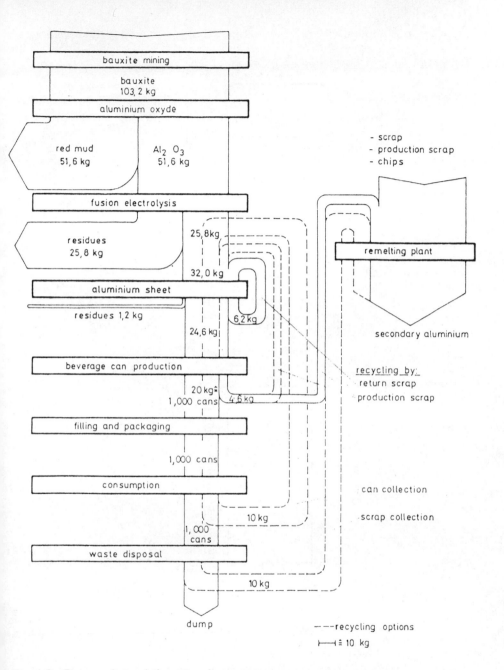

Fig. 4.3   Process chain of aluminium beverage cans.

production, no clearcut decision can be made as to which approach is the right one.

This chapter suggests that all technical, energy and cost inputs go into a process chain in order to produce and sell a product. In a free market economy, the revenue from selling the product covers all costs, including energy costs. The re-

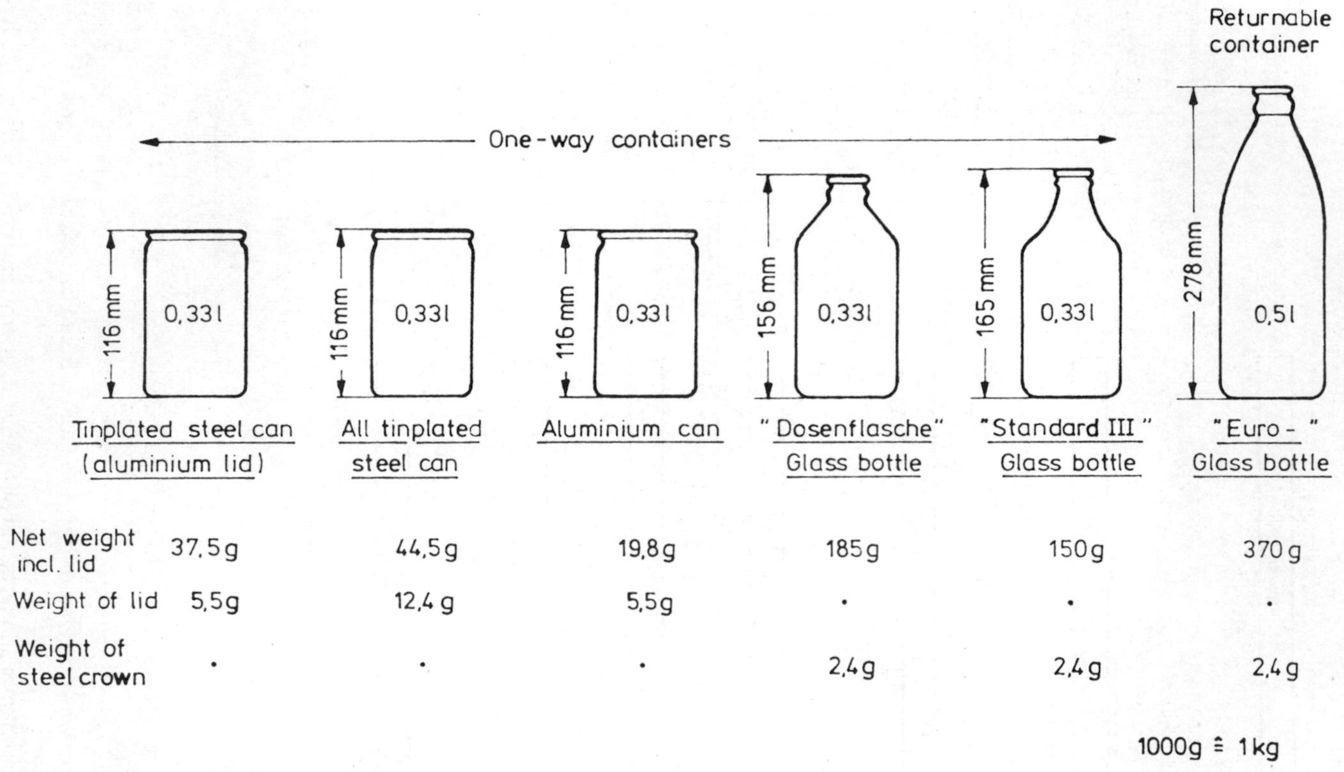

Returnable container

One-way containers

	Tinplated steel can (aluminium lid)	All tinplated steel can	Aluminium can	"Dosenflasche" Glass bottle	"Standard III" Glass bottle	"Euro-" Glass bottle
Size	116 mm	116 mm	116 mm	156 mm	165 mm	278 mm
Volume	0,33l	0,33l	0,33l	0,33l	0,33l	0,5l
Net weight incl. lid	37,5g	44,5g	19,8g	185g	150g	370g
Weight of lid	5,5g	12,4g	5,5g	•	•	•
Weight of steel crown	•	•	•	2,4g	2,4g	2,4g

1000g ≙ 1kg

Fig. 4.4   Beer container systems descriptions.

use of a product, if technically feasible, depends on the options for using recycled material and the efficiency with which these can be exploited. This also explains why the introduction of the concept of energy credit is unjustified. Hence, all products made from primary aluminium are charged with the high energy consumption involved in primary aluminium production, while products made of secondary aluminium are charged with the energy consumption involved in collecting, reprocessing and remelting scrap aluminium only.

A similar type of problem exists in the car industry which claims that, by increasing the proportion of aluminium built into the car, driving energy is conserved. The objection raised concerning the high energy demand of aluminium production is countered by the argument that the amount of aluminium built into the car is not lost and could be recovered from a scrapped vehicle and then reprocessed. However, detailed studies indicate that the types of aluminium used in automotive products are mainly malleable alloys of primary aluminium. There cannot, therefore, be a closed circuit in the production of primary aluminium and the recycling of scrap aluminium because of the inferior quality of secondary aluminium.

Cumulative or total energy analyses are mainly used for comparing the energy needed to make one product with the energy that goes into making an alternative product or using a different production process.

CASE STUDY: BEVERAGE CONTAINERS

Fig. 4.4 shows a selection of the most widely used disposable and re-usable containers for beer in the Federal Republic of Germany. The disposable containers include the 'Standard III' glass bottle and the 'Dosenflasche' (both can-sized) as well as three different types of metal cans for beer, i.e. aluminium can, tin can with aluminium cover, or tin can with tin cover. The re-usable container is the 0.5 litre 'Euro'-bottle. A study has investigated the overall energy required in the production of raw material, semi-finished goods and final consumption. In other words, the total energy consumption determined for packaging beer includes the amount of energy needed for producing the packing material, the container itself, filling and packaging.

Fig. 4.5 shows the final energy consumption per container, i.e. the total consumption of electricity and fuel. The surface area of all circles is proportional to the final energy consumption. A comparison of the disposable container systems shows that the tin can with aluminium lid and the Standard III bottle are about the same. If the specific final energy consumption for these two containers is set at 100% (at an average of 2850 kJ/container), then the can-sized bottle is 115% and the aluminium can 160% of the basic figure. The aluminium can, therefore, is the most energy-intensive disposable container. If, and when, the tin can with tin cover is launched onto the market, it will require only about 80% of the final energy presently needed for the lowest energy pack.

Compared to the aluminium can, even more energy is required for the re-usable Euro-bottle, when used only once. However, this assessment changes markedly if the bottled volume is set to a normalized quantity and the bottle is re-used (returned) as shown in Fig. 4.6. For a volume of one litre of beer, the 0.5 litre Euro-bottle used only once is as energy-intensive as the current disposable bottle. Only aluminium cans require about twice as much primary energy. The 0.5 litre Euro-bottle was conceived as a re-usable bottle. At 20 cycles, the primary energy

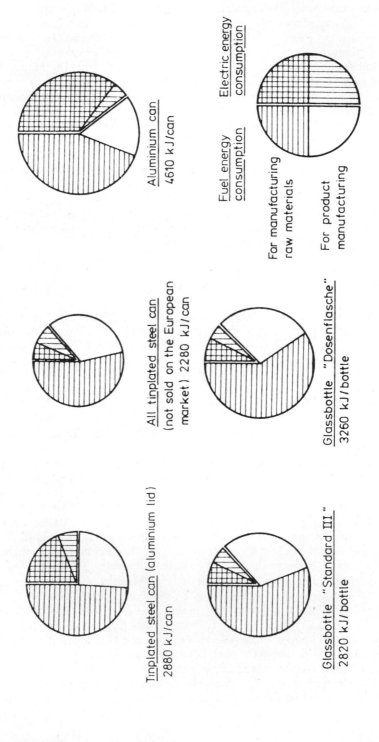

Tinplated steel can (aluminium lid)
2880 kJ/can

All tinplated steel can
(not sold on the European
market) 2280 kJ/can

Aluminium can
4610 kJ/can

Glassbottle "Standard III"
2820 kJ/bottle

Glassbottle "Dosenflasche"
3260 kJ/bottle

Fuel energy
consumption

Electric energy
consumption

For manufacturing
raw materials

For product
manufacturing

Fig. 4.5   Final energy consumption for one-way beer containers. All containers 0.33l two-piece cans.

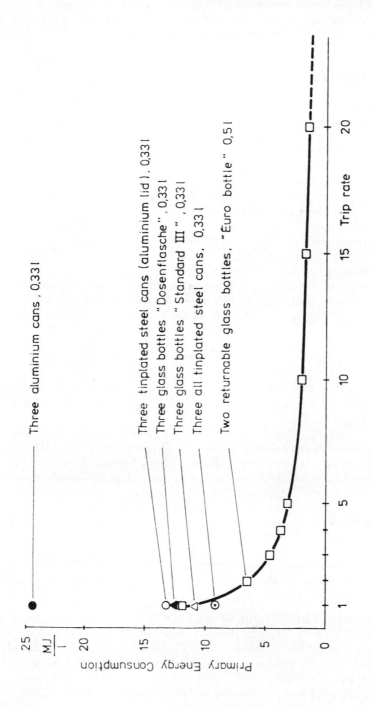

Three aluminium cans , 0,33 l

Three tinplated steel cans (aluminium lid), 0,33 l

Three glass bottles "Dosenflasche", 0,33 l

Three glass bottles "Standard III", 0,33 l

Three all tinplated steel cans, 0,33 l

Two returnable glass bottles, "Euro bottle" 0,5 l

Primary Energy Consumption

$\frac{MJ}{l}$

Trip rate

Fig. 4.6   Cumulated primary energy consumption for packaging 1 litre of beer.

consumption per cycle drops to one seventh of that of the disposable bottles, — all relating to the provision of one litre.

In addition to this energetic analysis, comparison of re-usable and disposable containers requires consideration of many additional aspects concerning different technical handling problems of these packaging systems.

CONCLUSIONS

The above discussion illustrates that the determination of the total energy consumption of industrial products raises a number of problems of definition. There are many studies and publications which are marred by the fact that they ignore or omit the basic prerequisites, and very often the figures presented are not even related to the type of energy consumption — useful, final or primary energy. A comparative analysis of energy consumption can, however, be based only on concise references and information on working conditions, etc. A thorough knowledge of the process chain and of the energy required to make a product provides useful clues as to where the total energy demand for the manufacture of a product can be reduced, for example by modifying materials, designs or process technologies.

In discussing questions of the total energy consumption, it must not be forgotten that energy consumption is only one aspect in the complex comparison of competing systems, and other technical, economical, ecological and social parameters have to be regarded as well, or even more.

REFERENCES

1. FLASCHAR, W., *Mikro- und makroanalytische Methoden zur Ermittlung des KSEV zum Herstellen von Verbrauchsgütern*, Thesis, Technical University of Munich, July 1979.
2. NIEHAUS, F., Nettoenergiebilanzen — Ein Hilfsmittel zur Analyse von Energienutzungsstrukturen, *Brennstoff-Wärme-Kraft* **27**, (10), 1975.
3. SCHAEFER, H., *Fundamentals and Methodology of Investigating Specific Energy Consumption*, Research Institute for Energy Utilization and Technology, Munich, 1975.
4. SCHAEFER, H., *Determination of Cumulative Specific Energy Consumption for the Manufacture of Tin-Plate Containers*, Research Institute for Energy Utilization and Technology, Munich, 1976.
5. SCHAEFER, H. and HARTMANN, D., *Kumulierter Energieverbrauch für das Verpacken von Bier und Dispersionsfarben*, Unveröffentlichte Studie der Forschungsstelle für Energiewirtschaft im Auftrag des Informations-Zentrum-Weissblech, Düsseldorf, 1981.

Professor Dr.-Ing. Helmut Schaefer studied light-current engineering at the Technical University of Karlsruhe and gained his doctorate in 1957 with a thesis on the energy demands of machine tools. He has been director at the Research Institute for Energy Utilization and Technology (now in Munich) since 1967. In 1969 he was appointed professor and director of the Institute for Energy Technology and Power Plant Engineering at the Technical University of Munich.

Dipl.-Ing. Detlef Hartmann studied mechanical engineering at the University of Stuttgart. From 1979 to 1980 he worked at the Research Institute for Energy Utilization and Technology in Munich. Since 1980 he has been a research assistant at the Institute for Energy Technology and Power Plant Engineering at the Technical University of Munich.

5 Energy Accounting for Aluminium

I. Wagner

INTRODUCTION

As a result of the energy crisis in 1973, the aluminium industry has suffered from growing criticism because of its high energy consumption. In order to counteract this criticism, the aluminium manufacturing and processing industry reacted with the moto 'Aluminium Saves Energy', which — to quote the journal *Metall* — was intended to 'give aluminium consumption a further boost'[1]. Many studies have delineated direct and indirect savings of energy, mainly in the areas of traffic, transportation and the packaging industry. The Austrian aluminium industry followed this general trend by trying to enter new markets by expanding and diversifying its range of products. An example is the planned manufacture of 400 million beverage cans per year by the nationalized Ranshofen Berndorf AG, 75% of whole output will be exported[2].

Since Austria has no bauxite deposits of its own, the raw material alumina is imported, primarily from the adjoining countries of Hungary, Yugoslavia and the Federal Republic of Germany. The electrolytic reduction, which is the most energy-intensive process, is carried out in Austria at the Ranshofen aluminium plant. This is Austria's biggest single consumer of energy, requiring 1.568 GWh_e in 1980 (4.88% of the country's total electricity production).

Tables 5.1 and 5.2 give some information on the Austrian aluminium and packaging industry. At present, no plans exist for any extension of primary aluminium pig capacity in Austria. Due to the small number of producers (three),

Table 5.1 The Austrian Aluminium Industry

Based on data from *European Aluminium Statistics* (1980) by permission of Aluminium-Zentrale E.V.

Capacity for primary aluminium pig (1980)		/tonne
Salzburger Aluminium GesmbH (Alusuisse)		12 000 t
Vereinigte Metallwerke Ranshofen-Berndorf AG		83 000 t
		95 000 t
	1979	1980
Production of primary aluminium	92 700 t	94 400 t
Production of secondary aluminium	8 700 t	14 300 t
+ Imports of aluminium	30 700 t	35 200 t
− Exports of aluminium	10 300 t	9 800 t
Apparent consumption of primary and secondary aluminium	120 800 t	116 400 t
Production of aluminium castings	12 400 t	13 000 t
Production of semi-fabricated aluminium products	95 000 t	88 200 t

Table 5.2   The Austrian Packaging Industry

Based on data from Österreichisches Institute für Verpackungswesen, Österreichische Verpackungsstatistik 1980, Vienna 1981 and information from Austrian firms.

	1979	1980
	Quantity/tonnes	
Total packaging production	844 688	890 450
Aluminium packaging (packages, foils, tubes, bottle caps, etc.)	21 777	20 950
Percentage of aluminium packaging group of total packaging production	2.6%	2.35%
	Value/million AS	
Total packaging production	11 609	13 336
Aluminium packaging	1 370	1 490
Percentage of aluminium packaging group of total packaging production	11.8%	11.2%

production figures are kept confidential, so that production groups are presented jointly in Austrian statistics. Certainly most of the foil production (more than 16 000 tonnes) has to be included in the figure. The packaging industry accounts for about 20% of the total aluminium consumption (crude metal) in Austria.

ALUMINIUM AS A PACKAGING MATERIAL

A primary demand of modern food distribution is long storage life with maximum preservation of quality. Aluminium can meet this demand, with its chemical resistance, low density, impermeability, good machining properties, deep-drawing qualities of sheets with inside coating, light package weight and lack of physiological toxicity. Fig. 5.1 shows the protective qualities of aluminium packages.

Disadvantages include formation of pores in thin foils, low ductility and susceptibility to corrosion. Aluminium-corroding agents include condenser water, glues and, especially, aggressive contents. High pH values as well as high salt contents, and several organic anions lead to aluminium corrosion. To control corrosion, the existing oxide layer is strengthened by anodic oxidation and lined with stoving lacquer, heat sealed varnish or synthetic foils, depending on the intended use. Cans for carbonated beverages are coated with vinyl resin[6]. Table

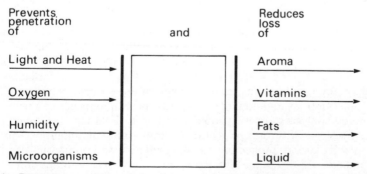

Fig. 5.1   Protective qualities of aluminium packages. (Data from Aluminium als Verpackungsmaterial[5].)

51

Table 5.3   Aluminium and Aluminium Alloy Packages

Reproduced from W. Hufnagel, Die Verwendung von Aluminium als Packstoff und Packmittel, *RGV — Handbuch Verpackung*, 1978.

Package	Material
foil, thin sheets	Al 99.5
tubes, cans and wrappings	Al 99.5
lightweight containers	Al 99.5; AlMn
cans and tins	AlMg 1; AlMg 2.5; AlMg 3; AlMn; AlMn 1 Mg 1
beverage cans	AlMn 1 Mg 1
can ends	same as cans and tins
tear-off lids	AlMn; AlMg 2.5; AlMg 4 Mn; AlMg 5
bottle caps	
table water	AlMg 1
tear-off caps	AlFeSi
wide-neck seals	Al 99.5; AlFeSi
packing wire	
for sealing clips	AlMg 3; AlMg 2 Mn 03
for tea bags	AlMg 2.5; AlMg 5
for staples	AlMg 5; high-tensile aluminium alloys

5.3 shows the range of packages produced from aluminium and aluminium alloys.

ENERGY ANALYSIS FOR ALUMINIUM PACKAGES

The considerable energy consumption for aluminium production must be set against the advantages of the package in protective and quality-preserving terms. The following energy analysis for aluminium packaging, and especially for foils, refers to Austrian conditions. The Gross Energy Requirement (GER) for this process analysis comprises direct energy inputs in the form of electricity and fuels, as well as indirect energy inputs for the production of raw materials consumed by the process and a proportionate share of working capital. The process flow GER depends significantly on the efficiency of electricity generation and of chemical processes, on the yield of ores, and on factors such as mode and route of transportation.

The analysis presented below used an efficiency of 47.3% for electricity generation in Austria. This rather high value, compared to the world average of 33.2%, is due to the high proportion of water power (70%) in Austria. In this analysis the GER is expressed in thermal and electrical kWh, as a high proportion of electrical energy is put directly into the process. This procedure facilitates comparison of energy requirements for each stage of the process between different countries. Although, as mentioned above, Austria is an importer of alumina, the present energy analysis starts with bauxite mining and alumina production.

Fig. 5.2 gives the GER for production of 1 tonne pure aluminium[8]. This starts with drilling and blasting, proceeding to shovel mining and preparation and transport of bauxite. At this stage the transport energy requirements are clearly dominant.

The following stage is the Bayer process, which includes the energy-intensive

52

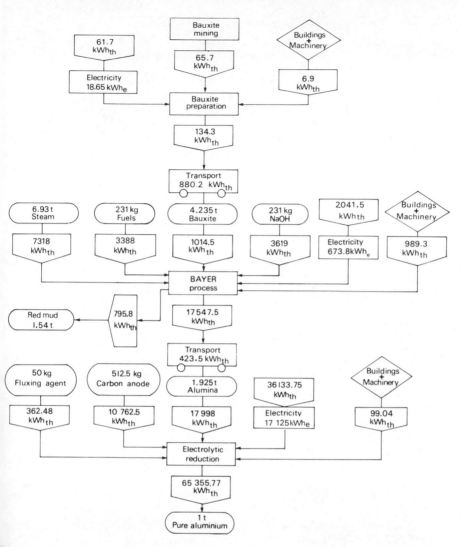

Fig. 5.2 Gross energy requirement: production of pure aluminium.

production of sodium hydroxide requiring the second highest energy input after steam generation. Production of 1 tonne of alumina generates 0.8 tonne of red mud as a by-product. Since generally only a small percentage (20%) of this is utilized, 80% of the GER for red mud disposal is added to the energy requirement for alumina. The GER of the Bayer process accounts for 26% of the total GER for pure aluminium production. New decomposition technologies, such as alumina calcination in a fluidized bed, could achieve considerable savings of energy.

The next stage gives the GER for electrolytic reduction. As expected, electricity accounts for the highest energy input, followed by the energy input for alumina and for the carbon anode. The GER for 1 kg of pure aluminium thus amounts to 65.36 kWh$_{th}$ or 235.3 MJ. For electrolytic reduction and the subsequent stages of the process an efficiency of power generation was calculated at 47.3%, this

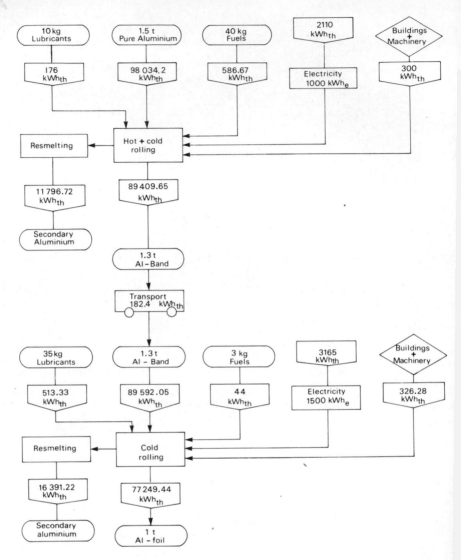

Fig. 5.3 Gross energy requirement: production of aluminium foil.

analysis being valid for domestic production of aluminium sheets and foils in Austria.

Fig. 5.3 shows the derivation of the GER for production of aluminium foil. Production of aluminium band is carried out at the primary aluminium production works, whereas aluminium foil is manufactured by the packaging industry. Production of 1.3 tonne of aluminium band requires one hot rolling and one cold rolling operation, generating 0.2 tonne of aluminium scrap, which is recycled after adequate treatment. The recoverable scrap provides aluminium band with an energy bonus minus energy requirements for treatment (5%) and accompanying losses (5%)[9]. Transportation of aluminium band to the foil manufacturer is effected by train.

Teich AG is the most important Austrian producer of aluminium foil, and has four rolling mills producing aluminium foils of 0.007 to 0.20 mm thickness. Additional cold rolling produces 1 tonne of foil with a thickness of 0.008 mm from 1.3 tonne of aluminium band. The resulting 0.3 tonne of scrap is fed to the resmelting process after baling, or processed to aluminium powder[9]. Again the foil may be credited with the energy value of the scrap, minus treatment and losses, resulting in an energy requirement of 77.25 kWh_{th}, or 278.1 MJ, for 1 kg of aluminium foil with a thickness of 0.008 mm.

Thus it is necessary to balance the energy and material requirements for the packaging material on the one hand and the advantages of the package on the other hand. A main factor is the ratio between the quantity of the packaging material and the value and quantity of the packed product.

An example for a favourable balance is the wrapping of butter[10]. Wrapping of 250 g of butter needs only 0.8 g of aluminium foil with a thickness of 0.008 mm, corresponding to a GER of 0.225 MJ. With the nutritional value of the butter being 8.15 MJ, the energy requirement for the wrapping accounts for 3% of the energy content of the packed product. By also considering agricultural inputs, the ratio between energy input for the package and the GER for the packed product becomes 1:100. However, when using extremely thin aluminium foil, its lack of strength requires bonding with other materials, such as paper and plastics, or the use of a second protective film, as in chocolate wrapping, so that the GER for the additional packaging material should be included in the energy requirement for the package. Furthermore, recycling of the used foil and composite material is rather difficult.

The cost/benefit relationship deteriorates with the rising volume of packaging material and diminishing value of the packed product. Examples are single portion packs for butter, and beverage cans.

MATERIAL AND ENERGY FLOW FOR ONE-WAY AND MULTI-WAY CONTAINERS

As a detailed illustration of the significance and variation of energy consumption, an example of beer packaging shows the various material and energy flows for returnable bottles, one-way glass bottles and aluminium cans (Fig. 5.4).

In 1980, Austrian beer consumption totalled 760 600 000 litres, of which

29%	was in barrels and kegs	
67.5%	was in re-usable 0.5 l bottles ⎫	70% in re-usable bottles
2.7%	was in re-usable 0.33 l bottles ⎭	
1%	was in 0.33 l cans[11]	

Multi-way Bottles   70% of beer is currently packed in re-usable glass bottles. The bottle weight is 340–345 g for a 0.5 l bottle and 310 g for a 0.33 l bottle, and average bottle circulation is 28–33 trips. The volume of beer bottles circulating in Austria is estimated to be 80–100 million, corresponding to 34 000 tonnes of glass passing between the filling industry, retailers and consumers, and embodying an energy content of 0.65 PJ (taking the energy content of 1 kg of glass bottles as 19 MJ[12]). Replacement of bottles is approximately 1% per year, corresponding to 0.0065 PJ/year. The net energy requirement is thus 0.66 PJ/year.

One-Way Bottles   If 70% of the beer were contained in one-way bottles (so-

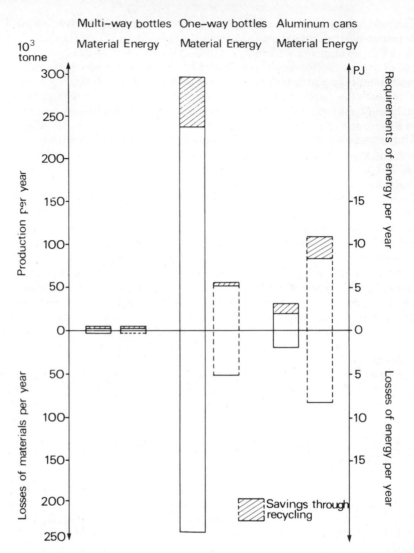

Multi-way bottles   One-way bottles   Aluminum cans
Material Energy   Material Energy   Material Energy

10^3 tonne

Fig. 5.4 Comparison of multi-way and one-way packaging systems: materials and energy requirements of beer containers.

called can bottles of 0.33 l, weighing 185 g), 1600 million pieces per year would be required, representing a glass volume of 296 000 tonnes with an energy content of 5.62 PJ. Assuming a recycling rate of 20%, as presently the case in Austria, energy savings of about 8% are possible in smelting by substituting old glass (cullet) for raw material[13]. This gives a net requirement of 5.1 PJ/year.

Aluminium Cans If 70% of the beer production were contained in 0.33 l aluminium cans, the annual can requirement would be 1600 million. Production of one 20-g can requires a GER of 6.88 MJ[12], so that this type of beverage package would consume a total of 11.01 PJ and 32 000 tonnes of aluminium. At a recycling rate of 38%, as achieved in the USA (1980)[14], 12 160 tonnes of aluminium waste would result, but about 12% of material and 5% of energy are lost by treatment and resmelting process. The energy bonus amounts to 22% (2.4 PJ) of the corresponding energy requirements of pure aluminium, giving a net requirement of 8.6 PJ/year. Depending on the quality of the waste, utilization is possible either in the same field or for producing casting alloys.

Comparing energy input and raw material requirements for the various packages, the difference between one-way and multi-way packages is found to be a factor of about 10. The comparison should also take into account that multi-way packages require increased energy input for transportation, washing and handling of returned bottles. Nevertheless, several studies have already shown the clear superiority, in terms of both energy and material consumption, of the re-usable system, even after a few cycles, depending on the method of calculation and various external factors[15] (see Chapters 4, 6 and 9).

Even for a partial change-over from multi-way packages to one-way packages (aluminium cans), a well organized recycling system is indispensible in reducing the enormous quantities of energy and materials involved. At present, relatively few beverage cans are used in Austria. Recently, however, major Austrian beverage producers seem intent on changing over to aluminium cans, which fits in well with the above-mentioned expansions plans of the Ranshofen aluminium plant. So far, energy considerations have made approval by the Austrian Minister of Trade and Commerce subject to presentation of a detailed recycling concept. More widely, the EC Commission is preparing proposals for guidelines to limit the use of disposable packages and to promote returnable packages and recycling material[16].

RECYCLING IN AUSTRIA

Processing and Energy Requirements

In Austria, wastes from aluminium production are also recycled. However, due to the small quantities of aluminium involved, recycling from household waste is not provided for, even at the recently opened Rinter AG waste separation plant in Vienna.

Aluminium waste is furnished primarily by scrap dealers and fed into the resmelting process. This process requires an energy input for transportation, electrical energy, buildings, and machinery for shredding. In addition, smelting and refining need fuel, fluxing agents and chlorine gas. The required rate of fluxing agent depends on the non-metallic proportion of the charge. The GER for 1 kg of secondary aluminium is typically 3.6 kWh_{th} or 12.96 MJ, representing 5.3% of the GER for 1 kg of primary aluminium (derived above as 65.36 kWh_{th} or 235.3 MJ)[8]. The analysis is based on ideal purity conditions. Collection and pre- and post-separation processes for heterogeneous materials would, however, increase energy requirements (and cost) significantly.

Mixed scrap from aluminium alloys may be re-used only as casting alloy, as the contamination tolerance values are too low for malleable alloys. Plastic-coated scrap requires initial thermal treatment. As mentioned above, foil scrap is often processed to aluminium powder. Laminated, enamelled or imprinted foil scrap is pretreated in a rotary kiln at temperatures between 300 and 400 °C to remove organic material[17].

Consumers and Recycling of Packaging

Large quantities of packaging materials such as glass, paper, plastics and metal are accepted by the consumer with the commodity purchased. For reasons of rationalization, the packaging industry and retail trade attempt to transfer the problems of packaging waste and material recovery (waste disposal, etc.) to the consumer or the community by pushing the introduction of one-way packages. The increased cost of these one-way packages and of waste disposal must be borne by the consumer. Thus, the ecologically aware consumer is given the responsibility of recycling materials which comprise a considerable energy input.

There are three ways to achieve recycling:

Re-use of containers   The well established system of multi-way containers offers the advantage of minimum loss of material and energy. By standardizing bottle shapes and sizes for table water and non-alcoholic beverages, this system would be as effective and advantageous as the Euro-beer-bottle by facilitating easy return of all containers by consumers, exchangeability of bottle crates and reduction of transport costs[18]. Some beverage producers are, however, fighting such standardization considering particular shapes to be company trademarks. However, the same companies are quite content to fill the same beverage into uniformly shaped cans and differentiate brands by affixing different labels.

Recovery by separate collection (source separation)   Increased use of one-way containers and the consequent growth of waste has, in some countries, resulted in separate collection of used materials such as glass, plastic and metal. In 1980, Austria achieved a recycling rate of 20% for used glass, with 90% of the population accessible to a glass collection system[19]. In the USA an aluminium can recycling rate of 38% could be reached in 1980 — with a market share of aluminium beverage cans of 83%[14]. The aluminium can and beverage industry has created aluminium waste can collection systems by paying up to 1.5 US cents per can to buy them back[20]. Use of the deposit system is another alternative to recover scrap as is practised in the national parks. Expansion of collection sites and activation of the 'environmentally sensitized' consumer should also increase the recycling rate. In general, separate collection of plastic material is not yet economical. However, by introducing the PET (polyester) bottle the Federal Republic of Germany intends to create a recycling system to recover polyester and use it for *other* purposes after adequate treatment. By providing adequate information to the consumer, the quality of the recovered material, and hence value, could be improved considerably by reducing the proportion of foreign substances.

Post-collection sorting of waste (central sorting)   Waste disposal is the easiest way for the consumer to eliminate waste, and post-collection recycling can be practised, such as incineration with recovery of heat, gasification and pyrolysis, and complex mechanical separation processes to recover valuable materials. Depending on the process configuration, various fractions such as ferrous and non-ferrous metals, fibres and plastics are separated and recycled as secondary raw materials. This practice, which so far is carried out only to a limited extent, produces materials at a much lower quality, and hence lower value, than those recovered from separate collection[21].

CONCLUSIONS

The general trend is to prefer one-way containers, because it is easier for the producer, the distributor and the consumer. A change from returnable containers to non-returnable containers is a very difficult move to reverse. From the point of view of resource conservation, re-use is preferable to recycling, especially for short-life products such as packaging. The most effective material and energy economics can be made by longevity of the products themselves and material-conscious design in products and packaging. To improve quantity and quality of recovered materials significantly, it is not only necessary to optimize collection systems by improving information and motivation for the consumer, but the package itself should be adapted to the recycling process.

REFERENCES

1. Aluminiumindustrie zwischen Hoffnung und Sorge, *Metall*, **32** (1978) 524-525.
2. VMW will auf Aludosen nicht verzichten, *Die Presse*, 2 April 1980.
3. ALUMINIUM-ZENTRALE (Ed.), *European Aluminium Statistics 1980*, Düsseldorf (1981).
4. ÖSTERREICHISCHES INSTITUT FÜR VERPACKUNGSWESEN, *Österreichische Verpackungsstatistik 1980*, Vienna, 1981.
5. Verband Schweizerischer Aluminiumfolien-Walzwerke, *Aluminium als Verpackungsmaterial*, Bern, 1978.
6. HEISS, R., *Verpackung von Lebensmitteln*, New York, 1980, pp. 97-98.
7. HUFNAGEL, W., Die Verwendung von Aluminium als Packstoff und Packmittel, *RGV — Handbuch Verpackung*, Berlin 1978, 4510 p. 6.
8. WAGNER, I. and GRITTNER, P., Die Aussagefähigkeit der Energieanalyse und die Grenzen ihrer Anwendbarkeit, *Proceedings of the International Congress on Commodity Science 'Natural Resources'* Triest/Italy, 1978, pp. 151-165; and GRITTNER, P., *Thermodynamische Betrachtung des Wertes und Energieanalyse von Aluminium und Kupfer*, Dissertation, Wirtschaftsuniversität, Vienna, 1978.
9. Ref. 5, p. 111, and information from Austrian firms.
10. SPRENG, D.T., Zur Aussagekraft produktbezogener Energiebilanzen, *Metall*, **31** (1977) 1357-1360.
11. Information from the Verband der Brauereien, Vienna.
12. BOUSTEAD, I. and HANCOCK, G.F., *Handbook of Industrial Energy Analysis*, Ellis Horwood, Chichester/John Wiley, New York, 1979, p. 319, 346.
13. TUROWSKI, R., Entlastung der Rohstoff- und Primärenergiebilanz der Bundesrepublik Deutschland durch Recycling von Hausmüll, *Berichte der Kernforschungsanlage Jülich*, No. 1455, Jülich, 1977, pp. 65 et seq.
14. TESTIN, R.F., Entwicklung bei Aluminiumrecycling in den USA, *Metall*, **35** (1981) 789-791.
15. ÖSTERREICHISCHES INSTITUT FÜR VERPACKUNGSWESEN, Systemvergleich Einwegverpackung — Mehrwegverpackung, *Schriftenreihe Verpackungsforschung* No. 7, Vienna, 1977.
16. WOOLFE, J. (Ed.), *Waste Management*, Commission of the European Communities, European Conference on Waste Management, Wembley UK, 1980, Dordrecht, Holland/Boston, USA/London, England, 1981.

17. SCHNEIDER, K., *Die Verhüttung von Aluminiumschrott, 3rd ed.*, Berlin, 1970.
18. BOJKOW, E., Studie zur Typenreduzierung bei 1.0 l und 0.35 l Pfandflaschen für alkoholfreie Erfrischungsgetränke, Heil-, Tafel- und Mineralwasser, *Ernährung/Nutrition*, **5** (1981) 336-337.
19. FISCHER, F. and SCHÄFER, E., *Abfall. Beiträge zur Darstellung der Umweltsituation in Österreich*, Österreichisches Bundesinstitut für Gesundheitswesen, Vienna, 1981.
20. ROCHOLL, P., Über die Verarbeitung von Aluminiumschrotten zu Knetlegierungen, *Metall*, **35** (1981) 792-795.
21. BRIDGWATER, A.V. and LIDGREN, K. (Eds.) *Household Waste Management in Europe: economics and techniques*, Van Nostrand Reinhold, 1981.

Ingrid Wagner graduated as Doctor of Chemistry from the University of Vienna. She is an assistant and lecturer for chemical technology and environmental protection at the Institute of Technology and Commodity Science of the Economic University of Vienna. Her research work centres on material and energy questions for technical products and studies of the flow of heavy metal contamination in the environment.

6 Comparing the Energy Requirements of Beverage Container Systems

I. Boustead

INTRODUCTION

Since the early work of Hannon[1,2] the energy associated with the production and use of beverage containers has received considerable attention[3-7]. In part this is due to the relative simplicity of the system in providing a useful model for testing analysis techniques, but by far the greatest spur to this activity has been the expressed desire of many national and international government agencies to regulate the use of certain types of container for environmental and conservation reasons. The preparation of such legislation should be soundly based upon accurate analysis of the environment impact of the different container types. Unfortunately, many discussions of proposed legislation have been fraught with arguments from both proponents and opponents often supported by totally opposite interpretations of essentially the same information.

This chapter therefore considers whether these disagreements arise because the basic data are incorrect or whether they arise from misinterpretations of essentially correct data. The chapter is in two parts. The first part considers some of the more important problems that arise in performing energy analyses and which are often forgotten or neglected when the results are subsequently used. The second part examines briefly some of the different types of comparison that can be made of different container systems using selected examples from a recent study of UK practices[7] in order to illustrate the use of energy data.

DEFINING THE SYSTEM

The methodology of energy analysis has been widely discussed elsewhere[8-10], but essentially *any* collection of industrial operations can be enclosed by a system boundary to form a production system, and the energy consumed *by this system* is the energy requirement of the process. Note that this allows *any* collection of operations to be considered.

Of crucial importance to the analysis is the definition of the system. This can be thought of in two parts. First, the component operations enclosed by the system boundary should be specified. This essentially defines the input and output materials and the processing route employed. This is vital in determining the extent of the system; for example, it will demonstrate whether all materials streams are traced back to the extraction of raw materials from the earth or whether some ancillary feeds are omitted. It is quite wrong to compare, say, a glass bottle system where all inputs are raw materials in the earth with an aluminium can system which starts with sheet aluminium, yet this has been done. Second, there is a need for a more abstract definition of the function of the system. For example, in the case of the beverage container industry, the aim of the system may be to deliver a single container to the consumer, or to deliver a volume of beverage. This second requirement may seem trivial, but it is surprising how many false results arise from comparing energy per unit volume for containers of different capacities; such comparisons are invalid because they involve two variables — the energy efficiency of the container system and the influence of container size on system energy requirements — factors which are considered later.

It must be emphasised that energy requirements refer to energy consumption *by a system* and not a product. There is convenient, but unfortunate, tendency to refer to 'the energy of the glass bottle' or 'the energy of tin cans', but these are misleading since the container itself is only one factor that must be specified in a proper definition of the system. As a result of considering the system variables within the beverage container industry it has been shown[11] that at least eight parameters must be specified to identify a container system adequately. These are.

(i)   *Container specification.* This requires a definition of:
       (a) container type (i.e. glass bottle, metal can, etc.),
       (b) container size (i.e. volume capacity),
       (c) empty container mass,
       (d) container composition in the case of cans and PET bottles (e.g. three-piece tinplate can, PET bottle with polyethylene base),
       (e) whether the container is returnable or non-returnable.

(ii)   *Beverage type.* The beverage type needs definition because it can significantly affect filling energy (e.g. beers are pasteurized whereas soft drinks are not).

(iii)   *Empty container delivery.* This must be defined because different packaging is used (hence affecting the energy associated with the production of ancillary packaging materials) and different forms of packaging affect stacking densities on lorries and hence transport energies.

(iv)   *Type of closure.* For bottles, a distinction must be made between crown closures, standard aluminium screw closures, large aluminium screw closures (for wide-mouth bottles) and rip cap closures, each of which possess different production energies.

(v)   *Outer packaging after filling.* The method of packing filled containers is a significant contributor to energy requirements because of the different energies required to produce the different packaging materials. This also affects the packing density, which influences subsequent transport energies.

(vi)   *Trunking.* The most significant variable affecting the energy associated with long-distance trunking (apart from container size) is the nature of the return load. Empty return loads can almost double delivery energies.

(vii)   *Retail distribution.* A distinction must be made between distribution systems with multiple dropping-off points, such as are needed for pubs, cafes and small shops, and systems with only one or two dropping-off points as with supermarkets.

(viii) *Retail sale.* The essential difference here is between consumption on and off the premises because this influences the energy required to operate the outlet.

Frequently the resource requirements of beverage container systems are discussed in relation to an 'average' system. It follows from the above considerations, therefore, that an 'average' system can only be specified by defining 'average' values for each of the above parameters. When expressed in this form it is clear how difficult, if not impossible, it is to refer to such 'average' systems; for example, what is the average mass and volume capacity of a returnable bottle? Despite this obvious complication, most discussions of container systems continue to be carried out at the level of 'returnable versus non-returnable containers'.

In addition to the need for precise definition of the main operations of a beverage container system, a further problem arises from the difficulty in deciding whether a particular operation should be included in the overall system. Examples of these marginal operations are the heating and lighting of factories and ancillary operations such as workshops, offices and sales operations, most of which do not contribute directly to the processing and handling of the materials flows within the system, but are nevertheless regarded as essential by the component companies to sustain their operations. Energy analysts differ on the need to include such functions, since there are no conclusive technical factors to act as a guide. Their inclusion is therefore largely a matter of choice but, whatever the decision, it should be clearly stated whether or not they are included.

Two ancillary operations of special interest are the energy of labour and the energy used to construct buildings and machinery (capital energy).

The energy of labour can be estimated by recognizing that the average energy extracted by a human being from food is of the order of 0.144 MJ per day per kilogram of bodyweight[12]. For a typical human, of mass 70 kg, this corresponds to an average daily consumptionof 10 MJ. Most of this energy is needed to sustain the human as a living organism and so, at most, the energy that can be attributed to his industrial activity is 5 MJ per day. As will be seen later, this is negligible compared with the energy consumed by the machines he operates and so can usually be ignored without introducing any serious error into the calculations.

The energy associated with capital plant is also frequently ignored, because detailed calculations for a variety of processes show that its contribution seldom exceeds 2% of the energy consumed in the direct processing operations[10, 13, 14]. There is, however, one area in which capital energy is very significant and that is transport. It has been shown, for example, that the construction of a 20 tonne payload lorry adds 15% to the energy directly consumed as fuel in running the vehicle[10]. In systems such as the beverage container system, which involve a considerable number of transport operations, omission of capital energy can introduce significant errors into results.

It is clear from the brief discussion above that there can be no 'correct' system to describe an industrial process. Thus, when energy requirements are calculated, a description of the relevant system should form part of the results so that it is quite clear which operations are included. Moreover, results should be presented in such a form that they can be readily revised to accommodate any desired changes.

METHODOLOGY OF ENERGY ANALYSIS

The procedure for calculating energy requirements of industrial systems is deceptively simple. Once the system is defined, the total system energy is simply the total energy passing into the system across the system boundary. This energy requirement can be made independent of throughput by normalizing with respect to some flow parameter. In many processing systems, this is frequently the mass of output product from the system. However, in the case of complete beverage container systems where all raw materials are drawn from the earth and the system includes all operations up to final disposal of container and packaging materials, the output is seldom known and it is usual to normalize with respect to an internal flow. This is usually chosen as either the number of containers or the volume of beverage delivered to the consumer. Note that the choice of either normalizing parameter will eliminate throughput dependence, but the final numerical results will, in general, be different.

FUEL-PRODUCING INDUSTRIES

Most energy analyses are intended to describe the total energy resource that must be extracted from the earth in order to support the system. Hence, included within the system will be those sectors of the fuel-producing industries which provide the fuels for the remaining operations within the system. In addition, it must also be remembered that the fuel-producing industries themselves consume fuels; i.e., of the total energy input to the fuel producing industries, only a fraction will reach the consumer. This is usually summarized by quoting a fuel production efficiency defined as the fraction of the total energy input which is delivered to the consumer. The value will change from one fuel to another and various estimates have been made for these efficiencies. Table 6.1 gives a set of values calculated for current UK practices. Thus, knowing the energy content of the fuel delivered to the consumer, the energy needed to produce and deliver this fuel can be readily calculated from Table 6.1.

Each of the entries in Table 6.1 is calculated by examining the sequence of processes through which the fuel must pass from extraction from the earth up to delivery to the consumer. It therefore depends not only upon the technology employed but also on transport distances and distribution practices. Thus the efficiency of fuel production will vary from country to country and an identical factory operated in two different countries will exhibit different total energy requirements which can be very marked indeed. Clearly, a set of energy requirements calcul-

Table 6.1   Energy Associated with Fuels (UK Practice)

Fuel	Unit	Fuel prod'n & delivery energy/MJ	Energy content of fuel /MJ	Total energy /MJ	Production efficiency %
Coal	kg	1.39	28.01	29.40	95
Coke	kg	3.93	25.42	29.35	87
Electricity	kWh$_e$	10.80	3.6	14.40	25
Natural gas	therm	8.67	105.44	114.11	92
Manufactured gas	therm	41.21	105.44	146.65	72
Heavy fuel oil	litre	8.57	40.98	49.55	83
Medium fuel oil	litre	8.50	40.92	49.42	83
Light fuel oil	litre	8.29	40.18	48.47	83
Gas oil	litre	7.42	37.84	45.26	84
Kerosine	litre	6.96	36.53	43.49	84
Diesel	litre	7.45	37.71	45.16	84
Gasoline	litre	6.85	35.97	42.82	84
LPG	kg	8.89	50.00	58.89	85
Lubricating oil	litre	8.29	40.92	49.21	83
Grease	kg	8.89	42.60	51.49	83

ated for a process operated in one country cannot be regarded as having universal application until the fuel production efficiencies have been modified.

Of particular importance in this regard is the efficiency of electricity production, and it is useful to consider this problem briefly since most systems are very sensitive to the choice of electricity production efficiency. A large proportion of the electricity demand in most countries is satisfied by thermal generation. Thermodynamic considerations alone indicate that with best possible practice the conversion from heat to electricity will have an efficiency of the order of 45%. Using the most efficient primary fuel (coal) as the source of thermal energy and allowing only 5% for all other losses in the production and distribution system, it is clear that an upper limit for the efficiency of thermally generated electricity will be of the order of $(0.45 \times 0.95 \times 0.95) \times 100 = 41\%$. However when oil is used this upper limit falls to 35%.

In practice two factors can significantly affect the average efficiency of electricity generation used in any process. First, if use is made of hydroelectric power, the average generation efficiency rises sharply to values as high as 90%[3]. The second modification is that when an industrial site can forecast a sustained demand, it is frequently economic to generate electricity thermally on-site. The advantage is the elimination of transmission losses, which can improve overall efficiency by up to 5%. One word of caution however; many one-site generation facilities co-generate steam and electricity. Such a practice is very efficient when there is a sustained demand for both steam and electricity and the *overall* efficiency calculated as the total energy output (steam plus electricity) as a fraction of the total energy input (as primary fuel at the facility) can be as high as 80%. However, the efficiency of electricity generation is still governed by thermodynamic considerations so that the efficiency of electricity generation is not 80%, but at best of the order of 45%. Making the erroneous assumption that electricity can be generated at 80% efficiency has led to some very strange results[15, 16].

Because of variations in fuel production and delivery efficiency from country to country, it is important that energy requirements of beverage container systems, calculated using the efficiencies of different countries, should not be compared without first correcting the data to the same base. If this is not done, the comparison has more to do with comparing the efficiencies of the different fuel production industries than with comparing beverage container systems. While this may seem obvious, it is one of the commonest problems in practice. Accepting that the need will arise to convert energy data to different bases for comparative purposes, it is clear that the two contributions to total energy associated with a fuel (i.e. production and delivery energy and energy delivered to the consumer) should be kept separate as in Table 6.1. Moreover, because of the different production efficiencies of the different fuel types, it is also necessary to keep separate the contributions from the different fuel types. Unfortunately, this latter requirement leads to unmanageably large tables, but one method that has been used successfully to simplify the presentation, while still retaining most of the essential information, is to aggregate the fuels into three groups — electricity, oil fuels and other fuels. This procedure has been adopted here and its usefulness can be judged in the later tables.

FEEDSTOCK ENERGY

One factor of special importance in packaging is the use of feedstock energy.

Plastics, paper, board and wood are all made from materials which could be used as fuels. If the energy requirements of a system is to represent the energy that must be extracted from the earth to support the industry, then the energy associated with the use of these materials must be included in the energy requirement. In accounting for feedstock there are two considerations to remember.

First, feedstock energy is the energy associated with *input* materials and not output materials. Thus, recorded feedstock energy will be influenced by materials losses within the process so that reducing losses will reduce feedstock energy. Because of this and because of possible changes in chemical structure of the material during processing, feedstock energy is *not* the energy that can be recovered from a material if it is subsequently reclaimed and burnt.

The second consideration concerns wood and wood products. It is often held that, because wood is a renewable resource, its feedstock energy should not be included in the energy required to produce these commodities. However, there are two arguments against this view. First, the paper and board industry use the by-products of pulp production as a fuel in integrated pulp and paper mills so that wood must be properly regarded as a fuel even though, in general, its use as a fuel is restricted. Second, many schemes which reclaim paper and board as a fuel (e.g. in the production of fuel pellets from domestic refuse) rely on the original input of feedstock energy. Advocates of such reclamation schemes readily point out the energy savings resulting from the recovery of such materials. However, if feedstock energy is omitted in the production of the original wood-based products, then it must also be omitted from the energy recovered in such reclamation schemes, and under such conditions reclamation of refuse-derived fuel appears to be singularly unfavourable from an energy viewpoint.

PARTITIONING

One major problem of energy analysis is the absence of detailed monitoring of materials and energy flows inside most factories. Frequently the best that can be achieved is the total consumption of energy and materials and the total output of different products. Under such circumstances the only way that the energy associated with the different production streams can be evaluated is by mathematical partitioning.

There is no general theory of partitioning and each case must be dealt with individually, but the aim is to attribute fuel consumption to each component sub-system in such a way that it represents as closely as possible the consumption actually used by the sub-system. A detailed example of a factory analysis is given in reference 10 to highlight the various techniques, but one relevant example that is useful here is the co-generation problem mentioned earlier.

A variety of different plant designs are in use, but the principles of the analysis are most easily demonstrated using the simple numerical example of Fig. 6.1. The primary aim is to provide a gross description of the system and for this reason no analysis of the component sub-systems is required. The numerical values shown in Fig. 6.1 represent energy flows (in arbitrary units) normalized to an input of 100 units of primary energy from the earth. In practice most, if not all, of the steam will be passed through the turbine before being distributed as steam. However, this mechanism may be illustrated schematically as shown in Fig. 6.1 in which the turbine extracts only 8 units of energy to satisfy the demand of the electricity production and delivery sub-system.

66

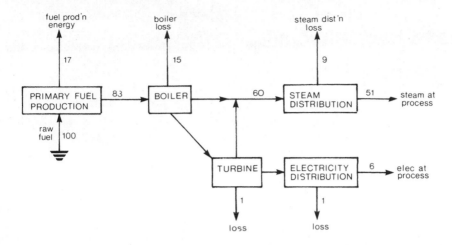

Fig. 6.1 Schematic flow diagram of typical energy flows (in arbitrary units) in a simplified co-generation system. See text for a more detailed explanation.

To demonstrate that the system of Fig. 6.1 satisfies the more commonly used criteria applied to such systems, the thermal efficiency of the boiler is $100 \times (60 + 8)/83$ or 82%, and the overall thermal efficiency of the cogeneration facility (excluding the production of the primary fuel) is $100 (51 + 6)/83$ or 69%. The production of the primary fuel is based on data for oil fuel production (83%, Table 6.1).

Of the energy losses from the system, the loss of 9 units in steam distribution can be directly attributable to the provision of steam. Similarly, the loss of 1 unit from the turbine and a further 1 unit from the electricity distribution system can be directly attributable to the provision of electricity. However, the boiler loss and the energy used to produce the primary fuel contribute directly to both steam and electricity production. The major difficulty lies in deciding the proportion of these 'losses' that are separately attributable to the steam and electricity supplies.

This dilemma can be resolved by assuming that a fraction, f, of these 'losses' is attributable to the production of steam. Hence the overall efficiency of steam production, η_s, is given by

$$\eta_s = \frac{51}{51 + 9 + f(15 + 17)} = \frac{51}{60 + 32f} \tag{1}$$

Similarly, the overall efficiency of electricity production, η_e, is given by

$$\eta_e = \frac{6}{6 + 1 + 1 + (1-f)(15 + 17)} = \frac{6}{40 - 32f} \tag{2}$$

The advantage of presenting the results in this form is that η_s and η_e can be displayed graphically as shown in Fig. 6.2 to highlight the influence of the factor f.

Fig. 6.2 demonstrates three important properties of the cogeneration system:

(i)   If no value of f is defined, the permitted values of η_s and η_e are bounded. In the present example, η_s must lie between 55 and 85% and η_e must lie between 15 and 75%. Moreover, the high values of η_e are accompanied by low values of η_s.

(ii) η_e and η_s are interdependent through the factor f, so that once a value is

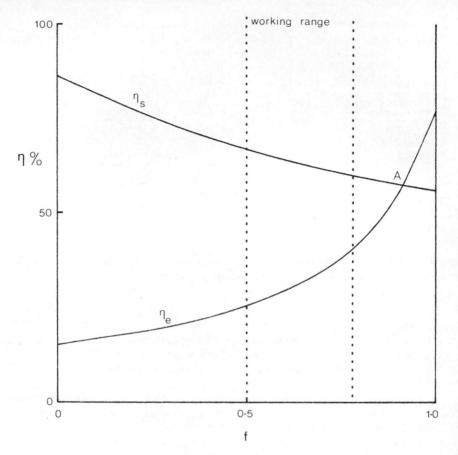

Fig. 6.2 Efficiency of steam and electricity generation as a function of f, the fraction of unattributable losses that are assigned to steam production. See text for a full explanation.

chosen for η_e, the value of η_s is automatically determined and vice versa.

(iii) With the exception of the unique point A in Fig. 6.2, the production efficiency for steam will always be different from the production efficiency for electricity.

Assumption (i) is not correct; the factor f is itself subject to some limits and two are of particular significance. First, there is a thermodynamic limit upon the thermal efficiency of electricity generation. Practical systems are expected to have a thermodynamic limit of the order of 40%[17]. When coupled with a primary fuel efficiency of 87%, the best that can be expected of electricity production would be typically of the order of 35%. With primary fuels of higher energy production efficiency (such as coal or natural gas) overall efficiencies closer to 40% are attainable.

Second, unless there are exceptional reasons, it is unlikely that electricity will be consistently generated at an efficiency lower than that achieved by the public supply. Hence a lower limit on production efficiency η_e of say 25% in the UK is applicable.

When these limits on η_e (i.e. 25-40%) are inserted on Fig. 6.2 as shown, they define a working range which limits steam production efficiency to the range 60-67%. With f lying in the range 0.50-0.78, a mean working condition can be defined by the average value of f (i.e. 0.64) and using Equations 1 and 2 leads to a value of 31% for electricity production and 63% for steam production. Note that these values take account of primary fuel production efficiency. At plant level, where this factor is usually ignored because it is outside the control of the plant operator, these efficiencies should be increased by a factor of $1/0.83 = 1.205$ to 37% for electricity and 76% for steam production. In all these calculations it is important to recognize the implicit assumption that all steam is used usefully.

This example is useful because, apart from reinforcing the earlier discussion of cogeneration, it illustrates the way in which reasoning must be applied in order to be able to obtain a useful solution. Again one common problem is the assumption of arbitrary partitioning, i.e. simply dividing total energy input by total product output.

CHECKLIST OF PROBLEMS OCCURRING IN ENERGY ANALYSIS

Because users of the results of energy analysis must frequently take data from a number of different sources, often relating to different countries, it is important before any comparative work is attempted to check that the data are consistent. The principal variations which lead to apparently differing results particularly for beverage container systems are discussed above and can be summarized as:

(i)   Are input and output materials to the systems the same?

(ii)   Is the same normalizing factor used?

(iii)   Are the same operations included in the systems? (This especially applies to marginal or ancillary operations.)

(iv)   Is capital energy included?

(v)   For beverage systems, are the container system specifications identical? If averages are used, were they derived in the same way?

(vi)   Are the same fuel production efficiencies used? (This is particularly important for electricity.)

(vii)   Has feedstock energy been calculated in the same way?

(viii)   Is wood feedstock accounted for?

(ix)   If partitioning has been carried out, are the procedures identical?

If these points are closely checked at the outset, and, if necessary, the data are suitably amended, many apparent disagreements disappear. The corollary of this, of course, is that analysts should present their results in a sufficiently detailed form to allow such checks to be made.

INTERPRETING THE RESULTS OF ENERGY ANALYSIS

Ten years ago, few detailed energy analyses based on actual operating practices had been carried out, and most of the available published information was derived from government and trade statistics usually collected for some quite different purpose and usually expressed in economic terms. There are two main consequences of deriving energy data in this way. First, the conversion from monetary to physical units is subject to considerable uncertainties. Since the original tables themselves contain errors, the final energy data are subject to considerable and often unknown errors. Second, energy requirements can be calculated from such data only as a single aggregated value. They cannot be broken down satisfactorily either by fuel type or by contributing operation (i.e. fuel production energy, energy content and feedstock). As a result, any comparisons of different systems could only be based on these single values for gross energy requirement.

As the results of increasingly more detailed analyses have become available over the last decade or so, new possibilities have opened up for more subtle and accurate comparisons to be made; not only is it now possible to compare the gross energy requirements of systems, but it is also possible to compare the dependence of different systems on specific fuels such as oil or electricity as well as to identify differences in practices not only from country to country but also from factory to factory. The penalty that has to be paid for increased accuracy and enhanced application possibilities is a destruction of the apparent simplicity of the earlier type of comparison, which arose from oversimplification of the whole concept of energy analysis. As a result, anyone wishing to use the results of energy analysis today must become acquainted with the methodology of the technique and the implications of the results in much the same way as an economist must be acquainted with accounting procedures. The earlier discussion highlights some of the more obvious factors that must be appreciated when examining the results of energy analysis and the following sections consider some of the implications of this more detailed work for the interpreter.

EXAMINATION OF SOME BEVERAGE CONTAINER SYSTEMS

To demonstrate some of the principles of interpretation, consider the energy requirements of five different beverage container systems using the results of a recent survey of UK practices[7]. The five container systems have been chosen not because they are in any way special, but simply because they allow some of the uses of energy analysis to be demonstrated. (Some 46 different systems are considered in reference 11.) The systems chosen here are:

(i)   9.68 fl.oz. (0.28 litre) returnable glass bottle to pack beer,
(ii)   9.68 fl.oz. (0.28 litre) non-returnable glass bottle to pack beer,
(iii)   35.2 fl.oz. (1.0 litre) non-returnable glass bottle to pack carbonated soft drinks,
(iv)   9.68 fl.oz. (0.28 litre) three-piece tinplate can to pack beer,
(v)   1.5 litre PET bottle to pack carbonated soft drinks.

In all cases the system boundary has been chosen to include all operations from the extraction of raw materials from the earth through to the final disposal of all materials as waste. The production of all packaging materials is included, as is the production of ancillary feeds such as glue, labels, carbon dioxide and water. Capital energy has been excluded with the exception of that involved in road transport.

To obtain the system energy requirements, further system parameters must be defined. These are:

(i)   *Bottle mass*
        9.68 fl.oz. (0.28 l) returnable glass; mass = 300 g,
        9.68 fl.oz. (0.28 l) non-returnable glass; mass = 200 g,
        1.0 litre non-returnable glass; mass = 630 g,

1.5 litre PET bottle; body mass = 60 g; base mass (PET) = 5 g.

(ii) *Empty container packaging* All bottles are assumed to be bulk palletized for delivery from container manufacturer to filler.

(iii) *Closure type*
9.68 fl.oz. (0.28 litre) bottles use crown closures.
1.0 and 1.5 litre bottles use aluminium screw closures.

(iv) *Outer packaging after filling*
Returnable bottles are packed in returnable plastic crates.
Non-returnable bottles are packed in shrinkwrapped trays.
Cans employ Hicone webbing and shrinkwrapped trays.
PET bottles are packed in cartons.

(v) *Retail distribution and sale* Returnable bottles are delivered via the brewery network, (multiple stops) and sold for consumption on the premises. Non-returnable bottles are distributed and sold by supermarkets.

The calculated energy requirements of these systems are given in Tables 6.2-6.6. Note that, following the earlier discussion, fuels are identified by three groups — electricity, oil fuels and other fuels. The detailed breakdowns shown in Tables 6.2 to 6.6 indicate the relative importance of the different contributing operations and also the sensitivity of the overall energy requirements to fuels of different types. Some of the operations listed contribute a significant fraction of the overall system energy requirements and in the most detailed work, the requirements of these operations needs further breakdown. Table 6.7, for example, shows the breakdown for the production of glass containers and Table 6.8 gives a typical breakdown for the production of the 9.68 fl.oz (0.28 litre) three-piece tinplate can.

For non-returnable containers, the total energy requirement is simply the sum of the individual contributions and can be readily calculated as shown in Tables 6.3-6.6. However, some of the contributions to the energy requirements of the returnable bottle system depend on trippage (i.e. the number of times the container is filled before it disappears from the system). The trippage-dependent terms are indicated by an asterisk in Table 6.2 and must be totalled separately from the trippage-independent terms.

The results of the above calculations give the system energy *per container* of beverage delivered to the consumer. However, an alternative expression of energy requirement is the energy required to deliver *unit volume* of beverage. This method of expressing energy requirement is most appropriate when considering the energy requirement of systems employing the larger sizes of container. Energy requirements *per litre* are also given in Tables 6.3-6.6.

THE ENERGY EFFICIENCY OF CONTAINER SYSTEMS

The simplest way of comparing the overall energy efficiencies of two container systems is on the basis of gross energy requirement. For equivalent non-returnable containers such as the 9.68 fl.oz. (0.28 litre) non-returnable glass bottle (Table 6.3) and the 9.68 fl.oz. (0.28 litre) tinplate can (Table 6.5), the comparison is possible simply by inspection. Here it is clear that the metal can system requires some 11% less energy than the glass bottle system.

Comparison of returnable and non-returnable container systems, must however take account of the effect of trippage. The most convenient procedure is to

71

Table 6.2   Energy Required to Produce and Use 1000 Returnable Glass Bottles of Mass 300 g to Package Beer

Bottle capacity 9.68 fl.oz. (0.28 litre). Trippage-dependent terms are indicated with an asterisk.

Operation	Electricity/MJ		Oil fuels/MJ			Other fuels/MJ			Total energy /MJ
	Fuel production & delivery	Energy content of fuel	Fuel production & delivery	Energy content of fuel	Feedstock energy	Fuel production & delivery	Energy content of fuel	Feedstock energy	
Bottle production*	1173	391	522	2543	—	183	1760	—	6572
Empty bottle packing*	114	38	21	106	30	—	39	70	418
Empty bottle delivery*	4	1	17	88	—	2	9	—	121
Filling & packing	540	181	133	641	76	30	298	43	1942
Trunking	7	2	33	169	—	1	18	—	230
Retail delivery	5	2	21	109	—	1	10	—	148
Retail sale	670	223	34	161	—	18	216	—	1322
Consumer use	—	—	260	1363	—	—	—	—	1623
Disposal*	40	13	19	102	16	2	12	1	205
Totals:									
trippage-dependent (*)	1331	443	579	2839	46	187	1820	71	7316
trippage-independent	1222	408	481	2443	76	50	542	43	5265

Table 6.3 Energy Required to Produce and Use 1000 Non-returnable Glass Bottles each of Mass 200 g to Package Beer

Bottle capacity 9.68 fl.oz. (0.28 litre).

Operation	Electricity/MJ		Oil fuels/MJ			Other fuels/MJ			Total energy /MJ
	Fuel production & delivery	Energy content of fuel	Fuel production & delivery	Energy content of fuel	Feedstock energy	Fuel production & delivery	Energy content of fuel	Feedstock energy	
Bottle production	782	261	348	1695	–	122	1173	–	4381
Empty bottle packing	114	38	21	106	30	–	39	70	418
Empty bottle delivery	4	1	19	99	–	2	10	–	135
Filling and packing	495	166	133	646	56	28	317	83	1924
Trunking	7	2	36	182	–	2	19	–	248
Retail delivery	4	1	17	88	–	1	9	–	120
Retail sale	684	228	–	–	–	–	–	–	912
Consumer use	–	–	260	1363	–	–	–	–	1623
Disposal	27	9	12	68	11	1	8	1	137
Energy/1000 containers	2117	706	846	4247	97	156	1575	154	9898
Energy/litre	7.56	2.52	3.02	15.17	0.35	0.56	5.63	0.55	35.36

Table 6.4 Energy Required to Produce and Use 1000 Non-returnable Glass Bottles each of Mass 630 g to Package Carbonated Soft Drinks

Container capacity = 1.0 litre (35.2 fl.oz.).

Operation	Electricity/MJ		Oil fuels/MJ			Other fuels/MJ			Total energy /MJ
	Fuel production & delivery	Energy content of fuel	Fuel production & delivery	Energy content of fuel	Feedstock energy	Fuel production & delivery	Energy content of fuel	Feedstock energy	
Bottle production	2463	822	1096	5340	–	384	3696	–	13801
Empty bottle packing	315	105	60	295	86	1	105	194	1161
Empty bottle delivery	12	4	56	286	1	5	30	–	394
Filling and packing	1116	404	246	1203	268	12	343	291	3883
Trunking	15	5	74	378	1	3	40	–	516
Retail delivery	10	3	51	258	1	2	27	–	352
Retail sale	684	228	–	–	–	–	–	–	912
Consumer use	–	–	260	1363	–	–	–	–	1623
Disposal	85	28	39	215	33	4	25	2	431
Energy/1000 containers	4700	1599	1882	9338	390	411	4266	487	23073
Energy/litre	4.70	1.60	1.88	9.34	0.39	0.41	4.27	0.49	23.08

Table 6.5 Energy Required to Produce and Use 1000 Three-Piece Tinplate Cans of Capacity 9.68 fl.oz. (0.28 litre) to Package Beer

Operation	Electricity/MJ		Oil fuels/MJ			Other fuels/MJ			Total energy
	Fuel production & delivery	Energy content of fuel	Fuel production & delivery	Energy content of fuel	Feedstock energy	Fuel production & delivery	Energy content of fuel	Feedstock energy	
Can production	1242	542	174	848	227	176	1383	1	4593
Empty can packaging	50	17	4	17	—	2	26	18	134
Empty can delivery	2	1	7	38	—	1	4	—	53
Filling and packing	345	115	76	369	47	9	156	73	1190
Trunking	5	2	23	115	—	1	12	—	158
Retail delivery	2	1	10	49	—	—	5	—	67
Retail sale	684	228	—	—	—	—	—	—	912
Consumer use	—	—	260	1363	—	—	—	—	1623
Disposal	6	2	3	15	2	—	2	—	30
Energy/1000 cans	2336	908	557	2814	276	189	1588	92	8760
Energy/litre	8.34	3.24	1.99	10.05	0.99	0.68	5.67	0.33	31.29

Table 6.6 Energy Required to Produce and Use 1000 PET Bottles of Capacity 1.5 litre for Carbonated Soft Drinks

Operation	Electricity/MJ		Oil fuels/MJ			Other fuels/MJ			Total energy /MJ
	Fuel production & delivery	Energy content of fuel	Fuel production & delivery	Energy content of fuel	Feedstock energy	Fuel production & delivery	Energy content of fuel	Feedstock energy	
Bottle production	4549	1516	950	4629	3028	—	—	—	14672
Empty bottle packing	172	57	33	161	45	—	59	105	632
Empty bottle delivery	6	2	27	137	—	2	15	—	189
Filling and packing	1850	648	376	1827	99	15	800	778	6393
Trunking	15	5	74	378	1	3	40	—	516
Retail delivery	10	3	51	258	1	2	27	—	352
Retail sale	684	228	—	—	—	—	—	—	912
Consumer use	—	—	260	1363	—	—	—	—	1623
Disposal	9	3	4	22	3	—	3	—	44
Energy/1000 bottles	7295	2462	1775	8775	3177	22	944	883	25333
Energy/litre	4.86	1.64	1.18	5.85	2.12	0.01	0.63	0.59	16.88

Table 6.7 Gross Energy Required to Produce 1 tonne of Saleable Glass as Containers from Raw Materials in the Ground

Operation	Electricity/MJ		Oil fuels/MJ			Other fuels/MJ			Total energy /MJ
	Fuel production & delivery	Energy content of fuel	Fuel production & delivery	Energy content of fuel	Feedstock energy	Fuel production & delivery	Energy content of fuel	Feedstock energy	
Production of:									
sand	90.0	30.3	37.9	174.2	—	—	—	—	333.3
limestone	20.8	6.9	6.9	34.6	—	—	—	—	692.0
soda ash	52.0	18.1	361.6	1853.2	—	58.8	872.4	—	3216.1
feldspar minerals	30.2	10.1	4.1	20.1	—	—	—	—	64.5
Calumite slag	9.9	3.3	3.8	18.2	—	—	—	—	35.2
sodium sulphate	1.9	0.6	1.4	6.9	—	—	—	—	10.8
calcium sulphate	3.6	1.2	neg	0.1	—	—	—	—	4.9
selenium	1.1	0.4	0.5	2.4	—	neg	0.3	—	4.7
alumina	1.1	0.4	3.3	16.2	—	0.6	6.9	—	22.5
water	15.5	5.2	—	—	—	—	—	—	20.7
Total energy to produce all raw materials	227.0	76.5	419.5	2125.9	—	59.4	879.6	—	4404.7
Delivery of raw materials	11.0	3.6	31.0	154.7	—	1.8	11.1	—	213.2
Fuel use in factory	3672.1	1224.0	1288.7	6195.2	—	547.6	4976.6	—	17904.2
Totals	3910.1	1304.1	1739.2	8475.8	—	608.8	5867.3	—	22522.1

Table 6.8 Gross Energy Required to Produce 1000 Three-Piece Tinplate Cans of Capacity 9.68 fl.oz. (0.28 litre)

Operation	Electricity/MJ		Oil fuels/MJ			Other fuels/MJ			Total energy /MJ
	Fuel production & delivery	Energy content of fuel	Fuel production & delivery	Energy content of fuel	Feedstock energy	Fuel production & delivery	Energy content of fuel	Feedstock energy	
Production & delivery of tinplate	179.8	71.9	59.6	287.8	—	98.1	668.8	0.9	1366.9
Printing & lacquering	18.5	6.2	—	—	—	3.9	47.7	—	76.3
Bodymaking	98.8	23.4	—	—	—	8.1	98.4	—	228.7
Scrap treatment	1.0	0.3	0.7	3.0	—	neg	0.2	0.1	5.3
Production of:									
lacquer	3.6	1.2	4.0	19.8	29.9	1.2	14.5	—	74.2
ink	0.1	0.1	0.3	1.4	2.5	—	—	—	4.4
varnish	1.6	0.5	1.8	8.8	10.1	0.4	4.2	—	27.4
lead solder	3.8	1.3	0.9	2.3	—	3.1	22.9	—	34.3
crystal flux	0.3	0.1	0.1	0.3	0.2	0.1	0.7	—	1.8
body flux	0.2	0.1	0.3	1.3	1.8	neg	neg	—	3.7
Sub-total	307.7	105.1	67.7	324.7	44.5	114.9	857.4	1.0	1823.0
Production of the tinplate end	125.6	47.8	34.6	168.9	22.9	43.1	306.1	0.1	749.1
Production of aluminium easy-open end	808.4	389.1	71.3	353.9	160.0	18.2	219.0	—	2019.9
Total/MJ	1241.7	542.0	173.6	847.5	227.4	176.2	1382.5	1.1	4592.0

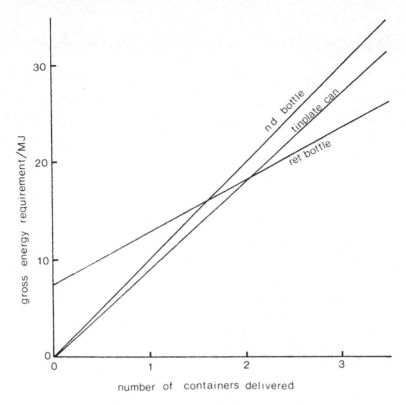

Fig. 6.3   Dependence of gross energy requirement on number of containers for beer packaging in containers of different types of capacity 9.68 fl.oz (0.28 litre).

plot a graph of energy requirement as a function of the number of containers delivered. Fig. 6.3 shows such a plot using the gross energy requirements from Tables 6.2, 6.3 and 6.5. For the non-returnable container systems, the total gross energy requirement must be expended each time a container is delivered and this gives a linear relationship passing through the origin of the graph. However, for the returnable container, the trippage-dependent component of gross energy requirement is expended initially and thereafter the trippage-independent component only is expended each time the container passes back to the filler. The graph is therefore linear but with a positive intercept on the energy axis as shown. The important feature of such graphs is that at low numbers of containers delivered, the non-returnable container systems require the lower energies. However, as shown in Fig. 6.3, there is a crossover point at which the energy required by the returnable system becomes lower than that of the non-returnable system.

This crossover provides a guide to the minimum trippage that the returnable container must achieve in order that the returnable system be the more energy efficient. In Fig. 6.3, for example, the crossover for the delivery of beer in glass bottles occurs at approximately 1.6 containers delivered. Remembering that only integral numbers of containers can be delivered, this implies that the returnable glass bottle must achieve at least two trips for the returnable system to be the more energy efficient. By the same type of argument, Fig. 6.3 also shows that the

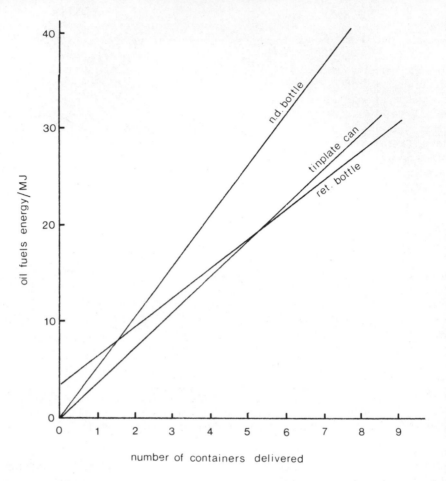

Fig. 6.4   Oil fuels energy as a function of the number of containers delivered for different types of container of capacity 9.68 fl.oz (0.28 litre).

returnable glass bottle must achieve at least three trips for the system to be more efficient than the three-piece tinplate can system.

Gross energy requirement is however only one criterion that can be used to compare the efficiency of container systems. For example, the relative oil dependence of the different systems may well be important. Using the detailed breakdowns of Tables 6.2-6.6, the technique used to construct Fig. 6.3 may be repeated but substituting oil energy requirement for gross energy requirement. In Table 6.3, for example, the oil-based energy requirement is the sum (846 + 4247 + 97) = 5190 MJ/1000 bottles delivered. By way of illustration, the oil dependence comparison for the same three systems used in Fig. 6.3 is shown in Fig. 6.4. Working in terms of integral trippages, the break even trippage for returnable and non-returnable glass bottles remains unchanged at two trips, but the metal can system, which uses significantly less oil fuels than the returnable glass bottle system, requires a trippage of six for break-even.

This comparison technique can be repeated using a number of different comparison criteria, such as electricity requirement, feedstock energy requirement, direct fuel requirement and so on. It is therefore important to decide which criteria are of greatest significance because, as can be seen above, the results of different comparisons are not necessarily the same. Much of the energy information available until recently has been insufficiently detailed to show comparisons other than on the basis of gross energy requirement. There is however no reason to suppose that this factor is any more important than, say, oil requirement; indeed, at the present time, minimizing oil dependence may well be the more important. It follows that once criteria other than gross energy requirement are given greater status, the minimization of gross energy requirement becomes less important. It is impossible, for example, for oil dependence of some systems to be minimized by substituting coal, but at the same time for the gross energy requirement to increase because of the less efficient way in which coal has to be used.

VARIATIONS IN THE SYSTEMS

The above discussion concentrated on specific systems, carefully defined to provide a specific set of materials flows within the overall system. Only by doing this are energy calculations at all possible. It is, however, misleading to assume that the results of such calculations are representative of all possible systems using the specified container type and size. When any system parameter is changed, the revised system must be regarded as a new system and a new energy requirement must be calculated, since not only will the gross energy requirement change but so also will the relative proportions of the different fuel types. Some notion of the effect of system variations can be gained from the following brief discussion.

Consider first the returnable glass bottle system. Table 6.2 was calculated using a bottle mass of 300 g. This lies at the lower end of the mass range for this type of bottle and in practice masses in the range 300–360 g are produced. Since the energy required to produce a glass container is directly proportional to the bottle mass, bottles at the upper end of this range require some 19% more energy than those at the lower end. Hence the value shown in Table 6.2 for bottle production would be increased by 19% if the heaviest bottle were used.

The values given in Table 6.7 for the energy to produce glass containers is the average of 16 glass container producing factories in the UK. When individual factories are examined, it is found that their energy use lies in the range ±19% about this mean value (note that this is an actual variation in energy usage). This factor will therefore introduce a further spread in the range of glass bottle production energies, to reflect the fact that the bottle may be produced in any one of the factories lying within the limits of the range.

Yet a further assumption in calculating Table 6.2 is that empty bottles are bulk palletized for delivery from glass factory to filler. However, other forms of packaging may be used. For example, the filler may send empty crates to the glass factory so that when new bottles reach the filling lines they may be treated in exactly the same way as bottles returned from retail outlets. This procedure reduces the energy associated with the production of packaging materials for empty bottles (i.e shrinkwrap film, layer pads and pallets) but increases the transport energy because fewer bottles can be loaded onto lorries in crates than in bulk packs. Yet another form of packaging is the occasional use of cartons, and this again will affect both the energy required to produce the packaging material and the transport energy.

In addition to the above physical variations in the system energy, there is also

Table 6.9 **Gross Energy Requirements per Container for Beverage Container Systems when Accuracy and Physical Variations in the Systems are Considered**

Container system	Gross energy requirement (MJ/container)	
	Minimum	Maximum
9.68 fl.oz. (0.28 litre) returnable glass bottle for beer	5.00 + 5.42/trip	5.53 + 11.30/trip
9.68 fl.oz. (0.28 litre) non-returnable glass bottle for beer	8.39	12.82
1 litre non-returnable glass bottle for carbonated soft drinks	18.81	30.85
9.68 fl.oz. (0.28 litre) three-piece tinplate can for beer	7.73	9.98
1.5 litre PET bottle for carbonated soft drinks	21.48	26.60

the accuracy of the results to be considered. When operational data are aggregated over relatively short periods (say 3 months), an accuracy of the order of ±5% is generally claimed. This error usually arises in the conversion of the delivery of materials and fuels, which are usually known accurately, to materials and fuels consumed, which are seldom monitored in any great detail within the factory. Any differences between deduced usage and actual usage are accommodated as changes in stock levels of raw materials and fuels held by the factory. When all of these factors are taken into account, the range of possible gross energy requirements for the returnable bottle systems using the 9.68 fl.oz. (0.28 litre) bottle for beer packaging, can be expressed by the limits of the range shown in Table 6.9.

Similar variations may be calculated in the other systems. In addition to the ±5% allowance for accuracy. Table 6.9 shows the limits of the ranges in gross energy requirements arising from considering the following factors:

9.68 fl.oz. (0.28 litre) non-returnable glass bottle for beer):
   Bottle mass variation up to +25%
   Glass factory energy variation ±19%
   Empty bottles delivered in packaging that is ultimately used as the outer packaging after filling
   Outer packaging may be shrinkwrapped trays, cartons or multipacks
1.0 litre non-returnable glass bottle for carbonated soft drinks:
   Bottle mass variation up to +19%
   Glass factory energy variation ±19%
   Outer packaging may be shrinkwrapped trays or cartons
9.68 fl.oz. (0.28 litre) three-piece tinplate can for beer:
   Energy variations in the can-making factory ±22%
   Variation due to rejection of defective coil ±5%
   Outer packaging may be Hicone or multipacks in conjunction with shrink-wrapped trays or cartons.
1.5 litre PET bottle for carbonated soft drinks:
   Bottle mass may be reduced from 60 g to 55 g
   Base materials may be PET or polyethylene
   Outer packaging may be cartons or shrinkwrapped trays

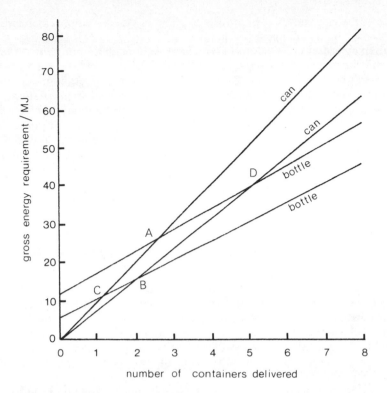

Fig. 6.5 Comparison of the gross energy requirements of the systems employing 9.68 fl.oz (0.28 litre) returnable glass bottles and three-piece tinplate cans for the delivery of beer when accuracy of data and variations in systems are taken into account.

If the gross energy requirements of the different container systems are compared using the maximum and minimum values indicated by Table 6.9, the results appear as shown in Fig. 6.5. The important feature of this graph is the replacement of the single crossover point in Fig. 6.3 by four separate intersections A, B, C and D in Fig. 6.5. Point A corresponds to a comparison of the most energy intensive systems for both containers and point B is the comparison of the least energy intensive practices. Points C and D represent comparisons of the least energy-intensive system for one container with the most energy intensive system for the other. It cannot be overemphasized that the systems which give rise to these different graphs and interactions are not some form of statistical variation but arise from actual physical variations within the systems themselves.

If, therefore, the energy requirements of different beverage container systems are to be compared without specifying the system parameters in detail, the best that can be achieved is the deduction that the crossover point will lie somewhere within the quadrilateral ABCD in Fig. 6.5. Hence, in the case of the returnable glass bottle and the three-piece tinplate can systems (9.68 fl.oz (0.28 litre)) for beer packaging, the returnable glass bottle must achieve a trippage of at least six before it can always be regarded as the less energy intensive of the two systems. Compare this with the value of three trips determined from Fig. 6.3 using the single specifications. In general, comparisons of container systems should always consider the influence of system variations; otherwise deductions made from such comparisons may be grossly misleading.

When considering variations in container systems, it is important to remember that the changes in the relative proportions of the different fuel energies will not necessarily be the same as the changes in the gross energy requirement. Suppose, for example, that the outer packaging were changed from shrinkwrapped trays to cardboard cartons. There will be an increase in the 'other fuels' component because of the increased use of wood products, i.e. board, but there will be a decrease in 'oil fuels' because of the elimination of the polyethylene shrinkwrap film. Even if the changes in the two different fuel contributions cancelled each other so that gross energy requirement remained unchanged, the individual fuel contributions would exhibit the changes indicated. Thus comparisons based on gross energy requirements will seldom give the same results as comparisons based on comparisons of specific fuel types.

EFFECT OF CONTAINER CAPACITY ON COMPARISONS

Comparisons of system energies are meaningful only when equivalent systems are compared. Obviously it would not be sensible to compare a 0.25 litre bottle system with a 1 litre bottle system because the functions of the two systems are different as mentioned earlier; the 0.25 litre system is designed to deliver a single 'drink' to the consumer whereas the 1 litre container is intended as a small bulk carrier of beverage. Hence, for small-capacity containers, comparisons are most effectively carried out by reference to the energy requirement *per container* delivered to the consumer. In contrast, for the larger container sizes (say greater than 0.5 litre) a more appropriate parameter is energy required *per unit volume* of beverage delivered to the consumer.

This change of normalization parameters (i.e. volume delivered rather than number of containers delivered) has no effect upon comparisons of containers of the same volumetric capacity (compare Tables 6.3 and 6.5). However, it does markedly affect the results for containers of different sizes. Tables 6.10 and 6.11, for example, give the energy requirements per container and per unit volume for carbonated soft drinks packed in 2.0 litre PET bottles. These have been calculated in the same way as the results in Table 6.6 for the 1.5 litre PET bottle system. Comparing Tables 6.4, 6.10 and 6.11, it is clear that the gross energy requirement *per container* is some 15% higher for the 2.0 litre system compared with the 1.5 litre system. Since the main function of both systems is the bulk delivery of

Table 6.10 **Gross Energy Required to Produce and Use 1000 PET Bottles of Capacity 2.0 litre Using the Same System as Described for the 1.5 litre Bottle**

Fuel type	Fuel production and delivery energy/MJ	Energy content of fuel /MJ	Feedstock energy /MJ	Total energy /MJ
Electricity	7990	2694	—	10684
Oil fuels	2029	10059	3770	15858
Other fuels	33	1321	1221	2575
Totals	10052	14074	4991	29917

Table 6.11   Gross Energy Required to Deliver 1 litre of Beverage to the Consumer Using 2.0 litre PET Bottles

Fuel type	Fuel production and delivery energy/MJ	Energy content of fuel /MJ	Feedstock energy /MJ	Total energy /MJ
Electricity	4.0	1.3	—	5.3
Oil fuels	1.0	5.0	1.9	7.9
Other fuels	neg.	0.7	0.6	1.3
Totals	5.0	7.0	2.5	14.5

beverage, the latter comparison is the more appropriate and so it can be deduced that the 2.0 litre system is the more energy efficient of the two.

PET bottles are relative newcomers to the beverage container market and it is inevitable that their energy requirements be compared with those of the well established glass container systems. Glass bottle systems for these types of beverages, using containers of capacities greater than approximately 1.0 litre, are seldom used and so the most sensible comparison that can be made is between PET bottles and the 1.0 litre non-returnable glass bottle system (Table 6.4) using volume delivered as the normalizing factor. For gross energy requirements the comparative values are:

1.0 litre non-returnable glass	23.1 MJ/litre
1.5 litre PET	16.9 MJ/litre
2.0 litre PET	14.5 MJ/litre

Clearly, on this basis, the PET bottle systems are more energy efficient than the glass bottle system and the 2.0 litre PET bottle system is more energy efficient than the 1.5 litre system. This conclusion remains unchanged when the system variations of Table 6.9 are considered. However, following the earlier discussion, it is important to recognize that a significant proportion of the energy advantage of the PET system arises from the greater volume capacities of these containers rather than from any intrinsic property of the polymer. Moreover, these reductions in energy with increasing volume is not a linear function of volume and so it follows that PET bottles of lower capacity would not necessarily retain their energy advantage over glass, a factor that must be watched closely if PET bottles of capacity less than 1 litre are introduced commercially.

One interesting feature which emerges from Tables 6.4, 6.6 and 6.11 is the oil dependence of the different container systems. Calculating oil energy requirements as (fuel + feedstock), the requirements of the three systems are

1.0 litre glass	11.6 MJ/litre
1.5 litre PET	9.2 MJ/litre
2.0 litre PET	7.9 MJ/litre

Thus, despite the expectation that the use of a hydrocarbon polymer to produce bottles would lead to a heavy oil dependence, it is clear that the economies achieved by using the larger container sizes offset this effect.

CONCLUSIONS

If the results of energy analysis are to be used successfully in policy making, all concerned with the production and use of such data must change their habits. Energy analysts must all stop producing only single aggregated values for gross energy requirements of systems and must provide detailed breakdowns by fuel type and contributing operation so that the validity of their calculations can be checked and so that the basis of their calculations can be changed if necessary in comparative exercises.

Similarly, those concerned with interpreting the results of energy analysis must stop expecting a single aggregated value for gross energy requirement and must start looking more closely at the way in which data have been calculated and appreciate the variations that are likely to occur.

It is hoped that this chapter will point the way for some of these changes of attitude.

REFERENCES

1. HANNON, B.M., *System Energy and Recycling: A Study of the Container Industry*, ASME Report 72 — WA/Ener-3, 1972.
2. HANNON, B.M., Bottles, Cans, Energy, *Environment*, **14** (2) (1972) 11-21.
3. SUNDSTROM, G., *Investigation of Energy Requirements from Raw Materials to Garbage Treatment for Four Swedish Beer Packaging Alternatives*, Report for Rigello Pak AB, 1973.
4. U.S. ENVIRONMENTAL PROTECTION AGENCY, *Resource and Environmental Profile Analysis of Nine Beverage Container Alternatives*, Report No. SW-91c, 1974.
5. RESEARCH TRIANGLE INSTITUTE, *Energy and Economic Impacts of Mandatory Deposits*, US Dept. of Commerce Report No. PB-258-638, 1976.
6. SEMA-METRA, *Elements d'Impact d'une Reglementation Europeene Concernant les Emballages de Boisson*, Report for the EEC Commission, 1978.
7. BOUSTEAD, I. and HANCOCK, G.F., *Beverage Containers and Resources (Final Report)*, Report to the UK Department of Industry, London, 1979.
8. INTERNATIONAL FEDERATION OF INSTITUTES OF ADVANCED STUDY (IFIAS) *Energy Analysis*, Workshop Report No. 6, Stockholm, 1974.
9. MADDOX, K.P., Energy Analysis, *Mineral Industries Bulletin*, Colerado School of Mines **18**, July 1975.
10. BOUSTEAD, I. and HANCOCK, G.F., *Handbook of Industrial Energy Analysis*, Ellis Horwood, Chichester/John Wiley, New York, 1979.
11. BOUSTEAD, I. and HANCOCK, G.F., *Energy and Packaging*, Ellis Horwood, Chichester/John Wiley, New York, 1981.
12. ODUM, E.P., *Fundamentals of Ecology*, W.B. Saunders Co., 1971.
13. SMITH, H., *Trans. World Energy Conference* **18**, Section E, 1969.
14. WALLER, R.F., *Primary Energy Requirements for the Production of Iron and Steel in the UK*, Open University Energy Research Group Report No. 11, 1976.
15. KINDLER, H. and NIKLES, A. Energy requirements in the production and processing of plastics, *Chem. Ing. Tech.*, **51** 1979 1-3.
16. MADDEN, W.F., High energy costs will continue to favour plastics, *Plastics and Rubber Weekly*, p. 12, 22 November 1980.
17. FRANCIS, W. and PETERS, M.C., *Fuels and Fuel Technology*, Pergamon, Oxford, 1980.

Ian Boustead is a Senior Lecturer in Materials in the Faculty of Technology in the Open University, having graduated from Birmingham University in 1960 with a B.Sc. (Hons.) in Physics, adding an M.Sc. and a Ph.D. in Physics in 1967 and 1969. Between 1960 and 1965 he was Physics Master at William Hulme's Grammer School, Manchester; and was on the research staff of the Royal Military College of Science, Shrivenham, until he joined The Open University in 1972. He is a Member of the Institute of Physics

7 Packaging Materials in Solid Waste as an Energy Resource

A. Heie and T. Halmö

INTRODUCTION

Solid waste as an energy resource has been known since mankind discovered fire. Organized utilization by burning in special incinerators with energy recovery is, however, quite a new technique. To our knowledge the first example is the Zürich incinerator which was put into operation in 1928. This plant had a design capacity of 240 tonne/day of refuse having a calorific value of 4.2 MJ/kg, and provided heat for the central railway station, a post office, a locomotive shed and 110 dwellings. Surplus heat was transformed into electricity by means of turbo-generators[1].

Today, incineration with energy recovery is a widely applicable solid waste treatment option. Waste usually has a much higher calorific value than the 1928 value of 4.2 MJ/kg, due to the increased use of combustible packing materials, increased newspaper volume and decreased use of fireplaces and ovens in households. Rising oil and energy prices also makes energy recovery increasingly profitable.

This chapter considers solid waste composition, energy content and recovery, and the significance of packaging materials. The figures given are strictly applicable only to Norwegian solid waste, but could easily be adjusted to other Western countries.

SOLID WASTE COMPOSITION AND ENERGY CONTENT

General Waste Composition

Solid waste is a general term that may include everything from household waste to wrecked cars and waste from mining. The solid waste that may be regarded a potential raw material for energy recovery is classified as municipal waste; the solid waste categories that are collected, handled and treated by the municipality or local authority. Typical compositions for a Norwegian city are given in Tables 7.1 and 7.2. The main solid waste categories are household, industrial, construction and demolition, and commercial and office waste; and about 75% of the waste is combustible.

Packaging Materials in Waste

Some of the waste arising is packaging materials. Table 7.3 shows the main combustible packaging material waste sources. When comparing Tables 7.2 and 7.3, it is evident that more than half of the paper and cardboard and most of the plastic in municipal waste is packaging materials. Also some of the metal present in municipal waste is packaging materials, mainly tins for food and beverages. This

Table 7.1   Typical Composition by Source of Municipal Waste in Norway[2, 3]

Category	Weight %
Household waste	40
Bulky household waste	4
Garden and park waste	2
Street sweeping	2
Commercial and office waste	11
Industrial waste	20
Agricultural waste	1
Construction and demolition waste	15
Institutional waste (hospitals, schools, etc.)	1
Hotel and restaurant waste	2
Ships and harbour waste	1

Table 7.2   Typical Composition by Components of Municipal Waste in Norway[2, 3]

Component	Weight %
Paper and cardboard	30
Food waste and putrescibles	20
Plastic and rubber	6
Other combustibles	20
Metals	9
Other non-combustibles	13
Fines (< 10 mm)	2

type of packaging constitutes only about 1% of the municipal waste, as tins for beverages carry a levy in Norway and are not widely used. Also glass packaging materials are a minor fraction of the waste, as a consequence of very efficient returnable bottle systems for soft drinks, beer, wine and liquors bottled in Norway. The main source of glass waste is therefore glass jars for jam, etc., medicine bottles and imported bottles, and the content in municipal waste is only about 1.5%.

Energy Content

The energy content of the different components in municipal waste and their contribution to the mixed waste energy content is shown in Table 7.4. Here it is

Table 7.3   Paper, Cardboard and Plastic Packaging Material Content in Solid Waste[2-5]

Category	Packaging materials, weight %	
	Paper/cardboard	Plastic
Household waste	9	4
Bulky household waste	20	4
Commercial and office waste	50	8
Industrial waste	35	10
Average construction and demolition waste	6	2
Average municipal waste	18	5

Table 7.4   Calorific Value for Typical Norwegian Municipal Waste[2]

Component	Fraction weight % (wet)	Dry matter weight %	Ash weight % of dry matter	Component gross calorific value MJ/kg (dry)	Contribution to overall gross calorific value, dry basis MJ/kg wet waste
Paper and cardboard	30	78	6	18.5	4.3
Food waste and putrescibles	20	34	18	18.6	1.3
Plastic and rubber	6	90	6	34.5	1.9
Other combustibles	20	79	6	19.0	3.0
Metals	9	94	100	0	0
Other non-combustibles	13	96	100	0	0
Fines (< 10 mm)	2	49	36	13.2	0.1
Total	100	73	25	—	10.6*

* or 14.5 MJ/kg dry waste.

expressed as gross calorific value, which shows the energy released when incinerating the waste. Dry matter and ash content are also shown. The gross calorific value of wet refuse is 10.6 MJ/kg, which is equivalent to 14.5 MJ/kg on a dry basis. The net calorific value corrected for water and hydrogen content for wet refuse is about 9.3 MJ/kg.

The total municipal waste generation in Norway is about 1.9 million tonnes/year. The energy content should then be about 17.6 PJ/year, which corresponds to about 450 000 tonnes/year of fuel oil. It also corresponds to about 3% of Norway's total energy consumption.

The corresponding calorific values for waste packaging materials are shown in Table 7.5. As may be seen from Tables 7.4 and 7.5, packaging materials make up about 29% of the municipal waste dry matter, 14% of the ash and 39% of the gross calorific value. Because of the high dry matter content,

Table 7.5   Calorific Value of Packaging Materials in Typical Norwegian Municipal Waste

Component	Fraction of total waste, weight %, wet	Dry matter weight %	Ash weight % of dry matter	Calorific value, dry matter, MJ/kg	Contribution to overall gross calorific value, dry matter MJ/kg wet waste
Paper and cardboard	18	78	6	18.5	2.6
Plastic	5	90	6	34.5	1.6
Metals	1	94	100	0	0
Glass	1.5	90	100	0	0
Total*	25.5	21	3.4	—	4.2

* All numbers given in relation to total municipal waste stream (see Table 7.4).

90

the percentage contribution to net calorific value is about 41%. The gross calorific value of the packaging materials on a wet basis is about 16.5 MJ/kg, which means that the rest of the waste has a much lower value of about 8.6 MJ/kg.

ENERGY RECOVERY FROM SOLID WASTE

The conventional energy recovery method is incineration with heat recovery. The process involves reaction between oxygen (which is supplied as air) and the combustible materials in the waste. Actually the process may be divided into five stages:

(i)   Drying of the waste (up to 200 °C).
(ii) Evaporation of volatile combustibles (200-300 °C).
(iii) Cracking of organic materials into volatile combustibles (300-500 °C).
(iv) Reaction between oxygen and the volatile combustibles with formation of primarily carbon dioxide and water (above 500 °C).
(v)   Reaction between oxygen and residual carbon in the ashes with formation of carbon dioxide (above 500 °C).

The heat released in the incineration gases can be absorbed in a heat carrier, such as water, to give hot water or steam. The energy thus recovered may be used for heating, as process steam in various industries, or to run a steam turbine producing electricity.

One alternative is to interrupt the process after the third stage. This is called pyrolysis, and the products are energy carriers in the form of solid char, oil and gas, which may be stored for later combustion. This pyrolysis process must be carried out in the absence of air to prevent spontanous combustion. A related process is gasification, in which insufficient oxygen or air is added for complete combustion, which gives a low calorific value fuel gas for combustion elsewhere[7].

Another possibility is to convert the raw waste to a storable fuel product, called RDF (refuse-derived fuel) or WDF (waste-derived fuel). This is done by shredding; removal of coarse material by sieving; removal of non-combustibles by one or more of the processes of magnetic separation, air classification and ballistic separation; drying; and finally pelletizing[8]. The product has a higher calorific value than raw waste, is storable and may be more economically transported if pelletized. It is suitable for firing in most industrial solid-fuel boilers[9].

The last energy recovery process to be mentioned is biogas production. The organic components are digested in a special reactor by microorganisms in the absence of oxygen. This also occurs in landfill and the gas can be collected[10]. The product is a mixture of methane and carbon dioxide, with a high calorific value.

Of these four techniques, incineration is the most widely used. A few RDF plants have been put in operation in Europe and the USA during the last five years, while pyrolysis and biogas production are still at an experimental stage.

EFFECTS OF SUBSTITUTION OF PACKAGING MATERIALS

General

For a number of applications packaging materials are interchangable. For example:

(i)   plastics and paper for wrappings and carrier bags,

(ii)   glass, plastic and aluminium/cardboard foil for semiconserved food (jam, pickles, etc.),

(iii)   glass bottles, plastic bottles and tins for soft drinks and beverages,

(iv)   glass bottles, plastic bottles, plastic bags and cartons for milk.

All such substitutions will affect the municipal waste amount, composition, calorific value and total energy content. For example, if half the glass packaging materials and 10% of the paper packaging materials were substituted by plastic materials, and if the amount of plastic required were 20% of the amount of glass and 30% of the amount of paper, the total amount of municipal waste would fall from 1.90 to 1.87 million tonnes/year (1.6% decline). The paper and cardboard content would fall from 30.0% to 28.9%, and the plastic content would rise from 6.0% to 6.7%. The moisture and ash content would be the same and the net calorific value would rise from 9.29 MJ/kg to 9.44 MJ/kg. The total energy content in the municipal waste would be about the same.

This shows that the waste stream and its energy content is fairly insensitive to interchanges in packaging materials. It also indicates that energy considerations regarding choice of packaging material should deal with other aspects rather than with the solid waste energy content.

Case Study: Milk Packaging Materials

Norway has experienced two drastic changes in milk packaging. The first was about 30 years ago, when returnable bottles were introduced. Until then every family had its own 1-5 litre milk pail, which was brought to the milk shop to be filled. When milk bottles came into use, grocery shops started to sell milk as well, and the milk shops faded away. The bottle system meant less work at the retail grocer level and better hygiene. The second change, about 15 years ago, was the introduction of milk cartons. This was welcomed both by the trade and the public for many reasons:

(i)   The carton is lighter than bottles.

(ii)   The carton is square and requires less storage space.

(iii)   No storage space for return bottles is necessary.

(iv)   Less breakage occurs.

(v)   No rinsing and storage of bottles is required in the household.

(vi)   Bottles do not have to be carried back to the shop.

Today 90% of the milk is sold in gable-top cartons. 44% of the milk volume is sold in 2-litre cartons. All sales are made through supermarkets and grocery shops. The growing interest in energy and resource conservation, waste problems and the development of new packaging materials has resulted in the milk carton being considered a sensible choice.

An analysis of different packaging systems for pasteurized milk has been performed by Nunn[6]. Three systems were evaluated:

(i)   gable-top cartons (cartons with polyethylene (PEL) lining),

(ii)   returnable glass bottles,

(iii)   returnable polycarbonate (PC) bottles.

The returnable bottles were assumed to be equipped with aluminium strip-off tops and paper labels containing product information.

Analysis

The following aspects were assessed:

(i)   total annual costs for package, distribution, sales, refuse disposal and consumer expenses,
(ii) total annual resource usage, with special emphasis on energy use,
(iii) number of jobs involved,
(iv) effects on refuse disposal.

Trippage

The calculations were carried out with different assumptions on returnable container trippage — 30 and 50 trips for glass bottles, and 50 and 75 trips for polycarbonate bottles. Present experience with returnable bottles for beer and mineral water is 30-35 trips. The attainable trippage with glass bottles is expected to be nearer 30 than 50, and for polycarbonate nearer 50 than 75. A deposit scheme was assumed in deriving these data. Further, it is assumed that the choice of packaging system does not affect sales of milk in any way. The calculations for glass bottles have been made on the basis that 2-litre bottles are not used, and that this share of the market is transfered to 1-litre bottles. 2-litre glass bottles were considered to be too heavy for the consumer to handle.

Energy Consumption

Table 7.6 presents a summary of energy consumption per million litres of milk sold in the three packaging systems. If just the total energy consumption is considered, it can be concluded that returnables use roughly half the energy consumed in the milk carton system. The returnable system with the lowest energy consumption is dependant on the trippage rate assumptions. The polycarbonate bottle has the lowest system energy if used 75 times on average. The polycarbonate bottle with a trippage of 50 still has a slightly lower energy consumption than glass bottles used 50 times, although the polycarbonate system uses the most oil in this case.

A more careful examination of the results shows that 44% of the milk carton system energy is derived from wood. If only the consumption of oil is considered, the carton system uses 19.8 tonnes of oil equivalent (toe) per million litres, while the returnable system uses between 13.6 toe/million litres (50 trip polycarbonate) and 10.4 toe/million litres (50 trip glass). A significant proportion of the system energy for both the carton and the polycarbonate alternatives is in the form of feedstock. This energy is liberated if the waste is incinerated and the energy is reduced by one third in the case of cartons. The results for glass bottles are not noticeably changed, whereas the system energy for the PC bottles is reduced by between 5% and 7% depending on the trippage. The reason that the figures for the polycarbonate system are not reduced by more is that energy consumption in distribution and sales dominates, rather than energy in the production of new bottles.

Jobs

Table 7.7 shows that the introduction of polycarbonate returnables would increase the number of jobs compared with today's cartons by 1.4 man years per million litres. The increase for glass is about 3.8 man years per million litres. Several factors should be taken into account when interpreting these results. Most of the increase in jobs occurs in shops, while the number of jobs in the industries which produce packaging materials, or deliver goods to these industries, is

Table 7.6 Energy Balance for Packaging 1 million litres of Milk in Different Systems (GJ/million litres of milk)

Reproduced from D.W. Nunn, *Alternative Milk Packaging — an Impact Analysis*, CMI report 790306-1, Bergen, 1980, by permission.

| | Carton | | | Glass | | | | | | Polycarbonate | | | | | |
| | | | | 30 trips | | | 50 trips | | | 50 trips | | | 75 trips | | |
	Electricity	Oil	Wood	Electricity	Oil	Wood	Electricity	Oil	Wood	Electricity	Oil	Wood	Electricity	Oil	Wood
Production of packaging	68	671	893	65	198	49	54	127	49	49	308	40	43	214	40
Dairy	22	30	—	30	102	—	30	102	—	28	101	—	28	101	—
Distribution	2	127	—	3	205	—	3	208	—	2	164	—	2	164	—
Sales	249	—	—	424	—	—	424	—	—	282	—	—	282	—	—
Consumer	24	—	—	73	—	—	73	—	—	56	—	—	56	—	—
Refuse disposal (landfill)	~0	4	—	~0	~0	—	~0	~0	—	~0	~0	—	~0	~0	—
Total	365	832	893	595	506	49	584	437	49	417	573	40	411	479	40
Total	2090			1150			1070			1030			930		

Table 7.7   Employment Requirements for each Packaging Alternative (man years per million litres of milk sold)

Reproduced from D.W. Nunn, *Alternative Milk Packaging — an Impact Analysis*, CMI report 790306-1, Bergen, 1980, by permission.

	Carton	Glass		Polycarbonate	
		30 trips	50 trips	75 trips	50 trips
Production of packaging	1.7	0.8	0.7	0.7	0.8
Dairy	0.8	1.1	1.1	1.0	1.0
Distribution	1.4	2.4	2.4	1.8	1.8
Sales	2.6	5.4	5.4	4.3	4.3
Consumer	—	—	—	—	—
Refuse disposal (landfill)	0.1	~0	~0	~0	~0
Total	6.4	9.7	9.6	7.8	7.9

reduced. The system chosen determines which industry will be affected. A move away from the milk cartons in use today would have severe effects on employment in companies who make the blanks and the board. The jobs created in the returnable systems would be significantly more decentralized than those they replaced in the companies producing packaging.

Costs

The cost calculations presented in Table 7.8 show that the single-trip system has the lowest total cost. Polycarbonate bottles represent the cheapest of the returnable systems, but the total cost per litre is increased by 0.13 NOK/litre — an increase of 19%. Glass returnables lead to costs which are 0.34 NOK/litre greater than today's cartons — an increase of 47%. Cost increases in distribution and sales are the most important explanatory factors. Cost savings in waste disposal are only a very small part of the total picture. Large investments will have to be made if dairies introduce returnable bottles — of the order of 1.2 million NOK per million litre capacity (one NOK is about 0.16 USD) for a medium-sized (5 million litre) dairy. Many of the smaller dairies may not have the means to make such investments.

Table 7.8   Cost of Selling Milk in the Three Packaging Systems (NOK/litre at 1978 price levels; 1 NOK ~ 0.16 USD)

	Carton	Glass		Polycarbonate	
		30 trips	50 trips	50 trips	75 trips
Production of packaging	0.175	0.101	0.092	0.092	0.084
Dairy	0.122	0.225	0.225	0.195	0.195
Distribution	0.160	0.263	0.263	0.207	0.207
Sales	0.237	0.459	0.459	0.352	0.352
Consumer	0.009	0.015	0.015	0.011	0.011
Refuse disposal (landfill)	0.014	0.002	0.001	0.002	0.001
Total	0.717	1.064	1.055	0.858	0.850

At present, there is no washing and bottling machinery on the market which can handle both 1-litre and 2-litre polycarbonate bottles. These bottles have different cross-sections. Dairies which would normally not have two bottling lines (i.e. dairies bottling less than 10 million litres annually) would therefore probably be forced to cut out the 2-litre size because of the necessary investment.

Single-trip cartons appear to be superior with regard to factors such as hygiene and consumer acceptability, although returnable systems may also be satisfactory in these respects.

Refuse Disposal

The introduction of returnable packaging will reduce the fraction of household waste resulting from milk packaging from 3.4% by weight at present to 1.1% if glass bottles (30 trips) are used, or to 0.2% if polycarbonate bottles (50 trips) are used. As household waste amounts to 40% of the municipal waste, the change in this stream will not exceed 1.3%. The energy content in the milk cartons used in Norway today corresponds to about 11 500 tonnes/year of fuel oil or 0.49 PJ/year, which is only 2.8% of the total energy content of municipal waste. The polycarbonate system would give rise to waste corresponding to 800-1200 tonnes/year of fuel oil or 0.034-0.051 PJ/year, depending on the trippage. The calorific value of municipal waste will not change by more than 1%.

REFERENCES

1. BALTENSPERGER, M., 75 years of refuse incineration at Zürich 1904-1979, *ISWA Journal*, **30** (1980) 1-2.
2. HALMÖ, T.M., *Solid Waste Treatment in Stavanger*, SINTEF report STF21 A79088, Trondheim, 1979. (In Norwegian).
3. MELÖY, H., WANGEN, G. and HALMÖ, T.M., *Solid Waste Received by Norwegian Landfills: Waste Categories, Amounts and Composition*, SINTEF report STF21 A76091, Trondheim, 1976. (In Norwegian)
4. NATVIG, K., KNAP, A. HJ. and HALMÖ, T.M., *Municipal Waste III: Chemical Analysis*, SINTEF report STF21 A77049. Trondheim, 1977. (In Norwegian)
5. BEKKEVOLD, S. and LUKKEDAL, B., *Recycling of Plastic Waste: Separation Methods and Product Specification*, SINTEF report STF21 A78081, Trondheim, 1978. (In Norwegian)
6. NUNN, D.W., *Alternative Milk Packaging — an Impact Analysis*, CMI report 790306-1, Bergen, 1980. (In Norwegian, with English summary)
7. BRIDGWATER, A.V., The technology and economics of thermal processing of refuse. In: BRIDGWATER, A.V. and LIDGREN, K. (Eds.) *Household Waste Management in Europe: economics and techniques*, Van Nostrand Reinhold, 1981.
8. BUEKENS, A.G., Materials recovery by central sorting of household refuse. In: BRIDGWATER, A.V. and LIDGREN, K., (Eds.) *Household Waste Management in Europe: economics and techniques*, Van Nostrand Reinhold, 1981.
9. ENHÖRNING, B., Incineration of refuse with energy reclamation. In: BRIDGWATER, A.V. and LIDGREN, K. (Eds.) *Household Waste Management in Europe: economics and techniques*, Van Nostrand Reinhold, 1981.

10. TABASARAN, O., Gas production from landfill. In: BRIDGWATER, A.V. and LIDGREN, K. (Eds.) *Household Waste Management in Europe: economics and techniques*, Van Nostrand Reinhold, 1981.

Dr. ing. Aage Heie is presently, after some years with chemical and biochemical research, leader of the 'Garbologists' (Garbage Scientist Group) at SINTEF in Trondheim, Norway. SINTEF is a non-profit organization performing research under contract to corporations, industrial association, public service agencies, government departments and other clients, and has a staff of about 1000, of which about 10 can be classified as garbologists. Dr. Heie's main projects at SINTEF have dealt with recycling of food waste, treatment and recycling of household, industrial and hazardous waste, regional solid waste management in rural areas, master plan for recycling in the Nordic countries and solid waste management in developing countries.

Dr. ing. Terje M. Halmö is Research Manager and Head of SINTEF's Environmental Engineering Division, which has research groups on gas cleaning, water and waste water treatment, solid waste management, industrial hygiene and applied biology. Dr. Halmö holds an M.Sc. and a Doctorate in chemical engineering, and has carried out research on absorption of pollutants on activated carbon, and material flow and treatment of solid wastes. He has been extensively involved in consulting projects on solid waste for international agencies like UNDP and the World Bank, in Kenya, Egypt, Ethiopia and the Phillippines as well as Norway. Dr. Halmö is senior lecturer in Solid Waste Management at the Norwegian Institute of Technology (NTH).

8 The Effect of Post-consumer Recycling on the Energy Requirements of Beverage Container Systems

I. Boustead

INTRODUCTION

The recovery and re-use of waste materials is widely practised within industrial systems. In the glass industry, for example, internally produced scrap is fed back to the melting furnace and tinplate scrap from the can-making industry is detinned and returned to the steelmaking process. However, by far the greatest amount of waste is generated by the domestic consumer. In the UK this amounts to some 18 million tonnes per year of all types[1], yet despite the very large mass and volume of this waste, as well as the presence of valuable raw materials and potential fuels, there is as yet very little reclamation practised in the UK when measured as a proportion of the total amount of waste generated. The same is true worldwide even though specific schemes show some promise.

The main reason why large-scale recycling is not practised appears to be economic, but attitudes are slowly changing as it is increasingly realised that domestic waste could yield many raw materials and fuels which may become scarce and/or expensive in the not too distant future. Moreover, the implementation of recycling schemes often leads to a reduction in the resource requirements of many practical systems such as the beverage container systems. While economic considerations will continue to play a large part in determining the viability of practical reclamation schemes, it is important to understand their resource implications.

THE GENERAL RECYCLING SYSTEM

The general features of a recycling system are shown in Fig. 8.1. Fig. 8.1a shows a typical linear sequence of operations in which materials of mass M are eventually disposed of in the ground. For simplicity, materials losses at individual processing stages have been omitted. The essential features of this system are that a materials input of mass M and an energy input $(E_1 + E_2 + E_3)$ are needed to sustain the system. Such a system clearly approximates to the beverage container systems if operation 1 represents all processing up to the point at which recycled material re-enters the production sequence. In the case of glass containers, operation 1 would be all operations up to the glass furnace; for steel cans it would represent all operations up to the steel making converter. Operation 3 would represent the collection and disposal of post-consumer waste and operation 2 would represent all other processes within the system. When recycling is practised as shown in Fig. 8.1b, a fraction of the materials leaving operation 2 are fed back into the production system via a recycling operation 4. The effect of this is to reduce the demand for

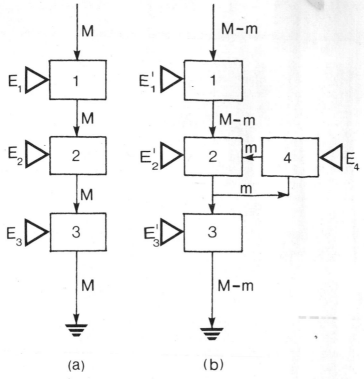

(a)   (b)

Fig. 8.1 Simplified flow diagrams of (a) a typical linear production system and (b) the same system when a recycling loop is included.

primary raw materials to $(M - m)$. The energy required to sustain the system is $(E_1'$ $+ E_2' + E_3' + E_4)$. It is immediately clear that by introducing the recycling loop the demand for raw materials has been reduced and this is invariably true for such systems.

However, it is not immediately clear whether such a system will save energy. The difference in energy requirements of the two systems is

$$(E_1 - E_1') + (E_2 - E_2') + (E_3 - E_3') - E_4 \tag{1}$$

This expression can be simplified for beverage container systems by making a number of assumptions. E_1' is expected to be less than E_1 because operation 1 is required to handle a lower throughput of materials when recycling is practised. Operation 2 is handling the same mass of materials in both cases and so E_2 and E_2' might reasonably be expected to be equal. The only important exception to this is the recycling of cullet, where an increased proportion of cullet in the furnace feed leads to a reduction in the furnace energy requirement[2]. Operation 3 is the disposal operation and, as can be seen from Chapter 3, this is usually a relatively small contributor to the total system energy. To a first approximation, therefore, let $E_3 = E_3'$. Thus, although expression 1 above is the more accurate form for calculating energy changes in this type of recycling system, a reasonable simplification for beverage container systems is

$$\Delta E_1 - E_4 \tag{2}$$

where

$$\Delta E_1 = E_1 - E_1'$$

For energy saving to occur, expression 2 must be positive and hence
$$\Delta E_1 > E_4$$
The magnitude of E_4 will depend on the type of reclamation scheme employed, but some notion of the energy limits within which such a scheme must work can be derived by considering the value of ΔE. For glass reclamation, recovered cullet replaces virgin raw material in the furnace feed. From Chapter 6, the energy required to produce and deliver the raw materials for the production of 1 kg of glass containers is 4.6 MJ. Hence, neglecting any changes in the furnace energy requirements, the maximum energy saving that could be achieved by reclaiming cullet is 4.6 MJ/kg and a net energy saving overall will occur if the energy requirement of the reclamation process, E_4, is less than this value. Similar calculations have been carried out for the other two main beverage container materials. For tinplate the maximum saving is 25.1 MJ/kg of recovered steel[3] and for aluminium the maximum saving is 308.3 MJ/kg recovered aluminium remelt ingot[4].

RECOVERY METHODS

The methods used to recover materials from post-consumer waste fall into three main categories:

(i) those in which domestic refuse is collected in the usual way and then passed through a mechanical separation plant which removes the desired materials as separate fractions, leaving the unwanted materials for disposal by conventional methods;

(ii) those in which the consumer is asked to keep separate the desired materials and these are collected separately from the consumer by door-to-door collections;

(iii) those in which the consumer is asked to keep separate the desired materials and also asked to deliver them to some central collection point.

The main advantage of mechanical sorting is that no reliance is placed on the often unpredictable behaviour of the consumer and, once in full scale operation, such plants should yield a constant supply of well characterized materials. The main problem with such processes is that they are expensive to construct and must handle heavily contaminated input materials so that extensive processing must often be carried out after a fraction has been separated from the main throughput. It is also important to remember that not all materials may be separated from domestic refuse with equal ease. Ferrous metal is the simplest to separate because of its magnetic properties and it is not surprising that most mechanical plants, no matter how small, extract this fraction. Aluminium and glass require more complex separation circuits. Moreover, since the amount of potentially re-usable aluminium present in much European domestic refuse is small, and because of the relatively low value of glass cullet, the large-scale extraction of these materials by mechanical separation plants is likely only where a suitably enriched by-product stream is available from some other separation operation.

Until recently, consumer-aided reclamation schemes were thought unlikely to succeed in the long term because of the gradual fall-off in interest by the consumer. Such schemes have, however, operated very successfully in the USA for many years, particularly for the collection of aluminium cans, where a financial incentive is usually offered to the consumer. More recently, experiences in the UK

Table 8.1 Energy Required to Recover 1 kg of Glass, Steel or Aluminium from Post-consumer Waste by Selected Recovery Schemes

Process	Electricity/MJ		Oil fuels/MJ			Other fuels/MJ			Total energy /MJ
	Fuel production & delivery	Energy content of fuel	Fuel production & delivery	Energy content of fuel	Feedstock energy	Fuel production & delivery	Energy content of fuel	Feedstock energy	
Glass (as clean cullet)									
Bottle bank (UK)*	0.08	0.03	0.05	0.26	—	—	0.02	—	0.44
York experiment (UK)**	5.17	1.72	3.13	15.65	—	0.01	4.41	4.74	34.83
BIRP (USA)*	0.05	0.02	1.98	9.38	—	0.01	0.14	—	11.58
Doncaster***	3.03	1.01	—	—	—	—	—	—	4.04
New Orleans (USA)***	2.28	0.76	0.11	0.54	—	—	—	—	3.69
Ferrous scrap (clean baled)									
Doncaster (UK)***	0.65	0.21	0.23	1.14	—	—	0.05	0.03	2.31
Material Recovery (Stoke)***	3.40	1.13	0.27	1.32	—	—	0.07	0.03	6.22
Byker (UK)***	1.46	0.48	0.21	1.02	—	—	0.04	0.03	3.24
New Orleans (USA)***	0.98	0.32	0.22	1.05	—	—	0.04	0.03	2.64
Ames, Iowa (USA)***	1.28	0.42	0.22	1.05	—	—	0.04	0.03	3.04
Aluminium (as remelt ingot)									
Alcoa, Edinburgh (UK)*	4.12	1.38	3.58	18.23	0.03	1.34	16.34	—	45.02
Alcoa, Dallas (USA)*	1.00	0.34	2.56	13.48	—	1.23	14.98	—	33.59
BIRP (USA)*	1.97	0.66	2.04	10.86	—	1.23	14.93	—	31.69
New Orleans (USA)***	5.16	1.73	0.12	0.60	—	1.23	14.93	—	23.77

* Consumers return containers to collection centre.
** Separated items are collected from the consumer.
*** Mechanical separation of collected domestic refuse.

101

Table 8.2   Energy Associated with Fuels (UK practice)

Fuel	Unit	Fuel prod'n & delivery energy/MJ	Energy content of fuel /MJ	Total energy /MJ	Production efficiency %
Coal	kg	1.39	28.01	29.40	95
Coke	kg	3.93	25.42	29.35	87
Electricity	kWh$_e$	10.80	3.6	14.40	25
Natural gas	therm	8.67	105.44	114.11	92
Manufactured gas	therm	41.21	105.44	146.65	72
Heavy fuel oil	litre	8.57	40.98	49.55	83
Medium fuel oil	litre	8.50	40.92	49.42	83
Light fuel oil	litre	8.29	40.18	48.47	83
Gas oil	litre	7.42	37.84	45.26	84
Kerosine	litre	6.96	36.53	43.49	84
Diesel	litre	7.45	37.71	45.16	84
Gasoline	litre	6.85	35.97	42.82	84
LPG	kg	8.89	50.00	58.89	85
Lubricating oil	litre	8.29	40.92	49.21	83
Grease	kg	8.89	42.60	51.49	83

with the bottle bank as a means of collecting glass cullet seem to suggest that they can be sustained without any financial incentive if properly organized.

The energy associated with the recovery of products from refuse using a number of different schemes in the UK and the USA has recently been examined[5] and the results are summarized in Table 8.1. These requirements have been calculated using the fuel production efficiencies of Table 8.2.

Bearing in mind the upper limits to the recovery energies for overall energy savings to occur (i.e. 4.6 MJ/kg for glass, 25.1 MJ/kg for steel and 308.3 MJ/kg for aluminium), it is clear that energy savings are most difficult to achieve in glass recovery. In contrast, the much larger savings arising with steel and aluminium are due mainly to the higher energy requirements for the production of these materials from primary sources. It is perhaps important to note that mechanical separation schemes are best operated with the recovery of a number of products; in this way the energy used per product is lower than when only a single product is extracted.

RECLAMATION OF FEEDSTOCK ENERGY

All beverage container systems generate waste, which involves the consumption of feedstock energy in the production of paper, board and plastics. The contribution of this component to the overall system energy is, however, small. There is one beverage system where feedstock energy is significant, namely the PET bottle system, and it is useful to consider this system in some detail because it highlights the more complex nature of feedstock recycling.

In common with all plastics waste, PET may be recovered from post-consumer waste for use as either a fuel or a material. The calorific value[6] of PET is of the order of 23 MJ/kg, so that if all PET used could eventually be reclaimed as a fuel, the net gross energy requirement for the production of this resin would effectively be reduced[7] from 154 MJ/kg to 131 MJ/kg, a reduction of 15%. On the other hand, if the polymer could be recovered for further use as a material, the energy required to produce it from crude oil would be spread over two applications. The net energy attributable to each application is then halved, giving an effective gross energy requirement for resin production of 77 MJ/kg. It is also important to note that the recovery of PET as a material does not exclude its eventual recovery at some later stage as a fuel. Thus if the materials were to be recycled once as materials and then recovered as a fuel, the net contribution that would arise from the use of the polymer is reduced to 65.6 MJ/kg compared with 154 MJ/kg for virgin polymer as at present used. This represents an overall decrease of 57% in effective energy requirement for polymer production.

The very significant potential energy savings outlined above do, however, rely upon two main assumptions. First, they assume 100% recovery of PET from post-consumer waste; and second, they assume that the polymer is recovered with the expenditure of no further energy. Neither of these assumptions is realized in practice, as discussed below. Nevertheless, the values quoted above do represent the *maximum* energy savings that could be achieved.

Consider first the recovery of PET as a fuel. A significant fraction of general domestic refuse consists of combustible materials which, when separated from the other components of waste, provide a useful fuel. By far the greater proportion of this combustible fraction is paper and board (approximately 28% by mass) but the calorific value of this component is substantially enhanced by the presence of plastics (approximately 6% by mass). Set against this, however, is the presence of moisture in domestic refuse which reduces the calorific value by about 30%. Thus, for the PET fraction of waste, an effective calorific value of 16 MJ/kg is probably more appropriate than the 'dry' value of 23 MJ/kg.

This effective value is further reduced since energy is required to separate refuse-derived fuel (RDF) from the bulk of refuse and the recovery rate of the combustible fraction is less than 100%. Detailed analysis of RDF plants operating in the UK[5] suggest that a reasonable average value for the energy required to manufacture RDF is 1.5 MJ/kg (Table 8.3) with a recovery rate of 85%. Taking the above factors into account and assuming that all domestic refuse is treated for RDF recovery, the net reduction in PET energy requirement, due to the recovery of used bottles as a fuel component in RDF, will be $((16 \times 0.85) - 1.5) =$ 12.1 MJ/kg PET; i.e. a saving of approximately half the 23 MJ/kg calculated for the ideal case discussed earlier.

Consider now the problems concerned with the recovery of PET as a *material*. Mechanical separation would be ideal because it could lead to a regular supply of recovered PET. However, it is well known[8, 9] that reclamation of re-usable plastic

Table 8.3 **Typical Average Energy Required to Produce 1 kg of Refuse-Derived Fuel (RDF) from General Domestic Refuse in the UK**

Fuel type	Fuel production and delivery energy/MJ	Energy content of fuel /MJ	Feedstock energy /MJ	Total energy /MJ
Electricity	1.12	0.38	nil	1.50
Oil fuels	nil	nil	nil	nil
Other fuels	nil	nil	nil	nil
Totals	1.12	0.38	nil	1.50

materials from general domestic refuse is difficult, principally because there is no physical property with sufficient variation to permit discrimination of different polymer types. The other major defect of mechanical sorting is contamination. These factors impose severe limitations on the reclamation of characterizable polymer fractions from general domestic refuse, and in the forseeable future it seems unlikely that PET will be recovered as a material from this source.

One factor which militates against the implementation of consumer-aided reclamation schemes for the recovery of plastics in general is the difficulty experienced by consumers in positively identifying specific polymer types. However, PET bottles as currently marketed have a distinctive appearance, so that the polymer can be identified by the layman using the product as the identifying feature. This advantage could be retained if the essential features of the design were to remain unchanged and so consumer-aided reclamation of PET as a material appears possible. In fact a pilot scheme has been started in Bradford in the UK.

A factor of particular importance in calculating the energy requirements of consumer-aided collection schemes is the bulk density of the collected containers. For PET bottles of total mass 63 g and capacity 1.5 litres, the bulk density is approximately 400 kg/m^3. This contrasts sharply with glass bottles where the bulk density varies from 630 to 1000 kg/m^3 depending on bottle size and assuming no breakage. Hence, in the worst case, the bulk density of PET bottles will be a factor of 25 times less than that for glass bottles. It is therefore expected that transport energies for collected PET bottles could be up to 25 times greater than the transport energies for glass bottles. In practice, this factor is unlikely to be as large as this because collected bottles would be crushed or granulated before being transported.

If PET bottles were collected by a consumer-aided scheme similar to the bottle bank, the energy requirements can be estimated by analogy with the bottle bank. For glass collection, the energy required to collect the containers and deliver them to the glass factory for processing has been estimated[5] as 0.27 MJ/kg. Adopting a 'worst case' approach, and assuming that the bulk density of PET bottles is a factor of 25 lower than for glass bottles, this would imply a gross energy requirement for PET bottle collection of 7 MJ/kg which is well below the potential saving of 77 MJ/kg.

The collected bottles would need to be treated to separate PET from any polyethylene, paper, glue and aluminium present. A pilot scheme which enables this to be done has been developed by Goodyear at Akron in the USA[10]. Based on experience with this pilot plant, a full-scale commercial plant has been designed and the energy requirements of the plant are given in Table 8.4. Assuming that 75% of the mass of the bottles collected is PET and that the process can reclaim 80% of the input PET, the data in Table 8.4 indicate a gross energy requirement for the production of recovered PET flake of $4.08/(0.75 \times 0.80) = 6.8$ MJ/kg. When combined with the collection energy of 7 MJ/kg, the total maximum energy required to recover PET is of the order of 13-14 MJ/kg giving a minimum net energy saving of $(77 - 14) = 63$ MJ/kg.

Thus the recover of PET material could lead to a practical reduction in energy of 63 MJ per kg of PET recovered. Remembering that the recovered PET is only $0.75 \times 80 = 60\%$ of the polymer originally used (assuming that all bottles are collected) then the net saving of energy per kg of polymer fed into the bottle making system is 38 MJ/kg, i.e. the effective polymer production energy requirement is reduced from 154 MJ/kg to 116 MJ/kg, a reduction of 25%.

104

Table 8.4   Estimated Energy Required to Separate the Components of PET Bottles Based on the Goodyear Process

Values are per kg of *input* bottles

Fuel type	Fuel production and delivery energy/MJ	Energy content of fuel /MJ	Feedstock energy /MJ	Total energy /MJ
Electricity	1.17	0.39	nil	1.56
Oil fuels	0.43	2.09	nil	2.52
Other fuels	nil	nil	nil	nil
Totals	1.60	2.48	nil	4.08

The production of PET resin contributes approximately 40% of the total system energy required in the production and use of PET bottles so the reclamation of PET as a *material* would lead to a reduction in the total system energy of the order of 10% and the recovery of PET as a *fuel* would lead to a reduction in the total system energy of the order of 3%.

ACKNOWLEDGEMENT

Part of the material contained in this chapter is taken from a report prepared for and financed by the Secretary of State, Department of Industry, London. The views expressed here are those of the author and do not necessarily coincide with those of the Secretary of State.

REFERENCES

1. PORTEOUS, A., *Recycling, Resources, Refuse*, Longman, London, 1977.
2. HUBERT, D., *Revista della Staz. Sper. Vetrol.*, No. 5., 1979.
3. BOUSTEAD, I. and HANCOCK, G.F., *Resources and Conservation*, **6** (1981) 29–45.
4. BOUSTEAD, I. and HANCOCK, G.F., *Resource Recovery and Conservation*, **5** (1981) 303–318.
5. BOUSTEAD, I. and HANCOCK, G.F., *Beverage Containers and Recycling*, Report to Department of Industry, London, 1980.
6. RESEARCH TRIANGLE INSTITUTE, *Energy and Economic Impacts of Mandatory Deposits*, US Dept. of Commerce Report No. PB-258-638, 1976.
7. BOUSTEAD, I. and HANCOCK, G.F., *Energy and Packaging*, Ellis Horwood, Chichester/John Wiley, New York, 1981.
8. THE PLASTIC BOTTLE INSTITUTE, *Energy Use and Resource Recovery — a Position Paper*, Society of Plastics Industry Inc., New York, February 1977.
9. BRITISH PLASTICS FEDERATION, *Technical Factors Governing the Recycling of Plastics*, London, July 1979.
10. GOODYEAR TIRE and RUBBER COMPANY, *Cleartuf Facts — Recycling Polyester Bottles*, Data sheet CT-17, Akron, Ohio (undated).

9 Beverage Packages and Energy — a Compilation of Different Investigation Results

M. Backman

INTRODUCTION

During the 1950s and 1960s, the number of single-use packages for beverages increased greatly. There are probably many explanations for this; in particular, increasing labour costs may have influenced the transition from the returnable bottle system, which may be described as labour-intensive, to the more capital-intensive single-use package systems. Furthermore, the rising real wages of consumers may have permitted the purchase of 'convenience' in the form of single-use packages. More recently, the growing problems of waste management, together with an appreciation of the finite limits to energy and mineral resources, have caused attention to be drawn to single use packages. These have been widely debated and blamed for much wastage of valuable resources. Many enquiries have been initiated, in the public and private sectors, to ascertain the energy consumption of beverage packages. This chapter summarizes the results from about 12 such enquiries.

On the subject of beverage packages, it should not be forgotten that there are wide-ranging technical demands — for example, gas and liquid tightness for carbonated drinks, compared with less stringent requirements for non-carbonated drinks such as milk. A single-use package solution for drinks such as milk may be made relatively 'simple' compared to a single-use package for, for example, beer. Consequently, in the remainder of this chapter, packages for carbonated drinks and non-carbonated drinks will be considered separately.

ENERGY CONSUMPTION

General

The manufacture, distribution and disposal of beverage containers are all processes in which resources in the form of materials and energy are used. Several investigations concerning the energy requirements of beverage packages have been carried out. A feature common to most of these investigations is that energy usage has been expressed in a single unit, for example kWh. However, the methods used to calculate this total supplied energy (gross energy) have not always been identical (more detailed accounts of the problems in energy analyses are included in Chapter 3) and, as a result, the calculation results vary widely and are difficult to compare, as will be apparent from the results below.

Carbonated Drinks

Beverage containers for beer and soft drinks are estimated to be responsible for about 0.25% of the total energy usage in Sweden. However, as was mentioned above, there is wide variation in published energy consumption figures. This is shown in Fig. 9.1, which is a compilation of results from a number of analyses relating to the energy requirements of beverage packages[1-5]. In all of these investigations, the energy input during the entire life cycle of the package is included; that is to say, packaging material manufacture, conversion, filling, distribution and waste management. In all investigations, energy consumption both at home and abroad has been included.

Fig. 9.1 illustrates energy usage as a function of the return rate for returnable bottles and aluminium cans. (The return rate is taken to mean the proportion of the containers returned or collected for re-use or recycling.) Since it is very difficult at the present time, both from a technical and economic point of view, to recycle metal cans having an aluminium lid, the energy usage of these items has been set out as independent of the return rate. As regards returnable bottles, the number of times which an average bottle is used (the usage rate) is a direct function of the return rate. If returnable bottles are thrown away in the same manner as single-use

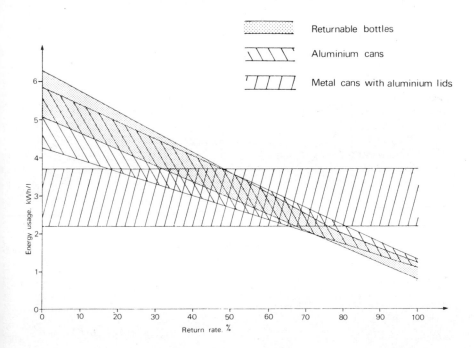

Fig. 9.1   The energy demands (in kWh /litre) of different beverage packaging systems as a function of the return rate (in %).

bottles, the return rate will be 0% and the usage rate 1. For purely physical reasons, i.e. that the bottles become worn out and break, the 'theoretical' maximum usage rate, i.e. 100% return rate, is probably about 45. Between the return rates of 0 and 100%, the usage rate increases exponentially. In Sweden, the usage rate for beer and soft drinks bottles is about 30 (return rate approximately 99%). For returnable wine and spirits bottles, the corresponding values are about 2.5 and 60%.

Fig. 9.1 can be summarized as follows:

(i)   Returnable bottles that are not returned are more energy-demanding than tinned steel cans with an aluminium top, and are as energy-demanding as, or slightly more energy-demanding than, aluminium cans which are not recovered. ·

(ii) In order that aluminium cans and returnable bottles be less energy demanding than tinned steel cans with aluminium tops, a return rate of between 50 and 60% will be required, i.e. for returnable bottles a usage rate of from 2 to 2.5.

(iii) At 100% return, the energy usage of returnable bottles is equal to or slightly less than that for aluminium cans.

Fig. 9.2 extends the scope by including two further recyclable containers — the all-steel can and the Swedish Rigello bottle. (A recyclable container is defined as a package which after use is utilized, for technical or economic reasons, as an input item in the production of new commodities. The term commodities is taken to mean both energy and physical products.) Because of difficulties in manufacturing a finger-pull opening of all-steel, the all-steel can is not available in Sweden,

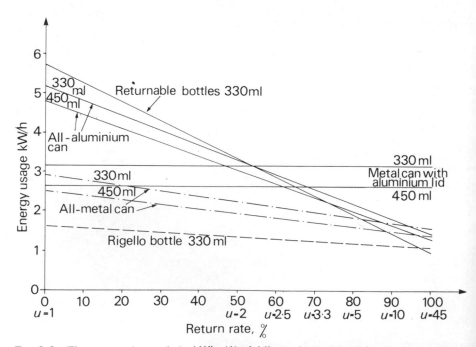

Fig. 9.2   The energy demands (in kWh /1) of different beverage packaging systems as a function of the return rate (in %). u = usage rate for returnable bottles.

108

and is available only in a restricted number of markets outside Sweden. For ease of reference the energy usage is indicated as averages of the energy values calculated.

It is clear from Fig. 9.2 that both the Rigello bottle and the all-steel can, on 100% return, have an energy requirement which is approximately equal to, or slightly higher than, that for the returnable bottle. It is also notable that the Rigello bottle has a lower energy consumption than other recyclable containers.

Non-carbonated Drinks

Milk cartons are estimated as being responsible for about 0.2% of Sweden's total energy usage. For containers for carbonated drinks, the margin of error in this estimate is relatively large. A compilation of energy analysis results from three different enquiries[6-8] is presented in Table 9.1. The calculations in these investigations have been carried out up to and including scope level III according to the definition presented in Chapter 3. Thus, the energy content in raw materials is included, irrespective of whether these are renewable (wood) or non-renewable (oil). It would seem to be a matter of opinion whether it is correct or not to do so — a policy which gives different answers in different studies.

Table 9.2 illustrates the effects of these different approaches concerning energy recovery[9], the scope of the energy analysis and the energy content of the wood. Five cases are represented in the table as follows:

(i)   (a) Direct energy supply in the form of electric power and non-renewable fuels.

      (b) The energy content of non-renewable raw materials bound in the products (such as gas, oil).

      (c) Electrical energy assumed to be marginally produced at an efficiency of 33%.

(ii) As Case (i) but with the assumption of 75% energy recovery by combustion of resultant waste product.

(iii) As Case (i), including the energy content of wood raw materials (renewable raw material) bound in the products.

(iv) As Case (iii) but with the assumption of a 75% energy recovery by combustion of resultant waste.

Table 9.1   The Energy Usage of Different Milk Packaging Systems in kWh_{th}/litre

Source	Carton	Glass bottle		Plastic bottle		Plastic bag
		20 trips	30 trips	50 trips	50 trips	75 trips 80 trips

Source	Carton		Glass bottle		Plastic bottle		Plastic bag
			20 trips 30 trips	50 trips	50 trips 75 trips		80 trips
CMI[6]							
Deposition	0.563			0.261 0.245	0.261 0.233		
Combustion	0.376			0.262 0.245	0.220 0.202		
Sundström[8]							
Deposition	0.670	0.420					
Combustion	0.540	0.420					
DMI[7]							
42% combustion with heat recovery	0.621		0.536			0.456	0.428

Table 9.2 The Effect of Different Approaches to Treating the Potential Energy in Trees and Plastics on the Energy Required for Packaging 3000 Quarts of Milk

Container	Case				
	(i) Base case	(ii) As (i) but with energy recovery from waste at 75% of potential	(iii) As (i) but considering trees as an energy source	(iv) As (iii) but with energy recovery at 75%	(v) Base case using GER*
3 quart jug — energy required: 10^6 BTU (use count: 200)	1.4	1.36	1.4	1.3	1.5
3 quart pouch — energy required: 10^6 BTU	3.6	2.6	3.6	2.6	3.9
1 quart carton — energy required: 10^6 BTU	4.1	2.5	7.8	6.2	4.6
1 quart bottle — energy required: 10^6 BTU (use count: 20)	3.5	3.5	3.5	3.5	4.0

* Gross Energy Requirement, which includes the energy required to produce petroleum, natural gas, etc.

(v)   As Case (i) but including energy inputs effected on production of supplied, non-renewable fuels.

One result from Table 9.2 is that the question of whether cartons are more or less energy demanding than returnable bottles can be reduced to a question of whether it is correct to include the heat value in wood raw materials supplied. One argument in favour of including such renewable raw materials in the calculation is the alternative use of wood as fuel. A counterargument is that wood, as opposed to coal, oil and gas, is a renewable resource which is used as an energy raw material to a limited extent. It might also be mentioned that the heat value in felled forest is never included in national energy balances. In Sweden, for example, inclusion of the energy content of felled pulp and timber production would increase the calculated annual energy usage by about 20%.

Table 9.3 shows a compilation of the results from two enquiries[10, 11] in which the energy usage has been calculated without regard to either the heat value in supplied wood raw materials or the energy consumption in transport and distribution. It should be noted that the German enquiry dealt exclusively with the disposal alternative for waste management, and that no final summation was carried out for electric power consumption and supply of fossil fuels (apart from wood).

Summarizing energy analyses relating to milk cartons leads to the following conclusions:

(i)   Cartons that are discarded make use of more energy than returnable bottles which are re-used.
(ii)   Cartons whose heat value is recycled are about as energy-demanding as returnable bottles which are re-used.
(iii) Plastic bottles which are re-used consume as much energy as, or slightly less energy than, returnable bottles which are re-used.
(iv)   Single-use bottles of plastic or glass, as well as returnable bottles of plastic or glass which are not re-used, are more energy-demanding than cartons.

CONCLUSIONS

The energy figures for beverage packages presented in different enquiries should be viewed against the background of the calculation problems related to energy analyses. Results presented with an accuracy of several decimal points are superficially impressive, but can always be said to be incorrect on the basis of different points of view and evaluations from those applied. By a different method of

Table 9.3   Energy Consumption Analyses in Germany and Austria

Source	Carton	Glass bottle	
		25 trips	60 trips
Kozmiensky et al.[10]			
Electricity	0.026	0.013	
Fuels	0.079	0.056	
ÖIV[11]			
Combustion	0.083		0.087
Deposition	0.146		0.088

Table 9.4   Containers for Carbonated Drinks — Energy Usage

Type of container	In relation to returnable bottles which are re-used
Aluminium cans, Rigello bottles and all-metal cans which are not re-used	use more energy
Metal cans with aluminium top	use more energy
Returnable bottles which are not re-used	use more energy
Aluminium cans, Rigello bottles and all-metal cans which are recovered	use as much or slightly more energy

calculation, the 'ranking' between the energy usages of different packages can be completely reversed. This effect is enhanced with small differences between individual products. A rough estimate of the order of magnitude of the energy consumption would seem in such cases to be of at least as much value as careful calculations.

For the establishment of 'large' energy balances relating to, for example, a whole country, the situation is different. The aim is then often to identify particularly energy-intensive sectors and/or to follow the developments of energy consumption through several years. The selection of calculation routines in such cases does not have the same decisive effect on the result as it has when individual products are compared.

Since the returnable bottle is to be found in all of the investigations which have hitherto been presented, this package constitutes a suitable point of reference in an attempt to correlate the investigation results. Such a summary is presented in Tables 9.4 and 9.5 for carbonated and non-carbonated beverages, respectively. Traditional so-called single-use or one-way packages, which are recyclable, such as aluminium cans and carton packages, are thus not associated with a higher energy consumption than returnable bottles, provided the rate of recovery is the same within both packaging systems. In Sweden, roughly 99% of all empty returnable bottles for beer and soft drinks are returned, which gives a recovery rate which is difficult to attain for other recyclable packages. However, this high figure must be viewed against the background that there are alternatives in the form of single-use containers for consumers who are not willing to undertake the work

Table 9.5   Containers for Non-carbonated Drinks — Energy Usage

Type of container	In relation to returnable bottles which are re-used
Returnable bottles of plastic which are re-used	use as much or slightly less energy
Single use bottles of plastic or glass, and returnable bottles of plastic or glass which are not re-used	use more energy
Carton packages which are not recovered	use more energy
Carton packages which are burned with heat recovery	use roughly the same amount of energy

112

nvolved in the handling of returnable bottles. If these alternatives were not avail-
ble, there is an obvious risk that a number of returnable bottles would assume the
lace of the single-use package among domestic waste, whence they cannot be
eparated and re-used.

If it is considered desirable that energy consumption in the beverage packaging
ector be reduced, the manufacture of re-usable and recoverable packages should
e stimulated, and at the same time it should be ensured that these packages really
re re-used or recycled. However, it is also worth highlighting the relatively low
nergy usage in these beverage packages in the context of national energy con-
umption. As far as Sweden is concerned at least, neither the above measures nor
ny others would be expected to result in perceptible changes of the total energy
onsumption of the country.

REFERENCES

1. HANSERUD, L., *Energy Analyses of Beverage Packages for Beer*, 1978.
2. MIDWEST RESEARCH INSTITUTE, *Resource and Environmental Profile Analysis of 10 Beer Container Systems*, 1975.
3. RESEARCH TRIANGLE INSTITUTE, *Energy and Economic Impacts of Manda-tory Deposits*, 1975.
4. SUNDSTRÖM, G., *Beverage Containers and Energy*, Lund, Sweden, 1974.
5. THE SWEDISH ENERGY SAVINGS COMMISSION, *Energy and Packages*, 1979.
6. CHR. MICHELSENS INSTITUTE (CMI), *Alternative Milk Packages — a Con-sequence Analysis*, Bergen, Norway, 1979.
7. DANISH MINISTRY OF ENVIRONMENT (DMI), *Report on an Investigation Con-cerned with Socioeconomic, Environmental and Resource Aspects on Alter-native Consumer Packages for Milk Products*, Copenhagen, Denmark, 1978.
8. SUNDSTRÖM, G., *Milchverpackungen und Energie in der Bundesrepublik Deutschland*, 1981.
9. ONTARIO RESEARCH FOUNDATION, *Energy Analysis of Milk Packaging*, 1976.
10. THOMÉ-KOZMIENSKY, K.J., FRANCKE, M. and BÖTTQE, H.-U., *Umwelt-auswirkungen durch Frischmilchverpackungen Systemvergleich*, Berlin, 1981.
11. ÖSTERREICHISCHES INSTITUT FÜR VERPACKUNGSWESEN (ÖIV), *Systemver-gleich Einwegverpackung — Mehrwegverpackung*, 1977.

10 Energy Utilization within the Beverage Sector as a Motive for Public Intervention

K. Lidgren

INTRODUCTION

Energy Consumption within the Packaging Sector

The manufacture, distribution and disposal of beverage containers are al
processes in which resources in the form of energy are consumed. A number o
investigations on different beverage containers' requirements of energy have
therefore been carried out. Regrettably, however, not all the investigations have
used the same methods to calculate this total input energy (gross energy). Results
therefore, are often difficult or impossible to compare.

This is by no means a new problem; it originated a few years after World War I
when so-called energy balances were first calculated. Since then there have been
wide ranging discussions about which model is best suited to convert differen
forms of energy into a common measuring unit. It is obvious that electrical powe
and fuel cannot be added directly, but there are differences of opinion as to how
the gross energy in the production of electricity should be calculated. How should
electrical production based on water power and nuclear power be evaluated
Depending on the model used, widely different values can be obtained for the
gross energy requirement.

The energy figures presented in the different investigations should be viewed
against the background of this calculation problem. Large numbers of significan
figures give a false degree of confidence, as the basis of the calculations is ofter
much less certain. An estimate of the order of magnitude appears to be of greate
value than a presentation of exact figures.

This chapter investigates whether politically motivated corrective action i
required in the beverage container sector because 'free market forces' do not auto
matically ensure optimal consumption of energy within this sector.

OVERCONSUMPTION OF ENERGY

To start with, it is quite clear that the prices paid for energy are determined by th
market. Certainly the processing of different energy resources can itself give rise to
negative external effects. (A negative external effect means that the production o
one or more firms and/or the consumption of one or more individuals influenc
the production possibilities of other firms and/or the living standards of othe
individuals in a negative, i.e. adverse, direction, without this effect being paid fo
by those who create it.) But if measures aimed at the types of environmenta
impact mentioned above are to be administered and really diminish the tota
pollution load, they must be general in the sense of being based on different kind
of pollution and not on the nature of the final product.

It is widely believed that we are undergoing a natural resource crisis and that every measure that decreases the consumption of natural resources should be considered. So the questions to ask are: Are we going through such a crisis? If so, how can it be attacked?

It would be unreasonable to deny that the world's total resources, known and unknown, of non-renewable natural resources, such as oil, continue to decrease. During the 1960s the known oil reserves increased by about 50 thousand million tonnes, to which can be compared the consumption of at least 15 thousand million tonnes. Thus for every tonne of oil used more than three times as much was found. This factor is of interest as, in spite of a decrease in total oil resources, there was concurrently a very considerable increase in the quantity that could be offered to the market. Increased supplies are not usually regarded as unpleasant crises by buyers — only by sellers. Thus it would be just as unreasonable to suggest that the price increases during 1973 and 1974 came about because the world's known oil reserves had suddenly decreased radically.

What in fact caused the price increases of these natural resources was initially a result of the change in the market structure, especially for oil. An effective cartel, OPEC, was formed by a number of the large oil-producing countries and limits were imposed on sales offers, which sent prices soaring. Those who favour limiting the consumption of natural resources are bound to approve of the oil producers for their monopolistic behaviour. But with a monopoly both higher prices and lower consumption usually follow. Yet the purchasers have also wrought changes. The formation of the oil club is one example.

Nevertheless the fact remains that non-renewable natural resources are continually being depleted. In a well known report from the Club of Rome, *The Limits of Growth*, it was shown — or, as many believe, 'proved' — that almost insoluble problems will appear in the not too distant future. One of the problems is that a number of natural resources will be consumed much too rapidly.

In this connection it is interesting to quote extracts from an article published in 1900 in the Swedish Economic Journal that dealt with the world's supplies of coal which were believed to be running out:

> The great rise in coal prices that arose towards the end of last year and which during this year have increased further, have, as is natural, made themselves unpleasantly felt in many different ways. For coal plays such an important and far-reaching role in all fields; nowadays of course it is included as a necessary means of production in all trades and also in a large part of the world constitutes the actual household fuel. A shortage of this article with an accompanying great price increase must therefore make its effect felt in the greatest degree.

> The present price increase of coal has produced a certain degree of uneasiness about western Europe's future supply of this article. The questions that have been considered in this situation are:
> 1. How shall it be possible to avoid such rapid increases in price in the future?
> 2. How long can the various producer countries' coal reserves last, and with regard to this, what measures should be taken?

> Even the question of the duration of the English coal deposits has been taken up again. Since Jevons' well known work *The Coal Question* appeared in 1865, this question has been taken up for new discussion repeatedly. Jevons has calculated that England's coal deposits . . . were 80 000 million tonnes and that these deposits would not last longer than 1960. In this he proceeded from the size of production in 1860, which was 80 million tonnes, and also that production . . . would grow on an average by 3.5% per annum.

115

It is quite natural that these views of the future of British industry and trade produced proposals to put off the expected catastrophe, at least for as long as possible. The means then considered were: excepting . . . export prohibition and export duties . . . to try to prevent waste of coal both in its mining and in its utilization. To achieve this it was suggested, among other things, to tax coal in order to make it dear, the intention being . . . coal consumers will be compelled to economize in its use.

1960 was passed by more than 20 years ago, and the world's total coal deposits are estimated today at about 65 000 thousand million tonnes. Coal has now been removed from the list of natural resources that are expected to run out in the next 100 years. The main themes of the article quoted from 1900 reappear, however, in various forms in articles written in 1973, but with the difference that coal was replaced by oil.

Thus the general debate on the future often ignores the likelihood that, as a commodity becomes less available and accordingly increases in price, its usage will be improved and the development and adoption of a substitute encouraged. Finally, price increases act as an inducement to find more of the commodity (an example being the Swedish Oil Prospecting Company Ltd.'s oil prospecting), and also to increase the degree of exploitation, for example by extracting North Sea oil. Taken together, these automatic corrections act as stabilizers which slow down the development of a resource crisis.

The decision of society to subsidize energy substitutes (for example energy-saving grants) in different ways and to place special taxes on energy and thus increase its relative price can be interpreted as a rejection of market price formation for energy. The introduction in Sweden of compulsory sorting of newspapers and magazines in households can also be interpreted as a protection of market pricing for raw materials to make paper.

In the general debate on future energy conservation, various reasons are advanced to save energy, including:

(i) environmental and safety aspects,
(ii) responsibility for future generations,
(iii) solidarity with developing countries,
(iv) an increased degree of national independence.

The weight to be attached to these arguments is a matter of evaluation, the answer being partly dependent on the perceived chances of finding new raw materials. The fact that value judgments are involved explains why individuals differ in the ideas they hold.

Reason (ii) above is one that usually appears: an 'overconsumption' of raw materials can be interpreted as a consumption of wealth that in fact should belong to the future. This wealth is considered to be prematurely used by those who have a shorter time perspective and employ a higher discount rate as the basis of their action. Others, however, consider that an 'overconsumption' of goods occurs, and set up a longer perspective in time and/or use a lower discount rate. From the latter point of view the market system then produces an imbalance as the time horizon is moved forward to include future generations. One way of correcting this imperfection in the market mechanism is to increase the price of the raw material and in this manner also create a balance between supply and demand in the long term. From a political point of view, the price increase can be seen as a way of simulating future generations' demand on their current market. An increase in demand leads to a price increase. Theoretically, this price increase can be achieved by imposing a tax on the raw material in question, a so-called 'raw material tax', but the implementation of this would create many problems in practice.

Without deciding whether, for any reason, it can be considered correct for an individual country to try to save energy, it will be presumed in the following discussion that energy should be saved on a national basis. Using this assumption initially, different measures to decrease the 'overconsumption' of raw materials in the beverage container sector are discussed.

BASIC PREMISES FOR ANALYSIS OF CONTROL MEASURES

In addition to direct demands that a certain production technology be used, action against the packaging sector in particular for the purpose of saving energy takes place in various ways:

(i) in the form of a ban on certain container designs or of extra levies on energy used in the packaging sector;
(ii) in the guise of information to consumers about how much energy the different containers require;
(iii) as a demand that special alternatives for disposal (including recovery) be utilized.

A container can be described by a number of characteristics of which one is its requirement of energy. To decide solely on this characteristic whether a container shall be allowed to remain on the market or be banned presumes that:

(i) the remaining characteristics can be ignored;
(ii) the raw material consumption really can be calculated. In spite of the great number of calculations that have started to appear, these are at best approximate and/or average figures which were applicable at a certain time.

Where it is considered that in some way the conditions mentioned can be fulfilled, this does not guarantee that a ban on containers will result in a corresponding decrease in energy consumption. For this presumes that there exists a difference in consumption between different types of containers. This is not always the case where energy is concerned.

Any suggestion for imposing extra levies on energy used in the packaging sector requires a demonstration of the energy consumption of that sector. The administrative feasibility must also be demonstrated. If, contrary to expectations, it is possible to fulfil both these demands, this still does not ensure that the total consumption of energy decreases. Other use of energy is still just as expensive and nothing stops the consumers from choosing other and more energy-demanding alternatives instead of beverage containers. Although deficiencies in the pricing system admittedly exist, it still seems unreasonable to interfere directly and solely in the production of beverage containers with bans or levies in order to save energy.

More general conservation measures should be taken instead. An example is a general 'energy tax'. The introduction of such a tax would clearly affect the packaging sector, but it would also permit energy to be saved at the pace and in the way that individual decision-makers (such as consumers and business executives) think best. At the same time the total result should be aligned with society's aims by variations in the amount of tax.

117

It has already been explained that it is a question of evaluation whether an over-consumption of energy is maintained. A more fundamental approach would be to inform the consumers about the energy requirements of the different packaging options, and ensure that this is done correctly: i.e. instead of making decisions centrally, decentralize them. Depending on the individual's valuation, he can then add a moral price to the shop price and then make his choice.

To achieve this objective, however, a basic condition must be satisfied that the consumer is able and willing to absorb and understand the additional information.

ENERGY DECLARATION OF CONTAINERS

According to a suggestion that the National Energy Conservation Committee has made to the Swedish Government, containers should be made to bear an energy declaration as an experiment. The Committee writes: 'At present every kind of energy declaration is missing. The main aim of such a declaration is to initiate the manufacture and use of less energy-demanding containers. Above all this should be of importance in the purchasing decisions of larger consumers'.

Apart from this proposal by the Energy Conservation Committee, an energy declaration would undoubtedly restore some order to the energy debate. A declaration is a more objective way of saying, for example, that from the energy viewpoint non-returnable containers of paper/plastic for non-carbonated beverages are equivalent to returnable bottles. Further, the declaration procedure should cause most of the different energy figures that are nowadays presented for one and the same container to disappear and be replaced by an 'official' figure.

For a *complete* energy analysis of a product, the whole of its life cycle must be taken into consideration. Whether any simplifications can be carried out in a final assessment becomes dependent on both the product's composition and the purpose of the analysis. Investigations have shown that the energy consumed in producing the material in a product forms a dominant proportion of the total energy used. For a container, the figure can be as high as 90%. To make a fair and comparable analysis the 'standard value' already discussed becomes an important consideration.

This implies that the processing industry is responsible for the dominating consumption of energy without actually belonging to the packaging sector. Paper and plastic, for example, have many other areas of use in addition to packaging, and therefore the processing industry's energy problem is not just a packaging problem. What the packaging industry can do, however, is use the material that will best fulfil the demands made on the respective container from the functional point of view, with regard to the conservation of energy. If, therefore, it is possible to fulfil the same packaging demand with different materials or combinations of materials, an energy declaration should guide the selection to the least energy-consuming alternative. But it must be clearly understood that the possibilities of saving energy are limited within the packaging sector and that factors other than energy, such as cost, influence the selection of the material that constitutes the packaging.

The recycling sector requires a relatively much smaller quantity of energy than primary material production and the differences between energy contents of different types of container are small, both relatively and absolutely. An accurate calculation naturally requires that these differences are taken into consideration. Generally, the number of recycling methods for producing a complete container from different materials is limited, and standard percentage surcharges can be used for different types of container, for example the production of cannisters from aluminium, and tin can production from steel plate. Here also, as with 'standard values' for materials, some kind of average value for current techniques must be applied. A further simplification of the energy calculation is obtained if the conversion part of the process is completely ignored, except in cases where the production and conversion of material is, in principle, one process — such as glass making. The acceptability of this simplification depends on the degree of accuracy required in the final result.

All packed products must be distributed from the producer to the retailer. The fact that containers may have different distribution structures, dependent on where and how the packed product is produced, is not primarily a packaging problem but rather a structural problem. Initially, therefore, the energy declaration of a container should not include the transport energy.

Another purpose of an energy declaration is to reflect differences in the consumption of energy between containers for the same product which have the same distribution structure. It is also necessary to differentiate between how the packed product is processed, for example deep frozen or preserved. Different processing methods have different requirements and containers, as in the two alternatives mentioned, and they cannot be compared without such further factors being considered. As the energy declaration must also be regarded as 'special accounting' for the respective container, the distribution energy can be regarded as a joint cost and therefore any comparisons between different containers must be excluded except in the cases where the returnable container system exists as an alternative to the non-returnable system. In these cases, transport energy must, of course, be compared to the energy required in manufacture with, among other things, the estimated trippage for the alternative returnable container.

It is possible only to speculate about the energy saving that this proposal will lead to. However, regardless of the size of this saving, the energy debate must be re-assessed: in this context, containers, and especially non-returnable containers for beverages, need particular consideration.

CONCLUSION

To summarize: while it is believed that 'free market forces' do not contribute sufficiently to desirable housekeeping, it is hardly worthwhile intervening directly and solely to either ban or place a levy on beverage containers on account of their energy content.

BIBLIOGRAPHY

BERGMAN, L. and MÄLER, K.-G., Framtidens oljepris och dess konsekvenser för Sverige (Future oil prices and their consequences for Sweden), *Ekonomisk Debatt* No. 1, Stockholm, Sweden, 1974.

BECKERMAN, W., *In Defence of Economic Growth*, London, England, 1974

BOHM, P., *Samhällsekonomisk effektivitet* (National economic efficiency), Uddevalla, Sweden, 1972.

FISHER, A. and KRUTILLA, J., *Economics of Natural Environments*, Baltimore, 1975.
FISHER, C. and PETERSON F.M., ·The Environment in Economics: A Survey, *Journal of Economic Literature*, USA, March 1976.
HJALTE, K., LIDGREN, K. and STÅHL, I., *Environmental Policy and Welfare Economics*, Cambridge, England, 1977.
JÖNSSON, B., LIDGREN, K. and SOMOGYI, L., *Stöd till energibesparande åtgärder i näringslivet — en samhällsekonomisk analys* (Support for energy saving measures in trade — a national economic analysis), Lund, Sweden, 1977.
KAY, J. and MIRRLEES, J., The desirability of natural resource depletion. In: *Economics of Natural Resource Depletion* (Ed. D.W. PEARCE). London, England, 1976.
LIDGREN, K., Naturresurskris — bluff eller verklighet? (Natural resource crisis — bluff or reality). *Teknisk Tidskrift*, No. 14, Stockholm, Sweden, 1975.
LIDGREN, K. and OLSSON, I., *The Macroeconomics of Environmental Protection*, The National Swedish Environment Protection Board, Stockholm, Sweden, 1978.
MEADOWS, D.L., MEADOWS, D.H., RANDERS, J. and BEHRENS, W., *Tillväxtens gränser* (The limits of growth), Stockholm, Sweden, 1972.
MÄLER, K.-G., Naturtillgångarna och miljön (Natural resources and the environment), *Ekonomisk Debatt*, No. 1, Stockholm, Sweden, 1973.
PAGE, T., *Conservation and Economic Efficiency*, Baltimore, 1977.
PEARCE, D.W., *Environmental Economics*, London, England, 1976.
RESEARCH TRIANGLE INSTITUTE, *Energy and Economic Impacts of Mandatory Deposits*, USA, 1975.
STÅHL, I., Vad är energipolitik? (What is energy policy?), *Ekonomisk Debatt*, No. 8, Stockholm, Sweden, 1974.
STÅHL, I., Energiskatten — värd en diskussion (Energy tax — worth a discussion), *Ekonomisk Debatt*, No. 2, 1975.
Departmental Memorandum, The Swedish Ministry of Industry, 1977: 15, *Styrmedel för en framtida energihushållning* (Control measures for a future economy of energy), 1977.
Departmental Memorandum, The Swedish Ministry of Agriculture, 1974: 5, *Avfall som energikälla* (Waste as a source of energy), 1974.

Karl Lidgren holds a Ph.D. in Economics and is Professor in Recycling Economics at the University of Lund, Sweden. During the last ten years he has worked as an expert in a number of governmental investigations, principally about environmental and energy questions. As author or co-author, he has participated in the publication of some 20 books in such fields as energy, packaging, the environment and transport.

11 Some Observations on the Use of Energy Analysis in Public Policy Making

R.A. Bradley

INTRODUCTION

The 1970s were, in some respects, the decade of the energy problem. Two major crisis periods resulted in rapidly rising energy prices, and a concomitant heightened public awareness of energy matters. This higher level of public consciousness was translated into a demand for action on the part of political authorities. As a result, almost every western industrial nation has enacted regulations designed to conserve energy and alter the composition of energy supply.

Energy production and use has, however, not been the only problem on the public mind. For example, during this same period the public was demanding a higher level of environmental quality, as evidenced by the number of pro-environment demonstrations. The most important of these events was the Earth Day celebrations in the early 1970s. This public pressure resulted in passage throughout the industrialized world of environmental legislation mandating controls on discharges into each of the environmental media.

Public pressure has been exerted upon governments to resolve both types of problem in addition to many others, even though some specific issues may not be resolvable, and resources are not forthcoming to adequately respond to all problems. The number of competing claimants for public funds places a new burden on governments to perform quality analyses which compare alternative actions in terms of a multiplicity of objectives. The response of the analytical community to this demand has been an explosion of new techniques designed to assist the policy-maker in this task of comparison. One of those techniques was energy analysis, which is the subject of this chapter.

The scope of energy analysis has grown from a methodology used mostly by engineers in design work into a complex policy tool. In other words, energy studies which were limited to purely technological assessment, e.g. the design of a coal combustion plant, are in some cases now assessing impacts external to the energy facility, e.g. the altered energy flows in natural environments. In fact, some supporters[1-7] believe it can provide insights into economic, social, environmental and political questions. But is this analytical tool up to the challenge presented by these types of problem? Or, perhaps a more useful question, what types of question might energy analysis reasonably expect to provide the decision-maker with cost-effective information? These are the questions of interest to this chapter. In the process of addressing these questions, perhaps some light will be shed on the desirability of the extension of energy analysis from an engineering tool to a policy tool.

THE POLICY-MAKING ENVIRONMENT AND THE ROLE OF STRUCTURED INFORMATION

This chapter proposes to analyse the role(s) energy analysis might play in government decision making from the perspective of decision maker needs. To do so requires an understanding of the public policy-making environment and the role professional analyses play in it. Energy analysis is but one type of structured information, i.e. information about states of the world which has been organized according to specific rules; but some of its limitations for public policy purposes are shared by other analytical techniques. This section will discuss briefly two general perspectives on the role professional analyses may play in government decision making. Later sections will apply one of these conceptions to energy analysis specifically.

Evaluations of comparative assessment techniques, of which energy analysis is one, have been done from several different perspectives. For example, techniques have been evaluated in terms of normative properties, i.e. from theoretical perspectives which specify how a government should make decisions. At the heart of most such theories is the concept of rational government decision making as a desirable property of analytical techniques. Rationality is defined in terms of certain mathematical properties like transitivity. Comparative assessment techniques are therefore evaluated according to whether the choices they identify exhibit transitivity.

In all perspectives used to evaluate those techniques, however, there is either an implied or an explicit conception of the decision-making environment and of the decision maker. Differences in the conceptualization of the decision maker, especially as they relate to his autonomy, is the focus of this chapter. In this regard, two broad views of the decision maker can be identified. In one case, he is clearly a prime mover in the policy-making arena: the person who sends his analytical staff on information gathering forays, armed with the most sophisticated of information structuring tools. He seeks, albeit imperfectly, the public interest; either because of personal preference, or because of an incentive system which enforces behavior consistent with it. The public interest is usually thought to be associated with such goals as efficiency, distributional equity or national security, or some combination of these.

In this conceptualization, the decision-maker reviews the results of the study he commissioned, and on the basis of the study, and perhaps certain 'other' considerations, makes a decision. The presumption is that the structured information about efficiency, distributional equity or national security helped him to decide, and that the choice is the best one for the public given the state of knowledge.

This conceptualization misrepresents the role and importance of formal, structured information in 'real' public decision making. In part this is true because it focuses on a decision maker as the cynosure of problem solving and therefore fails to consider the complex relationships which actually work to solve public problems.

In reality there is no single decision maker, but rather a multiplicity of interested parties with different amounts of power, and this interaction may, but does not necessarily, produce a resolution to the problem. In some cases, the strength of conflicting parties does not produce a policy directed at a problem, but rather a stalemate. This is usually an unacceptable political result, therefore the contending parties must give the impression of moving towards a solution even though they are not able in fact to resolve it. One way to do so is to resolve to study

122

the problem further. An example is the plethora of legislative and executive commissions which are appointed with much fanfare to study a problem. Rarely, however, is the information generated in this process conclusive and sufficiently authoritative to persuade all, or even most parties of the 'correct' course of action. What they contribute towards problem solving is not influential information but time for contending parties to sort out differences. (An excellent description and documentation of this process is a case study on the US National Commission on Water Quality[8].)

An alternative view of public problem solving, therefore, portrays it as much more interactive than the other conception of government. This process of problem solving is best viewed as a 'game' in which contending parties create strategies utilizing a range of actions (some of them information gathering in nature) to 'win' for their interests. The relative importance of player objectives, which may be very self-interested, is subordinated to organizational environment and rules of the game in explaining the relationship of government activity and the public interest. Public objectives are served if the 'rules' of the game and the competitive environment are such that the outcome of the game is consistent with them. This is not to say that public-spirited civil servants do not exist, or even that this is unimportant, only that it is relatively less important. It should be noted, however, that one observer has contended that the internal workings of a bureaucracy will subvert the public spirited individual.

> It is impossible for any one bureaucrat to act in the public interest, because of the limits on his information and the conflicting interests of others, regardless of his personal motivation. This leads even the most selfless bureaucrats to choose some feasible, low-level goal, and this usually leads to developing expertise in some narrow field. The development of expertise usually generates a sense of dedication, and it is understandable that many bureaucrats identify this dedication with the public interest.[9]

While the brief sketches of both views is certainly stylized, and not comprehensive, for the purpose of this chapter it is the implied autonomy and power to determine choices of actions which are important. To the extent that decisions result from an interactive process (where participants differ in power but none is so powerful as to dictate policy), the interest in comparative assessment methods becomes less a concern for their purely 'scientific' characteristics, or their ability to identify 'correct' choices in terms of decision-maker objectives; than for their ability to meet participant needs in a conflict oriented atmosphere. These needs are based only in part on the above characteristics, which have been thought necessary to give 'authoritativeness' to studies. In other words, it was believed important for studies to follow scientific conventions so that rational individuals could discern the accuracy of the analysis, and therefore be persuaded. Studies rarely seem to be authoritative in this sense, and appreciating why this is true requires a perception of decision making which is more interactive.

There are several reasons which explain why professional analyses cannot be authoritative in this sense. Lindbloom and Cohen[10] have identified two of the most important as the lack of widespread acceptance of rules for evaluating policy alternatives, and the complexity of policy questions and the 'real world'.

Evaluation Rules

The rules for accepting and rejecting analyses in the arena of public policy making are not well established. This is certainly true of social analyses, and of methods for using physical analyses. The rules of science may be sufficiently widely accepted to make analysis of physical phenomena authoritative in the scientific community, but that does not imply that sufficient agreement could be found concerning their role in a public policy arena. Energy analysis presents an interesting example of this distinction. A particular energy analysis may be widely accepted as a description of energy flows into and out of a system, providing it follows common engineering practice. However, some of its advocates would extend its implications, applying them to broad public policy questions[1, 3, 7, 11-14]. Presumably there are at least two advantages over social science analysis:

(i) It is based upon immutable physical laws, especially the first law of thermodynamics. In that sense it serves as a fundamental constraint upon the extremes of human behavior, and provides a certainty to results not found in social science analyses.

(ii) Since energy is embodied in all matter and the energy content of systems can in principle be measured, it can represent a measure of value not subject to human vagaries. It provides therefore a useful 'scientific' device for aggregating disparate phenomena into common units of energy inputs and outputs. This can then serve as a ranking function, as in its representation of net energy.

These advantages are not, however, widely accepted, nor are the policy implications which are drawn from an energy analysis, even though the analysis may be scientifically credible. For example, immutable ranking functions like the net energy criteria are not considered desirable by many policy analysts. Most social scientists believe public policy ranking functions should be anthropocentric in nature. In other words, valuation of consequences is done in units incorporating human values. Additionally, the socio-economic-political implications drawn from energy analysis have been criticized[15, 16]. Some of these criticisms will be discussed later in the chapter. The point is that energy analyses do not generate anthoritative results when extended to non-physical phenomena because the rules for accepting and rejecting policy implications are not commonly accepted.

Problem Complexity

Most policy problems are quite complex, embodying a range of considerations. Energy policy, for example, has implications for national defence, employment, inflation, distributional equity, environmental quality, institutional forms, profits, etc. Analysing such a multiplicity of factors, or even the most important ones, is a heroic task, if not impossible. The number of variables is enormous, and knowledge gaps concerning the functional forms are sufficiently great to render any analytical result contestable. Formal analysis may provide useful information, but it will not be authoritative. Contending parties, even those of good will, will find in any analysis weaknesses sufficient to justify legitimate disagreement with portions of the results which do not conform to their previously held perspective.

Specifying a role for energy analysis in decision making requires a recognition of these limitations. Professional studies may not be authoritative, but that does not preclude their being useful in ways not generally appreciated.

INTERACTIVE DECISION MAKING AND ENERGY ANALYSIS

The role of professional analysis in this game-like decision process is two-fold.

124

First, it can help the decision maker to formulate his position on the policy issue. However, since the policy-making world is interactive, he is constrained in his choice by what is possible to achieve. In a game, participants develop strategies and tactics which reflect expectations about the responses of contending parties to each other's actions. In such a world the participants make their own policy proposals, not exclusively on what is the 'correct' course, but what will be a successfully adopted policy. Selling and convincing others of the desirability of ones position takes on an importance not recognized in the naive theory.

Methodologies

This aspect of the interactive process will help to define a second role for professional analysis, namely to assist in the process of persuasion. There are several features to successful selling, including developing a proposal that has benefits for the party one is trying to persuade. Another important aspect, however, is to structure information provided to other parties in a manner they will find acceptable. In other words, if a study is to be used in negotiations to support one's position, the methodology (which structures the information signals) should be acceptable to other parties. Contending interests will be swayed by analyses only if there is agreement on the method of acquiring and organizing the information. Even this may not be enough, however, since studies cannot be authoritative. Legitimate disagreements can exist about the results and methodology of any study, for the reasons mentioned above. When interests conflict, disagreement on the validity and meaning of an analysis is assured even among parties of good will. Agreement on a broad range of methodological issues reduces the scope of possible disagreement, and makes it more likely that a particular study will persuade.

It should be noted that the importance of a methodology having properties associated with scientific methodology has a different character in the light of this changed perspective. 'Scientificness' is no longer desirable because policy analysis should be done according to rules of science, but only because some subset of the contending parties believe it is important. In a policy arena there will in all likelihood be several opinions on the correct methodology for social science analysis and therefore methodology will frequently be a point of dispute among contestants.

When is agreement on methodological approaches most likely? It would seem that at least one factor which affects acceptance is the disciplinary training of the contestants. Economists seem to find economic methodologies more acceptable; engineers and sociologists likewise seem to find information-structuring tools with which they are familiar more acceptable.

Perhaps a more important determinant of methodological acceptability is the type of policy query. Economic methodologies seem more appropriate for questions which are economic in nature, e.g. unemployment. This may seem to be self-evident, but there are many examples in which a methodology of one discipline is applied to a set of questions outside its traditional framework. The issue here is not whether such a transcendency generates new insights from its application in foreign intellectual territory where there have been successful applications; the issue is whether the use of methodology in an unorthodox manner is likely to yield an enhanced bargaining position for a contestant. It does not seem likely, since a new ingredient of disagreement has been added. Participants rarely find it advantageous to experiment with a new methodology in the policy-making arena. Only when the application of a new methodology has gained acceptance within the discipline generally is its introduction into policy making likely.

Thirdly, a methodology must express itself in and about magnitudes which have policy relevance, i.e. those of relevance to the public. If a policy is to be explained to the public, and especially if a professional analysis is to be used to justify the policy selection, it must address those things of interest to the public. The inflation rate, unemployment rate, numbers of accidents, prices, crime rate, etc., are magnitudes of interest to the public.

Value

These three factors which affect methodological acceptability are important in explaining the acceptance of energy analysis as a policy tool. Consideration of the disciplinary training of contestants and the types of policy question leads to the conjecture that it will more easily find acceptance in policy making which addresses narrow engineering questions. These usually arise in the technical bureaucracy of a government, and the responsible offices of that bureaucracy are usually headed by professionals with engineering expertise. Representative questions which are faced by this sector of a government include technical issues about alternative technological designs, and the application of R&D support for technological systems and components. These are the areas in which energy analysis is most likely to be used and has in fact played a role in the past.

When it is applied outside this narrow area it has a number of difficulties, because of the three factors mentioned above. One needs to be clear about what is meant by 'applying' it. There are two possible categories of use:

(i)   where it is to be the sole analytical response to a policy question, and the net energy criteria is meant to affect the policy decision;
(ii) where it is one indicator among many of system health and function.

In the first case it would play a major role in determining public policy. In this application it functions as a decision rule, i.e. a rule which relates certain information signals to the choice of an action. In other words, it is meant to identify the 'correct' policy alternative in terms of some objective function. With energy analysis, system performance is optimized by choosing alternatives in accordance with the net energy criteria. This decision rule corresponds roughly with the notion of thermodynamic efficiency.

Odum and Odum[7] make the most elaborate case for energy analysis and the net energy criteria, and also argue for its broadest application. Basically their argument is an extension of the principles of systems ecology to socio-economic systems. Socio-economic activity is conceptualized as an ecological system, the most important factor in its operation being energy. War, poverty, growth, etc., are all explained on the basis of energy analysis. It should be noted that the linkage between energy production and uses, and economic vitality of a country is merely postulated by Odum and Odum without careful analytical and statistical support.

There are several problems with this analysis. First, it is not likely to be widely used in policy making because of the factors listed above. Except in the narrow field of engineering, national policy makers are not acquainted with this information tool, expecially in its broader applications. Most policy makers are not ecologists or even engineers, and this framework will not be as appealing as those they are more familiar with. Additionally, decision makers prefer not to have

126

decision rules, or even ranking functions, as part of an assessment tool, since it limits their effective choices. It can be politically difficult to choose alternatives ranked below the first two or three.

Second, its usefulness in addressing questions broader than engineering and ecological questions is suspect. Several people have discussed the weaknesses of energy analysis with respect to resource allocation questions[13, 15-17]. Not all those arguments will be repeated here, but they do demonstrate why energy analysis will probably not gain acceptance among social scientists. Basically, when net energy is used as the sole input into decision making, it is too narrow a criterion. Energy analysis excludes a whole set of socio-economic behavior, which social scientists believe important. If its broader applications to socio-economic problems are attempted, e.g. as in Odum and Odum, the lack of a demonstrable linkage between net energy and socio-economic behaviour will pose a problem for its use in policy analysis.

Deficiencies

For government allocation decisions, social scientists would claim it has a number of missing elements. For example, little, if any, attention is given to technological change, nor are the possibilities of technological change fully appreciated by net energy advocates. While it is undeniably true that man's productive and consumptive activities accelerate the degradation of high-quality energy, it does not necessarily follow that dire consequences are in the offing for the human race. At many times in the past, pundits have prognosticated difficult times because of man's use of a finite resource. At the end of the 19th century, for example, William Stanley Jevons predicted decline for England in a book called *The Coal Question*. British dependence on coal was considerable, and its exhaustion imminent. What Jevons did not foresee was the technological changes that led to the switch to oil. None of this is meant to imply that public decisions should be made ignoring possible environmental degradation or exhaustion, only that policy analysis tools must effectively account for and utilize technological change. Net energy analysis does not adequately incorporate technological change.

Technological change may respond to a variety of factors, e.g. prices, risk preferences of economic agents, uncertainty. Some of these may be influenced indirectly by energy flows; however, net energy itself is not a direct consideration of business firms. If public policy prescriptions are to be accurate, they need to reflect potential technologies, which depend on factors other than energy flows. In fact, modelling of potential energy flows requires a specification of technologies that may be used, the determination of which requires an understanding of factors other than energy. In other words, to make reasonable energy analysis predictions one must have considerable information, including technologies to be used, input options and prices. These are determined by the socio-economic system. Since both energy and economic analyses must include modeling of this system, it would appear redundant to do energy analysis, because energy usage is incorporated in the economic system though prices.

Another closely related weakness is the failure to account for substitution behavior in the economy. The phenomenon of substitution is well known. As relative prices change, consumers and firms change the composition of their purchases. When the price of oil has risen in real terms, gasoline consumption has declined and electric power companies have switched to coal. If energy analysis is to be useful, it must account for these possibilities. It cannot do so.

Energy analysis also fails to incorporate adequately or effectively assess the most important aspect of most public policy choices, namely uncertainty. In fact, it does not appear that its founders have considered uncertainty, which results from several sources. For example, data utilized in assessment may be in error, or at least not be exact measures, and there may be ignorance of the relationships between phenomena. Human knowledge is incomplete, and decisions must be made before total knowledge is available. Choices, for example, between certain types of development projects, or on the desirability of any development, are continually made before a complete understanding of the effects on local ecosystems are known. The central question for the policy analyst is how to incorporate and represent uncertainty. There are methods that aid in this problem, but energy analysis is not one of them. It offers no distinctive insights into the nature of uncertain events.

Limitations

Evaluating energy analysis in its second application as an information signal, to be used in an assessment with other measures, is much more difficult. Inevitably, our determination must be 'it depends'. If information were free, more information would be better and no complaint could be lodged against energy analysis. Unfortunately, information is costly to acquire, and decision-making resources, like all resources, are limited.

In policy analysis, the resource which is frequently the most binding is time. Many problems compete for access to the policy-making 'game'. Only the most pressing, in terms of urgency or public attention, successfully enter that arena. When they do, the contestant rarely has the luxury of extended information gathering exercises. Time becomes of the essence, and the information used in such cases is frequently that which is readily available. In an interactive policy process, victory often goes to those who can marshall evidence for their argument earliest, and thereby build momentum for their position by capturing undecided elements.

What does this imply for energy analysis? An energy analysis of a technological process or system is time-consuming and the time requirements of such analysis do not match well with the time constraints of the policy process. To the extent therefore that time is a constraint, new energy analysis can rarely be done in time to be used by participants.

On the other hand, the relative unchanging nature of technological processes and energy flows implies that previously performed energy analysis may be easily applied. Technological system components may change, but once a configuration has been characterized in terms of energy flows it is unchanging. Additionally, energy flows are relatively easier to quantify then most socio-economic phenomena, which makes them especially amenable to modelling exercises which facilitate the evaluation of multiple alternatives. Both models of technological processes and those of energy flows within sectors of an economy will be highly accurate. What changes in such models is the socio-economic interface with the technological basis.

In the policy-making arena, reliable information is highly valued. Information which is quantified and certain frequently has disproportionate influence compared to information which is of uncertain accuracy. This can be true even when the information is about largely irrelevant considerations. In part highly reliable information is valued because it is incontrovertible. So much analysis is subject to disputation that professionally derived and uncontestable evidence which supports decisions is highly valued.

Applications

As noted above, energy analysis would seem to offer an advantage in this regard, at least to the extent that it is limited to technological processes and systems. Energy analyses have been done on specific processes, and can be expected to remain unchanged in their results[18-20]. In addition to process analysis, models have been developed which describe energy flows in an economy[21-23]. The controversy surrounding these efforts is in their significance for a broad range of policy issues, not their increase of energy flows.

Energy analysis may have a number of weaknesses for analytical purposes because of its omission of technological change and uncertainty about the socio-economic systems, but it may well be a good indicator of technological system function. In that regard, with adequate analytical resources, there may be occasions where energy analysis offers interesting information to decision makers. One such occasion has been identified above as technological design questions or R&D support questions. Since the decision-making process is interactive, it is possible that energy analysis would prove useful in a broader context. This occurs when energy analysis is valued by an opponent, and the results are consistent with the study originator's negotiating position.

One promising method of using energy analysis is as part of a system of indicators designed to monitor the performance of the economic, ecological and technological systems. A systematic collection of indicators could be devized and organized into a system of accounts. Energy flows would then be taken as one indicator of the performance of technological and ecological systems. Developing a system of consistent indicators is a complex task, but a suggested framework for doing so is found in Stearns and Montag.[24].

If an indicator system were developed it would presumably function as a continuing monitor of the function or dysfunction of these systems. Maintenance of such systems can be quite expensive, and as yet most countries have chosen not to build them either because of the cost or because of professional disagreements about the appropriate indicators. If theoretical, statistical and financial problems can be resolved with respect to indicator systems, this is a promising use of indicators. Energy analysis should be limited to indicators of technological and ecological system performance, however, for the reasons identified above.

CONCLUSIONS

In summary, an alternative methodology to the traditional approach for evaluating comparative assessment techniques would focus upon the policy-making environment and the ways professionally developed information is used. Such a world solves problems through an interactive process which requires information structured to meet the needs of game-like situations.

Energy analysis will therefore probably receive a favourable reception only in technical bureaucracies responsible for technological analysis. When applied to broader social questions, it fails to address a number of concerns of policy makers, and is at variance with the analytical perspective of a significant part of the analytical community, namely social scientists. It is therefore too risky a methodology to be applied exclusively by a policy arena contestant.

If it is to play a role in broader types of policy analysis, it will probably be as part of a system of indicators. In such circumstances, it would represent one indicator of technological and ecosystem health. When incorporated into an indicator framework, a conceptually coherant scheme can be offered the decision maker, in the sense that the relationship of socio-economic and technological variables is explicitly stated. Modelling frameworks which encompass technological and economic systems in an integrated manner have been developed[25], and incorporated into indicator systems[24]. However, elaborate indicator systems have not been developed, and that may be because they do not meet the needs of the policy making environment.

ACKNOWLEDGEMENTS

The opinions expressed in this chapter are not necessarily those of the OECD or its Member countries.

The author wishes to acknowledge his indebtedness to Dr. Peter House of the US Department of Energy for conversations which helped in the formulation of this chapter, without of course ascribing any errors to him.

REFERENCES

1. GILLILAND, M.W., Energy Analysis and Public Policy, *Science*, **189** (4208), 1975.
2. GILLILAND, M.W., (Ed.), *Energy Analysis: A New Public Policy Tool*, Westview Press, Boulder, Colorado, 1978: chapter entitled The Kinds of Information It Provides Policymakers.
3. GILLILAND, M.W., (Ed), *Energy Analysis: A New Public Policy Tool*, Westview Press, Boulder, Colorado, 1978.
4. ODUM, H.T., Energy, Ecology and Economics, *Ambio* 2(6), 1973.
5. Combining Energy Laws and Corollories of the Maximum Power Principle with Visual Systems Mathematics. In: *Ecosystem: Analysis and Prediction*, Proceedings of a SIAM-SIMS conference held at Alta, Utah, July 1-5, 1974.
6. GILLILAND, M.W., (Ed.), *Energy Analysis: A New Public Policy Tool*, Westview Press, Boulder, Colorado, 1978: chapter on Energy Analysis, Energy Quality and Environment.
7. ODUM, E.C., *Energy Basis for Man and Nature*, McGraw-Hill, 1976.
8. OUTEN, R.B., *The National Commission on Water Quality: A Case Study in Congressional Policy Analysis*, Ph.D. dissertation, University of Texas at Dallas, 1980.
9. NISKANEN, W.A. Jr., *Bureaucracy and Representative Government*, Aldine Atherton, 1971.
10. LINDBLOOM, C.E. and COHEN, D.K., *Usable Knowledge: Social Science and Social Problem Solving*, Yale University Press, 1975.
11. *Energy Basis for the United States*, June 1979. DOE Contract No. EV-76-S-05-4398, Systems Ecology and Energy Analysis Group, Department of Environmental Engineering Sciences, University of Florida, Gainesville, Florida.
12. *Energy Analysis of Models of the United States*, December 1977, DOE

Contract No. EV-76-S-05-4398, Systems Ecology and Energy Analysis Group, Department of Environmental Engineering Sciences, University of Florida, Gainesville, Florida.
13. BRADLEY, R.A., A Comparison of Four Methods for Assessing National Energy Policy, paper presented at 1979 Annual Meetings of American Institute of Chemical Engineers, Houston, Texas, April 1-3, 1979.
14. PERRY, A., et al., Net Energy Analysis of Five Energy Systems, Oak Ridge National Laboratory, ORNL/IEA (R) 77-12, 1977.
15. HUETTNER, D.A., 'Net Energy Analysis': An Economic Assessment, Science, **192** (4235), 1976.
16. WEBB, M. and Pearce, D., The Economics of Energy Analysis, Energy Policy, 3(4), 1975.
17. PENNER, P.S., A Dynamic Input-Output Analysis of Net Energy Effects in Single Tool Economics, Energy Systems and Policy, **5**(2), 1981.
18. CHAMBERS, R.S., HERENDEEN, R.A., JOYCE, J.S. and PENNER, P.S., Gashol: Does It or Doesn't It Produce Positive Net Energy, Science, **205**(4420), 1979.
19. HERENDEEN, R.A., Kary, T. and Rebitzer, J., Energy Analysis of the Solar Power Satellite, Science, 205(4405), 1979.
20. INSTITUTE FOR ENERGY ANALYSIS, Minimum Energy (Thermodynamic Limit) to Obtain Oil from Oil Shale, IEA (M)-76-6.
21. HANNON, B., Energy Conservation and the Consumer, Science, **189**(4197), 1975.
22. HANNON, B., Herendeen, R.A. and Penner, P., An Energy-Conservation Tax: Impacts and Policy Implications, Energy Systems and Policy, 5(2).
23. MILON, J.W., An Economic and Energetic Framework for Evaluating Dispersed Energy Technology, Land Economics, **51**(1), 1981.
24. STEARNS, F.W. and MONTAG, T. (Eds.), The Urban Ecosystem: A Holistic Approach, Halstead Press, 1974.
25. KNEESE, A., AYRES, R. and D'ARGE, R., Economics and the Environment: A Materials Balance Approach, Resources for the Future Inc., Washington, DC, Johns Hopkins University Press, 1970.

Dr. Bradley is currently on leave from the US Department of Energy to the Environment Directorate of the OECD. Both comparative assessment methodologies and their application to energy and environment policy issues has been the focus of his research, with particular attention given to the relationship between the requirements of policy-making participants and the choice of the comparative methodology. While at the OECD he has developed an environmental assessment of energy efficiency technologies in the space heating-cooling sector.

12 Packaging Waste as an Energy Resource in Switzerland

L. Silberring

INTRODUCTION

The information included in this chapter has been collected from many sources, both published and unpublished, and is in many cases based on estimates. The reliability of the figures has been improved as far as possible by cross checking, but nevertheless many uncertainties remain. Action to improve statistical information on energy and the contribution of residential and industrial waste to local and national energy balances was initiated a few years ago, and it can be expected, therefore, that the completeness and reliability of data will significantly improve in the course of the next few years.

Unless otherwise stated, all numerical information included in this chapter refers to the calendar year 1979. Essential data about the year 1980 were still unpublished at the time of writing, but the evidence is that little change occurred.

ORIGIN AND QUANTITIES OF PACKAGING WASTE

Paper and cardboard packagings provide the major contribution to packaging waste in Switzerland. The Swiss paper industry produces nearly one million tonnes of paper and cardboard per year. About 30% of this output is exported, but this is counterbalanced by imports. In summary, the domestic consumption of the paper and cardboard slightly exceeds one million tonnes per year.

About 28% of the above domestic consumption (against 20% in the USA) is recycled to domestic paper mills and used mostly for the production of cardboard and lower quality paper, and an additional 12% of the recycled consumption is exported. Recycling of the paper and cardboard waste is more economic in Switzerland for the above-mentioned products than the use of additional wood as a feedstock, due to the relatively high prices of the latter. The fate of the exported part of the recycled material is unknown, but some experts claim that it is burned abroad. This would, of course, be a misuse of the enthusiasm of the recycling promotors. If domestic recycling possibilities are limited, domestic combustion with energy recovery for which surplus capacity is available is preferable to transport over long distances followed by combustion abroad.

The remaining part of the domestic consumption of paper and cardboard, namely 650 thousands tonnes per year, appears in waste, with the exception of a small part destinated for prolonged use. Of this figure, about 300 thousand tonnes per year originate from packaging waste and a similar amount from newspapers, periodicals, sales promotion leaflets, etc. A full material and energy balance of the Swiss paper and board industry is shown in Fig. 12.1.

The quantities of other packaging waste suitable for use as fuel can be deduced from the published average composition relating to 1975[1]. Table 12.1

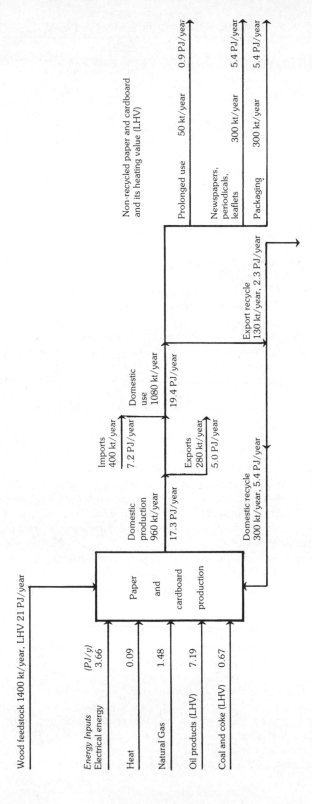

Fig. 12.1 Material and energy balance of the Swiss paper and cardboard industry, showing the proportion of packaging. Material flow data in 1000 tonnes per year (kt/year); energy flow data in 10^{15} J per year (PJ/year); energy content expressed as lower heating value (LHV).

Table 12.1   Composition of Packaging Waste (by Weight)

	Switzerland[1]		USA[2]
	%	thousand tonnes per year	%
Paper and cardboard	80	300	84
Wood	8	30	10
Plastics	12	45	6

summarizes these data and compares them with the corresponding data for the packaging waste in the USA in 1976[2].

ENERGY USED FOR THE PRODUCTION OF PACKAGING

The average feedstock requirement for the production of paper packaging and cardboard is 1.5 tonnes of dry wood substance per tonne of product. Air-dried wood contains 12-25% of water and has an average lower heating value (LHV) of 15 MJ/kg. It follows from the above that the heating value of the feedstock is 25-30 GJ per tonne of product. The LHV of the paper and cardboard packaging waste, as delivered to the incinerator, is about 18 GJ per tonne[2]. It is obvious from the above that a significant part of the heating value of the wood feedstock is lost during its transformation into packaging material.

Feedstock consumption is reduced when packaging waste is recycled. Up to 80% of new paper or cardboard can be made from waste originating from these products, but there are restrictions on the acceptable characteristics of the waste and possible qualities of the products. One Swiss manufacturer of cardboard products is using exclusively recycled material as feedstock. Half or more of the previously mentioned 300 thousand tonnes per year of paper and cardboard packaging used in Switzerland could originate from recycled material.

Paper mills need driving power for their machinery and a considerable amount of heat at various temperature levels[3-7]. Modern paper mills generate all their electric driving power requirements within the plant, usually by back pressure steam turbines. Extraction and exhaust steam cover the heating power requirements. High-pressure steam is generated in fired boilers, for which a significant part of the fuel requirement is sometimes met by the paper mill wastes, such as bark, sawmill residues and black liquor. Heat is required not only for the paper production process, but also for various auxiliary services, in particular for effluent treatment[7]. If everything is taken into consideration, the external fuel requirements can vary between 7 and 20 GJ per tonne of product. Energy supplied[8] to the Swiss paper and cardboard industry in 1979 are summarized in Table 12.2.

It can be assumed that the fabrication of paper and cardboard packaging contributes to the figures in Table 12.2 in the same proportion as the weight of the total product, i.e. about 30%.

The heating value of the wood is conserved in wood packaging, such as crates and pallets, provided the wastes appearing during their fabrication are not rejected. On this basis, the energy in wood packaging (which eventually appears in the waste as discussed above and in Table 12.1) is about 0.4 PJ/year (0.4 × 10^{15} Joule per year or 400 000 GJ/year).

Plastic packaging consists mostly of polyethylene and PVC products having

Table 12.2   Consumption of Externally Supplied Energy by the Swiss Paper Industry in 1979[8]

	TJ/year	GJ/tonne
Electrical energy (including energy supplied by paper mill-owned hydroelectric plants)	3664	3.8
Heat from district heating	91	0.1
Natural gas	1483	1.5
Oil products	7193	7.5
Coal and coke	666	0.7

lower heating values (LHVs) of 43 MJ/kg and 38 MJ/kg respectively. The amount of energy necessary to produce them depends mainly on the kind of feedstock and the nature of fabrication processes, in particular for the ethylene production process, which does not take place in Switzerland. Most of the European ethylene plants use naphtha as feedstock and fuel. In this case no more than 40% of the heating value of the naphtha appears in the final product. The energy requirement expressed as LHV of feedstock and fuel necessary for the production of plastic packaging waste, estimated in Table 12.1, may be therefore about 5 PJ/year.

A rough estimate of energy spent in producing combustible packaging, which appears eventually in the municipal and industrial waste in Switzerland is summarized in Table 12.3.

Adding different forms of energy has become common in many statistical tables published in recent years, but is intentionally avoided in Table 12.3. Such additions imply ability of replacement and interchangeability which are seldom possible without significant losses.

Table 12.3, besides being a rough estimate, cannot be considered as complete. It does not include, for example, the energy directly or indirectly used for the

Table 12.3   Estimates of Total Energy Used to Produce Combustible Packaging which Eventually Appears in Municipal and Industrial Waste in Switzerland

Values include lower heating value (LHV) of waste and production energy. Derived from Tables 12.1 and 12.2.

Feedstocks and fuels	LHV (10^{15} J/year)			
	Paper and cardboard	Wood	Plastic	Total
Wood	4.0	0.4		4.4
Coal and coke	0.2			0.2
Natural gas	0.4			0.4
Oil products	2.2		5.0	7.2
Total	6.8	0.4	5.0	12.2
Electrical energy	1.1	0.1	0.4	1.6

135

transport of packaging and waste. It does give, however, some indication of the quantities of energy involved in the production of packaging.

TREATMENT OF RESIDENTIAL WASTES

The total amount of residential wastes in Switzerland is estimated to be 2.2 million tonnes per year or 350 kg per resident per year. Of this, packaging waste has been previously estimated to be about 0.38 million tonnes per year[9, 10].

Regional waste treatment plants process residential waste from 95% of the Swiss population. These plants may be classified into the following types:

19 incineration plants with heat recovery,
22 incineration plants without heat recovery,
 8 combined plants for composting and incineration,
 2 composting plants without incineration,
32 sanitary landfills.

Small plants having an incineration capacity up to 5 tonne/h are generally well charged with an average capacity factor of 80%. The same factor for the 8 largest plants, having incineration capacities between 10 tonne/h and 50 tonne/h, is only 55%. These latter plants have sometimes been constructed on the basis of overestimated predictions about increases in the amount of waste.

ENERGY RECOVERY IN WASTE INCINERATION PLANTS

Of the total amount of residential waste processing described above, incineration plants with heat recovery treat 55% or 1.2 million tonnes per year. The average LHV of this waste is estimated to be 10 MJ/kg, on an as-received basis, which agrees with values reported elsewhere[2]. Hence the potential heat recoverable from incinerated waste is about 12 PJ/y.

Waste incineration leads to some difficulties in comparison to the combustion of most fossil fuels. As a consequence, the heat recovery boilers associated with incinerators are quite different from industrial boilers using conventional fuels. Because of corrosion and ash problems, both air excess and stack gas temperature must be higher than usual when waste is used as a fuel, and the boiler efficiency cannot, therefore, be as high. Also, more moderate steam parameters are usually selected for downstream heat recovery from incinerators, mainly due to the moderate unit size. This leads to only a moderate cycle efficiency when steam is used for electrical energy generation.

Typical steam conditions upstream of the steam turbine are 30-40 bar and 400-430 °C. Downstream, the turbine steam is often condensed at a pressure of about 0.1 bar using air-cooled condensers. The condensate is then deaerated and preheated in one stage to a temperature between 110 °C and 140 °C prior to its use as the boiler feed water.

Heat recovery boilers associated with the waste incinerators in Switzerland generated 3 million tonnes of steam in 1979. The corresponding heat recovery is about 8 PJ, i.e. about two thirds of the LHV of the waste introduced to the corresponding 19 plants.

Some plants are selling heat in the form of steam originating either directly from the heat recovery boilers or from a turbine extraction. The condensate is recycled in most cases to the plant at a temperature slightly below 100 °C. The total sales of energy from waste incineration plants in 1979 were:

| Heat in the form of steam or hot water | 2.81 PJ |
| Electrical energy | 0.85 PJ |

In the case of electricity generation, it can be assumed that the amount of heat rejected to the condensers is two or three times greater than the amount of electric energy sold. The remaining heat (to the balance of 8 PJ — about 3 PJ) can be assumed to have been used for the internal requirements of the waste incineration plants, including generation of electrical energy for plant auxiliairies.

Essential technical data on two Swiss waste incineration plants with heat recovery and electric power generation are summarized in Table 12.4. The first of

Table 12.4   Essential Technical Data of Two Swiss Waste Incineration Plants with Heat Recovery and Electric Power Generation

		KSW (1 new unit only)	SATOM
(a) Technical Description			
Number of communities served		47	54
Weigh-scales			
Number		1	2
Width	m	3	3
Length	m	12	12
Maximum weight	tonne	40	50
Number of waste reception gates		10	8
Number of traveling hoists		2	2
Incinerators			
Number		1	2
Incineration capacity of each	tonne/h	15	7.5
Steam boilers			
Number		1	2
Steam pressure at superheater outlet	bar	40	32
Superheated steam temperature	°C	390	430
Feedwater temperature	°C	140	140
Maximum steam flow rate	kg/s	12.3	4.72
Stack gas temperature	°C	230	300
Steam turbines			
Number		1	1
Speed	rev./min	9600	3600
Maximum steam extraction			
at 11 bar (non-controlled)	kg/s	3.06	—
at 4 bar (non-controlled)	kg/s	8.33	—
Electric generators			
Number		1	1
Speed	rev./min	1500	1500
Tension	kV	6.4	5.2
Power rating	MW	8.5	10.7
Rated power factor		0.83	0.80
Condenser cooling fluid		Air	Air
Feedwater heating stages		1	2
Make-up water demineralization			
Number of units		2	2
Maximum flow rate (of each)	kg/s	4.2	4.2

Table 12.4   *(continued)*

		KSW (1 new unit only)	SATOM
Flue gas system			
Maximum content of solids in the flue gases downstream of electrostatic precipitators	mg/kg	54	77
Height of chimney	m	81	85
(b) Operating Results in 1980			
Waste and steam (thousands of tonnes)			
Waste input		57.3	
Used oil input		0.38	
Combustion residue output		16.6	
Steam generation (by the new unit only)		166	
Steam outputs			
to the steam turbine		142	
to the throttling valve (for sale, when extraction pressure is too low)		22	
during starting-up operations		2	
sales of extracted steam			
from extraction at 11 bar		19.3	
from extraction at 4 bar		8.8	
Electrical energy (GWh)			
Gross output		22.2	
Sales		17.9	
In-plant requirements		4.3	

these plants is installed in Winterthur (Kehrichtverbrennungsanlage Stadt Winterthur, abreviated below to KSW), while the second, sited near Monthey, belongs to the Société pour le traitement des ordures du haut bassin lémanique et de la vallée inférieure du Rhône à Monthey, abreviated to SATOM. The KSW is composed of two old units and one larger new unit. The data in Table 12.4 refer to this latter unit only.

CONTRIBUTION OF PACKAGING WASTE TO ENERGY RECOVERY

The LHV values of packaging materials have been specified above. On this basis, the average value of the LHV of the packaging waste mix assumed in Table 12.1 is about 20 MJ/kg, i.e. about twice as high as the average value of the LHV of the total residential waste. Hence the packaging waste contributes about 34% to the heating value of the total residential waste, in spite of its much smaller contribution to the weight, namely only 17%. If packaging waste were absent or significantly reduced, some kinds of other waste material would not burn properly in the incinerators.

Looking again at the total sales of energy by the waste incineration plants, it can be deduced from the above considerations that the contribution of packaging waste to these sales in 1979 was:

Winterthur plant.

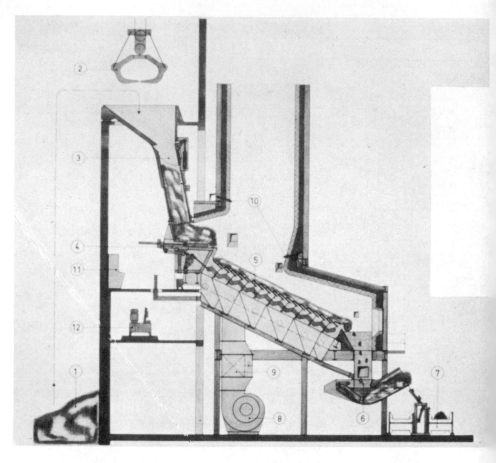

Cross-section through an incinerator.

Sales of heat as steam	0.96 PJ
Sales of electrical energy	0.29 PJ

The first of the above contributions represents 0.32% of the heat requirements for industrial and space heating in Switzerland, deduced[8] to be 301 PJ/year. The ratio of the above electrical energy to the overall delivery of this energy (122 PJ) is even lower, namely 0.24%.

It is also interesting to compare the above yields of heat and electrical energy with the energy consumed in the production of combustible packaging, as specified in Table 12.3. Such a comparison shows that 8% of the heating value of the feedstocks and fuels used for production is eventually delivered for sale by burning the product packaging in waste incineration plants with heat recovery. Also, 18% of the electrical energy consumed for the production of the combustible packaging has been eventually recovered from these plants using packaging waste as the energy source.

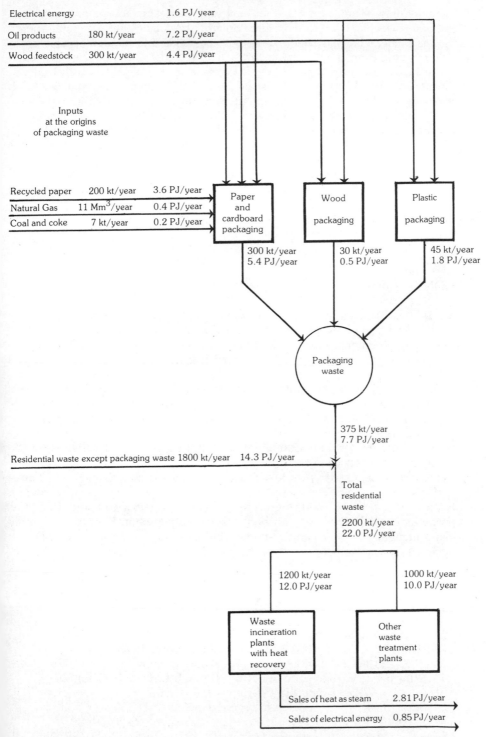

Fig. 12.2 Material and energy balance of residential waste in Switzerland, showing the proportion of combustible packaging. Material flow data in 1000 tonnes per year (kt/year); energy, flow data in 10^{15} J per year (PJ/year).

Taking into account the fact that each unit of electric energy produced in a thermal power plant needs about three units of LHV of any fuel, an overall energy recycle rate can be calculated for the activities related to the combustible packaging up to and including their incineration. The feedstocks and fuels specified in Table 12.3 can be used to produce 4.1 PJ of electrical energy, to which 1.6 PJ of directly consumed electric energy are to be added, leading to a total of 5.7 PJ. If the heat sold by the incinerating plants were to be transformed into electrical energy instead of being sold, about one fifth of this medium-grade heat could be available as the latter energy for additional sales, yielding a total of 0.48 PJ.

A full material and energy balance of residential waste in Switzerland is provided in Fig. 12.2.

The overall energy recycling ratio of the packaging business in Switzerland, calculated in this way, becomes 8%. This is neither negligible nor magnificient. It could be raised to about 15% if all wastes were incinerated with heat recovery, and if this heat could be delivered for purposes which would otherwise need combustion of fossil fuels.

CONCLUSIONS

Incineration of packaging waste represents an improvement compared to sanitary landfill. The heat recovered from such incineration currently provides 0.32% of the heat requirements and 0.24% of the electrical energy delivery in Switzerland. Both above figures could be nearly doubled if all incinerators were equipped with heat recovery boilers.

The size of electricity generation units, associated with waste incineration plants will remain small and their specific cost will remain high. Therefore, heat delivery by such plants is preferable to electrical energy generation by condensing turbines, provided useful application of this heat can be found near its source and purchase of fuels can be restricted. Combined heat and power (CHP) systems are too complicated and costly in such situations.

The overall energy recycle rate of the activities associated with the production of combustible packagings, up to and including their incineration with heat recovery, is about 8% in Switzerland at present and could be raised to about 15% if all incinerators were equipped with heat recovery equipment. However, a significantly higher recycle rate can be achieved by increasing the direct recycle of packaging waste as a feedstock to its production process.

REFERENCES

1. MOSER, W., *Synthetic*, No. 5, 1977.
2. MANTELL, C.L., *Solid Wastes*. Wiley, New York, 1975.
3. WESTERBERG, E.N. and Asantila, R., *Pulp and Paper Int.*, May 1976, p. 43.
4. STRAUSS, R.W. and Carmon, R.E., *Tappi*, **59**, 6 (June 1976), 80.
5. WILSON, W.B., *Tappi*, **60**, 8 (August 1977), 99.
6. SCHMIDT, W., *Wochenblatt füe Papierfabrikation* **1** (1976) 6.
7. SCHMIDT, F.E., *Wochenblatt füe Papierfabrikation*, **2** (1979) 39.
8. *Schweizerische Gesamtenergiestatistik 1979*, Bull. SEV/VSE No. 12, 1980.

9. BRAUN, R., *SIA*, H. 26, 1979.
10. OBRIST, W. and Braun, R., *Müll- und Abfallbeseitigung*, **58**, XII/1980.

L. Silberring received his M.Sc. in mechanical engineering from the Polytechnical Institute in Wroclaw and his D.Sc. from the Swiss Federal Institute of Technology in Zurich. Most of his activities are related to the development and design of thermal energy equipment and systems and of selected equipment and processes for chemical industry, in particular for the production of hydrogen, ammonia and heavy water. Since 1975 he has operated his own engineering firm in Zurich. He is author of over 40 publications and holder of several patents.

13 The Composition of Municipal Refuse and Energy Recovery through Waste Incineration in the Federal Republic of Germany

O. Tabasaran

INTRODUCTION

Any discussion concerning the composition of municipal wastes must include such wastes as household refuse, bulky refuse, industrial solid waste and, in some cases, excavated soil and debris. The term household refuse covers the solid substances which arise primarily in households. They may also occur in administrative buildings, schools, sales outlets, trading companies and, in isolated cases, in small industrial enterprises. Household refuse is generally collected in locally available refuse containers and is disposed of regularly by either the party responsible or its agent. Waste originating from households which is bulky, and therefore cannot be put into the locally available waste containers, is called bulky refuse.

Litter on roads and pavements and in parks usually consists of leaves, branches, grit, particles abraded from tires and road surfaces, animal droppings and such small litter as cigarette ends, fruit peels and paper. Such litter is usually collected and disposed of together with household refuse.

Waste occuring on the marketplace is solid; it includes primarily vegetables and packing material, and is usually disposed of together with household refuse.

Non-production-specific solid waste from sales outlets, trading companies and industrial enterprises, and in particular from kitchens, canteens and the shipping departments of companies, is called business waste or industrial solid waste, and is disposable together with household refuse. Industrial waste which cannot be disposed of together with household refuse for reason of public safety due to its nature and/or quantity is referred to as 'special waste'.

COMPOSITION OF MUNICIPAL REFUSE

Household Refuse

The most common constituents of household refuse are: organic substances such as left-over food; kitchen and garden waste; paper; cardboard; cartons; glass; metals; textiles; plastics; wood; leather; rubber; bones; stone; porcelain; and ashes.

The quantity and composition of household refuse varies depending on geographical situation, climate, living standard, style of living, economical struc-

Aerial view of refuse incinerator with heat recovery showing environmental considerations.

Table 13.1 Composition of Household Refuse in Germany

Variations can be explained by several socio-economic, seasonal and geographic factors.

Material group	Counties					Cities			
	Reutlingen 1974/75	Tübingen 1976/78	Wetterau-kreis 1981	Tuttlingen 1980	Schwarzwald-Baar-Kreis 1981	Stuttgart 1974	Heidelberg 1976	Karlsruhe 1978	Ulm/D 1980
Organics (kitchen waste, left-over food, garden waste)	46.5	53.9	62.3	56.6	58.8	52.4	31.4	43.0	40.5
Paper, cardboard, packaging material	13.3	16.7	13.6	11.9	14.5	14.7	22.7	21.9	22.7
Glass	12.7	9.8	5.2	9.0	8.5	9.9	14.0	11.7	14.0
Plastics, textiles	6.4	8.3	5.4	10.6	8.8	6.2	8.0	10.5	7.7
Fines (<8 mm or <10 mm)	10.1	4.6	6.5	5.4	3.5	6.2	4.9	7.0	9.7
Leather, wood, cardboard, rubber	5.0	1.4	3.1	2.5	1.1	4.1	11.0	1.6	1.2
Metals	4.6	4.1	2.6	3.4	3.9	5.3	4.8	3.4	3.8
Inert materials	1.4	1.2	1.3	0.6	0.9	1.2	3.2	0.5	0.4
Total (percent by weight)	00.0	100.0	100.0	100.0	100.0	100.0	100.0	100.0	100.0

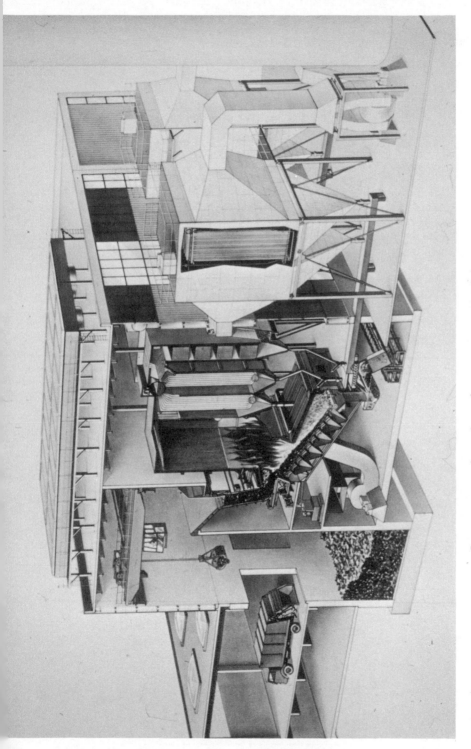

Cross-section through a refuse incinerator with heat recovery.

ture, social standing, availability of containers, local regulations, fashion trends, etc. These contributory influences may be characterised as follows (which offers sufficient accuracy for preliminary planning purposes in depending only on the number of people living in the area concerned). The Federal German averages are as follows:

	Population	kg/capita/year
Large towns	>300 000	300
Medium-size towns	50 000–300 000	250
Small towns	<50 000	225
Communities	<1000	180
	1000–5000	200
	>5000	210

The specific refuse quantity may also be expressed as a function of the specific gross national product. An increasing gross national product (which covers the market value of all goods manufactured and the value of all services rendered) is prompted by an increase in the private per capita consumption and, as a result, in the amount of household refuse.

Table 13.1 shows the material composition of household refuse determined by analysing the refuse of several selected counties and towns. It appears that organic substances (by weight) account for 31.4-62.3%, followed by paper and card-board accounting for 11.9-22.7%. Glass, accounting for 8.5-14.0%, holds the third rank and plastics including textiles account for 6.2-10.6%. Table 13.2 compiles the results of several additional detailed household refuse analyses, and shows that (by weight) polyethylene accounts for more than 70% of all plastics,

Table 13.2 Detailed Analysis of Some Components of Household Waste

	Weight %
(a) Plastics	
Polyethylene	70.2
Polystyrene	15.3
PVC	11.7
Others	2.8
	100.0
(b) Glass	
white	35–62
green	23–40
brown	14–20
mixed	8–20
(c) Ferrous-metals	
food cans	67.9
beverage cans	16.3
spray tins (aerosols)	6.0
others	9.8
	100.0

Table 13.3   Significance of Packaging Materials in Household Waste Regarding the Heat Value (Analysis Ulm, 1980)

Component	Proportion by weight (%)	Dry solids (kg)	Water (kg)	Ignition loss (kg)	Heat value (MJ)	Heat content (MJ/dry kg)
Organics	40.5	206.0	199.0	145.2	2735.6	13.28
Paper	17.7	145.1	31.9	127.7	2426.3	16.72
Cardboard	5.0	43.0	7.0	38.7	802.1	18.65
Plastics	6.0	55.0	5.0	51.8	1951.8	35.49
Textile	1.7	13.6	3.4	12.4	246.6	18.13
Glass	14.0	140.0	0.0	0.0	0.0	0
Metals	3.8	38.0	0.0	0.0	0.0	0
Wood, leather, rubber, bones	1.2	11.0	1.0	10.0	101.0	9.18
Inerts (rocks, ceramics etc.)	0.4	4.0	0.0	0.0	0.0	0
Balance (<10 mm)	9.7	77.6	19.4	46.6	936.6	12.07
Total	100.0	733.3	266.7	432.4	9200.0	12.55

followed by polystyrene. Polyvinylchloride (PVC) accounts for approximately 11.7%. The amount of white glass accounts for the majority of scrap glass, followed by green and brown glass waste. Cans account for almost 68% by weight of all ferrous metals.

The data shown in Tables 13.1 and 13.2 demonstrate the important role that packaging materials play in connection with refuse composition. Table 13.3 refers to the refuse composition of Ulm/Danube and shows the calorific value attributable to the individual refuse components. It thus follows that such packing materials as paper, cardboard and plastics contribute most to the calorific value of refuse. The calorific value of Federal German refuse has risen steadily during the last few decades, mostly because of the increasing proportion of packaging material. An investigation was conducted into the calorific value of refuse arising from different sources. The results, shown in Fig. 13.1, reveal that the mean calorific value of refuse as received is approximately 8500 kJ/kg (wet basis), which fluctuates by as much as 2000 kJ/kg.

Bulky Refuse

Bulky refuse is usually placed in the street by the inhabitants of almost every community for collection by refuse collectors, and has a different composition depending upon a number of factors. Generally it has high proportions of such combustibles as wood, cardboard, plastics, leather and textiles. The quantities also vary depending upon local conditions such as community structure, size of containers, local regulations, and living standards. The specific quantity lies between 20 and 50 kg/capita/year depending on the household refuse container system. Due to its heterogeneity, the density of bulky refuse is difficult to determine. As an average it may be assumed to be approximately 100 kg/m³. A suggested composition of such bulky waste is proposed in Table 13.4.

Litter

This type of waste occurs in communities having regular street sweeping activities. Otherwise it becomes part of household refuse. Its quantity depends on the frequency of sweeping and the length of streets to be kept clean. 1400 kg/m³ is an average density for litter.

Table 13.4   Example of the Composition of Bulky Wastes

Material group	Mean values (% by weight)
Paper	28
Wood	27
Cardboard	16
Metals	9
Plastics	7
Glass	4
Textiles	3
Porcelain, rocks	2
Balance	4
Total	100.0

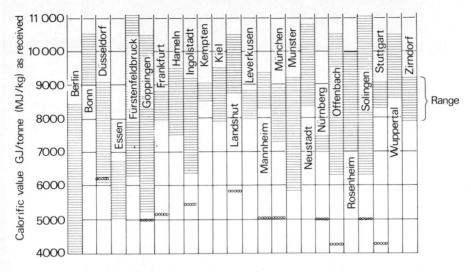

Fig. 13.1   Calorific value ranges of refuse (wet basis) in a number of incinerator plants in the Federal Republic of Germany. Dotted lines represent the lower limit values for unassisted incinceration.

Marketplace Waste

Waste arisings from marketplaces and similar activities is usually collected by the regular waste collecting system. Therefore, the quantities are often counted in with household refuse. A description should not be necessary.

Industrial Waste

Only that part of industrial waste which is normally treated and collected together with household refuse is relevant to this chapter. Waste coming from kitchens, canteens and offices of industrial enterprises resembles that of household refuse as far as its composition is concerned, whereas refuse coming from incoming goods departments and shipping departments is more likely to resemble bulky refuse except that such typical household appliances as used furniture, refrigerators, etc., are unlikely to arise. Empty packaging made of paper, cardboard, plastics and wood account for most of such industrial waste. Quantity and composition of production-specific industrial waste are influenced by the type of production, the applied technology, the company management and similar factors.

Experience has shown that approximately 10% by weight of industrial waste and 35% by weight of waste coming from service enterprises are collected and disposed of together with household refuse. The bulk density of industrial refuse varies considerably. For rough estimation, a mean value of 130 kg/m³ is believed reasonable. Examples of industrial waste composition are given in Table 13.5.

HOUSEHOLD REFUSE INCINERATION

General

There are 42 incineration plants in the Federal Republic of Germany which

Table 13.5 Example of the Composition of Industrial Waste

Material group	Mean values (weight %)	
	Counties of Reutlingen/Tübingen	County of Tuttlingen
Packaging materials	26.3	40.7
Wooden wastes	12.6	11.9
Paper	10.4	7.5
Textiles	7.7	6.4
Plastics, leather, rubber	7.1	15.5
Production waste	20.1	1.7
Balance	15.8	16.3
Total	100.0	100.0

Table 13.6 Refuse Incineration Plants in the Federal Republic of Germany (July 1980)

Reproduced from L. Barniske and H. Voßköhler, Abfallverbrennung in der Bundesrepublik Deutschland, *Müll und Abfall*, **9** (1980), 263–274.

Locality	Start of operation	Manufacturer	Number of furnaces	Theoretical throughput (tonne/h)	Hours of operation (h/week)	Annual throughput × 1000 t	Inhabitants served × 1000	Steam parameters bar/°C	Flue-gas purification
Bamberg	1978 (E 1981)	VKW/VKW	2	6 without sludge	7 × 24	86	220	26/227 sat. steam	E-Filter
Berlin	1967 (E 1971/72)	Borsig/Borsig	3	12.5	7 × 24	400	1100	73/470	wet-scrubber
			4	16					E-Filter
Bonn-Bad Godesberg	1966	Koppers-Wistra/Buckau-Wolf	2	5.5	6 × 24	29	80	10/250	Cyclone
Bremen	1969	Dürr-Werke/Bremer Vulkan	3	15	7 × 24	240	600	21/215	E-Filter
	E 1978		1	20					E-Filter
Bremerhaven	1977	von Roll/Seebeckwerft-MAN	3	10	7 × 24	150	250	40/400	E-Filter
Darmstadt	1967	von Roll/MAN	2	8.5	7 × 24	136	320	38/430	wet-scrubber
	E 1978		1	11				38/350	E-Filter
Düsseldorf	1965	VKW-Dürr/VKW-Dürr	4	10					
Essen-Karnap	1.E 1972	VKW-Dürr	1	12.5	7 × 24	360	770	80/500	dry-sorption
	2.E 1980	VKW/Lentjes	1	12.5					E-Filter
Geisselbullach	1960	Babcock/Dürr-Werke	5	20	7 × 24	355	1400	100/500	E-Filter
(Krs. Fürsten-feldbruck)	1970	Keller-Peukert/Baumgarte	1	2	5 × 24	42	165	24/220 sat. steam	E-Filter
	E 1975	Keller-Peukert/Baumgarte	1	6 without sludge					
Göppingen	1975	VKW/VKW	2	12	7 × 24	104	230	39/410	E-Filter
Frankfurt/M.	1966	von Roll/Baumgarte	4	15	7 × 24	330	1000	60/500	E-Filter
Hagen	1967	VKW/VKW	3	6	7 × 24	112	335	14/196	E-Filter
Hamburg I (Billbrook)	1.E 1953	von Roll/Oschatz-Walther	3	7.5 ⎫	7 × 24	182	600	21/340	E-Filter
	2.E 1967 (3.E 1981)	Martin-Walther	1	12 ⎬					

153

Table 13.6 *(continued)*

Locality	Start of operation	Manufacturer	Number of furnaces	Theoretical throughput (tonne/h)	Hours of operation (h/week)	Annual throughput × 1000 t	Inhabitants served × 1000	Steam parameters bar/°C	Flue-gas purification
Hamburg II (Stellinger Moor)	1973	Martin-Walther	2	19	7 × 24	264	600	40/410	dry sorption
Hamburg III (Stapelfeld)	1978	Steinmüller/ Steinmüller	2	19	7 × 24	260	600	28/380	E-Filter wet scrubber
Hameln	1977	VKW/VKW	1	10	5 × 24	70	200	40/450	E-Filter
Heidelberg	1974	Lambion/-	1	5	5 × 24	23	150	—	E-Filter
Ingolstadt	1978	Alberti Fonsa/-	2	7 without sludge	7 × 24	95	340		E-Filter wet scrubber
Iserlohn	1970 E 1974	K.K Ofenbau Zürich/Babcock Babcock/Babcock VKW/VKW	1 1 2	8 8 16	7 × 24	157	300	16/250	{ E-Filter wet scrubber
Kassel	1968 E 1968	Dürr-Werke/ Dürr-Werke	2	10	7 × 24	115	350	42/450	E-Filter
Kempten/ Allgäu	1975 E 1976 (E 1982)	von Roll/Wamser	1 1	4 5	7 × 24	65	250	25/225 sat. steam	E-Filter
Kiel-Süd	1975 E 1980	{ VKW/VKW	2 1	5 10	7 × 24	96	260	14/197 sat. steam	E-Filter wet scrubber
Krefeld	1975 (E 1982)	{ VKW-BSH/VKW	2	12 without sludge	7 × 24	162 without sludge	330	22.5/ 375	E-Filter wet scrubber
Landshut	1971 E 1974 (E 1981)	von Roll/Wamser	2	3	7 × 24	31	160	20/380	E-Filter
Leverkusen	1970	von Roll/MAN	2	10	7 × 24	130	360	20/305	E-Filter
Ludwigshafen	1967	von Roll/Baumgarte	2	10	7 × 24	90	250	42/420	E-Filter
Mannheim	1965 E 1973	{ EVT/EVT	2 1	12 20	7 × 24	172	330	120/500	E-Filter

Location	Year	Manufacturer	No.		Operation			Temp.	Filter
Marktoberdorf	1974	Dr. Pauli — Lurgi/-	1	2 without sludge	4 × 24 1 × 12	10 without sludge	30	—	wet scrubber
München-Nord	1964 E 1966 (E 1982)	Martin-Babcock	2 1	25 40	6 × 15 7 × 24	223		205/540	E-Filter
München-Süd	1970 E 1971	Martin/ VKW-Babcock	1 1	40 40	6 × 24 7 × 24	265	1500	231/355	-Filter
Neufahrn/Freising	1970 E 1978	Keller-Peukert/Ten-Horn Steinmüller/Wamser	1	3	7 × 24	33	140	16/203 16/250	E-Filter
Neunkirchen	1970 E 1977	Martin/Wamser	1 1	3 5 10	7 × 24	100	280	20/180 28/350	E-Filter
Neustadt/Holstein	1964	Maschinenfabrik Esslingen/ME	1	4.5	5 × 24	19	50	Recuperator	Multiple cyclone
Nürnberg	1968 E 1980	von Roll/MAN Martin/EVT	3 1	12.5 20	7 × 24	200	485	80/450	E-Filter
Oberhausen	1972 (E 1982)	VKW/Babcock	3	22	7 × 24	320	1100	55/480	E-Filter
Offenbach	1970	VKW/VKW	3	10	7 × 24	180	530	16/250	E-Filter
Pinneberg	1974	Claudius Peters/-	2	5	5 × 24 1 × 12	50	260		E-Filter dry sorption
Rosenheim	1964 E 1970	VKW/VKW	1 1	4.5 6	6 × 24	40	210	16/200 sat. steam 70/500	E-Filter
Solingen	1969	von Roll/MAN	2	10	7 × 24	100	255	42/450	E-Filter
Stuttgart	1965 E 1971	Martin/KSG VKW/VKW VKW/EVT	1 1 1	16 16 20	7 × 24	245	600	64/510	E-Filter
Wuppertal	1976	VKW/VKW	4	15	7 × 24	250	550	30/350	E-Filter wet scrubber
Zirndorf	1971 E 1977	von Roll/MAN Widmer + Ernst/Baumgarte	1 1	4 4	7 × 24	52	190	20/200 5/150	E-Filter wet scrubber

NOTES

E = Extension   E-Filter = Electrostatic Filter

incinerate primarily municipal waste. Table 13.6 lists the most important data on these plants. According to this information, refuse of approximately 18 million people, or about 29% of the total population, is incinerated. Because of the number of plants under construction, it may be expected that the percentage will increase to 33.4% by 1985. Nearly all of the incineration plants use the calorific value of the refuse for steam generation. As an average, 1 tonne of refuse produces a little more than 2 tonnes of steam, which are used for heating purposes, or as a process heating medium which enables the generation of approximately 500 kWh of electricity.

In larger plants high-pressure steam having temperatures up to 500 °C is primarily generated. In smaller plants, lower-pressure steam is produced at temperatures up to about 250 °C. For economical reasons combined production of electricity and heating steam is preferred.

The fact that the calorific value of German household refuse is about 8500 kJ/kg and often reaches 10 000 kJ/kg and more, and is still increasing slightly, is due to the constantly increasing use of packaging made of paper, cardboard and plastics. The outlook is that a noticeable decrease of the heating value is not to be expected within the foreseeable future even though pre-separation of paper may be increased.

Costs

The widespread belief that incineration counts among the most expensive methods of refuse disposal can no longer be upheld considering the increase in energy prices in recent years. Because of the increasing proceeds from energy production, the net costs of incineration in Germany have fallen to a point (typically 45 DM/tonne) which is almost economically acceptable compared to modern landfill (typically 30-35 DM/t). The difference is anticipated to reduce in the future. This development can be explained using the example in Table 13.7.

SUMMARY

Changes in the composition of Federal German refuse have been characterized during recent decades by a steadily increasing share of packaging material and decreasing proportion of ashes and other inerts. Therefore, the calorific value has consistently increased. The current mean calorific value is estimated to be 8500 kJ/kg, and often approaching 10 000 kJ/kg.

In 1980 there were 42 incineration plants in the Federal Republic of Germany for the primary purpose of incinerating municipal waste and generating energy in the form of steam. In 1985 it is anticipated that 33.4% of the total population of the Federal Republic of Germany will be serviced by incineration plants. The specific costs of refuse incineration have a tendency to decrease as demand and prices paid for recovered energy increase.

Professor Tabasaran is Head of the Department for Solid Waste Techniques and Chair-Professor for Solid Waste Management in the University of Stuttgart, Faculty of Civil Engineering.

Table 13.7   Example: Parameters for a Modern Refuse Incinerator

Municipal solid waste quantity	240 000 tonne/year
Furnaces (grates)	3
Capacity of each grate	11–12 tonne/h
Temperature in the furnace	820–950 °C
Boilers	3
Steam pressure	25 (28) bar
Steam temperature	275 (375) °C
Flue-gas purification	Wet absorption
Chimney height	70–120 m

Typical Expenditure

Investment	million DM
Mechanical and electrical equipment	70
Installation	30
	100
Amortization at 12% over 20 years	
Equipment ⎫ Installation ⎭	13.39/year
Operating costs	
Labour, 40 × 3 shifts	2.0/year
Repairs and maintenance	2.0/year
Miscellaneous	1.5/year
Total annual cost	18.89/year

		Assumed future (1991)		
Income	1981	A	or	B
Electricity, unit value DM/kWh	0.08	0.12		0.16
Generation at 10 000 MWh/year: value, million DM/year	0.8	1.2		1.6
Thermal energy (steam), unit value, DM/MJ	0.015	0.0225		0.03
Generation at 120 GJ/h, 24 h/day, 250 days/year = 720 000 GJ/year: value, million DM/year	10.8	16.2		21.6
Scrap metal, unit value DM/tonne	30	30		30
Generation at 3% metal content on 240 000 tonne/year value, million DM/year	0.22	0.22		0.22

Cost Balance				
Total income, million DM/year	11.82	17.62		23.42
Total annual cost (from above), million DM/year	18.89	18.89		18.89
Net annual cost (credit), million DM/year	7.07	1.27		(4.53)
DM/tonne refuse treated	29.5	5.3		(18.9)

Note: Future A or B has alternative electricity values in 1991.

157

14 Energy Considerations in Thermal Conversion of Refuse

A.V. Bridgwater

INTRODUCTION

Refuse has an appreciable energy content due to the paper, plastic, and vegetable constituents. A typical analysis of European refuse can be represented as in Table 14.1, although the composition can vary considerably with time and place.

The energy contents of the various constituents are shown in Table 14.2, with a summation to give the heating value of the typical refuse of Table 14.1 as 9.92 GJ/tonne dry refuse. This can range from 8 to 12 GJ/tonne according to composition.

Table 14.1   Typical European Refuse Characteristics

	Wet basis	Dry basis	DAF basis*
Paper	27	39	58
Vegetable and animal wastes	15	21	32
Rag and textile	2	3	4
Plastics	3	4	6
Metal	6	8	
Glass	6	9	
Dust and cinder	11	16	
Water	30		
	100	100	100

* DAF: Dry and ash free.

Table 14.2   Energy Content of Constituents of Refuse

	GJ/tonne	Typical composition (%)	Contribution to total dry refuse heating value
Paper	16.5	39	6.44
Vegetable and animal waste	13.5	21	2.84
Rag and textile	18.0	3	0.54
Plastics	36.0	4	1.44
Metal	—	8	—
Glass	—	9	—
Dust and cinder	12.0	16	1.92
Heat energy content of dry refuse:			13.18 GJ/dry tonne
			(= 9.23 GJ/wet tonne at 30% moisture)

This energy may be realized in a variety of ways, as summarized in Table 14.3[1]. Also included is an energy efficiency of a typical complete system to convert refuse into the appropriate energy containing product. This includes *all* energy inputs into the process, not only in the feed material but also for heating, power, etc. Only the energy content of the main or primary product is included — waste

Table 14.3 Methods for Realizing Energy Potential from Refuse, and Efficiencies of Conversion (derived from Ref. 1)

Method	Product	Approximate overall energy efficiency (%)
Incineration[1]	Heat	70
	Power	—
	Electricity	21[a]
Gasification	Fuel gas	70
(oxygen)[1]	Methanol	50
	Methane (SNG)	50
Pyrolysis[1]	Fuel gas	
	'Oil'	see text
	Char	
	Methanol	35-40
	Methane (SNG)	33-38[b]
Liquefaction	'Oil'	40-60[c]
Mechanical separation[1]	Refuse-derived fuel (RDF)	60-75[d]
Digestion[2]	Methane (SNG)	60[e]
Fermentation[3]	Ethanol	20[f]
Methanol from natural gas by reforming and synthesis	Methanol	65-70
Coal conversion	Methanol	50
	Methanol and methane (SNG)	60
	Methane	55
Methanol to gasoline	Gasoline	85
	Gasoline and LPG	95

NOTES

[a] 30% efficiency assumed in converting thermal to electrical energy.

[b] Including compression to about 25 bars.

[c] Liquefaction is still at a very early stage of development. The efficiency is dependant on the extent of conversion and quality of products. See also discussion on pyrolysis products.

[d] More complex, and hence more costly, processes give a higher yield of RDF with a higher process energy efficiency but at a higher cost.

[e] This figure is for small-scale processes and local use of methane without gas clean-up and compression. Moderate compression for distribution would reduce the figure to about 55%, and with gas clean-up to about 50%. Large scale processes have a much higher energy requirement for materials handling and reactor agitation.

[f] For low efficiency processes an alternative and complementary method of expressing energy efficiency is to compare the net process energy requirements — after deducting in-house energy credits from by-products and excluding feedstock — to the energy available in the final product. For ethanol production from many forms of biomass, more energy is consumed in the process than is available in the product. This is only acceptable when fuel is 'free' (e.g. as wastes such as bagasse) or for strategic reasons. In the case here of ethanol from refuse, the Net Energy Production is + 3.9 GJ/tonne dry sorted refuse[3].

streams, for example, are excluded and it is assumed that energy recovery/recycling is practised according to conventional practice. Equipment and plant availability is not included due to lack of data. The energy efficiency is expressed (see also Chapter 1) thus:

$$\frac{\text{Energy in main product(s)}}{\text{Energy in feed + All other energy inputs}} \times 100\%$$

which is an orthodox method.

This is, however, not necessarily a useful way of defining efficiency, as the most efficient method is that which does nothing — an energy efficiency of 100%! The value of the end product must be also considered therefore. Also included in Table 14.3 are comparable efficiences of a conventional process for making methanol from natural gas; analogous coal conversion processes; and a recent

Table 14.4 Characterization of Energy Quality — Thermal and Chemical Fuels

Availability	Is it available continuously? If not, when is it available?
Conversion efficiency	How efficiently can the energy be used?
Energy density	What is the energy value per unit volume?
Environment	Do any problems arise from production or use?
Hazards	Is it poisonous, dangerous, or toxic? Does it require special precautions?
Market	How can it be sold? Who would buy it? What price does it command? What quantities can be sold? Where can it be sold?
Phase	Is it gas, liquid or solid?
Physical properties	Are there special problems of handling or use?
Production	Is the process producing the energy available? Is it flexible? Is it dependent on scale? Are there any by-products?
Quantity	How much is available?
Storage	Can it be stored? Is special equipment needed?
Temperature	What is the temperature?
Use	What can it be used for? How easily can it be used? Can it be readily converted into a more valuable product? Is special equipment or modification needed? Can it be assimilated into existing distribution networks? Can it be blended?
Value	What is it worth? Can it be upgraded? Is upgrading valuable?

Table 14.5 Assessment of Energy Product Quality

Energy product	Form	Uses	ED	H	IN	ST	US	Value £/tonne	£/GJ
Primary									
Heat	Hot water	District heating	L	L	—	N	L	—	2.8
	Steam	District heating, power, industry, electricity generation	L	M	P	N	L	10	5.5
Gas (low heating value)	Fuel gas	Local use by industry	L	M	N	Y	M	—	2.0
"Oil"	Liquid (unstable)	Uncertain	H	M	P	Y	L	110[a]	2.2
Char[b]		Solid fuel[b]	H	L	P	Y	L	40[b]	1
Secondary									
Power		Electricity, industry	—	L	N	N	H	—	—
Electricity		Direct	—	L	Y	N	H	—	8.5
Methanol	Liquid	As methanol, fuel extender	H	L	Y	Y	H	110[c]	4.8
Methane	Gas	As methane/natural gas	L	M	Y	Y	H	140[d]	2.5
Ethanol	Liquid	As ethanol, fuel extender	H	L	Y	Y	H	285[e]	9.6
Gasoline	Liquid	As natural gasoline	H	L	Y	Y	H	220	4.5
Comparative									
Coal			H	L	—	Y	H	40	1.6
Fuel oil			H	L	—	Y	H	140	2.7

[a] 20% less than fuel oil to allow for special handling problems (q.v.).
[b] Assumed similar to coal.
[c] Contract price; spot price about £130.
[d] Uninterruptible supplies.
[e] Very approximate European price as not widely traded.

ED—Energy Density, HZ—Hazard, IN—Integration into existing use patterns, ST—Storability, US—Usefulness and marketability.
L—Low, M—Medium, H—High, Y—Yes, N—No, P—Possible.

development for high-yield conversion of methanol to synthetic gasoline. These are included not just for comparison, but to show the energetic cost of product or high grade/high value product.

Background to Current Activity

Most investigations up to around 1978 had been devoted to developing a refuse *disposal* system, with inadequate attention being paid to the usefulness and value of the products (see Tables 14.4 and 14.5). The high cost of developing a new technology combined with the relatively low value of the end product (for example a low heating value fuel gas from Purox) inevitably proved a barrier to commercial implementation.

With such a pessimistic prognosis attention turned to biomass as a renewable energy source in the wake of the oil problems subsequent to 1973. For biomass-based processes the objective turned to producing a high value, commercially viable fuel, preferably in liquid form to satisfy the premium transport market. Examples include ethanol, methanol, methane, and more recently synthetic gasoline (see Table 14.3). There are many examples of implementation of synthetic fuel policies, notably synthetic crude oil from coal gasification in South Africa, and ethanol by fermentation from cassava and sugar cane in Brazil. The latter option of fermentation of suitable forms of biomass is now being quite widely introduced, particularly in less developed countries where a high technology is not required, labour is cheap, and mineral oil is prohibitively expensive. In a total system from biomass production to end product marketing, the thermal processing reactor is an essential but relatively minor part, and therefore does not dominate the process. The significance of this has been largely ignored in both coal and biomass conversion studies.

As in many countries, extensive studies have been carried out in the UK on the potential of biomass as a renewable energy resource[7]. One part has concentrated on production of biomass and the other on conversion to useful fuel products.

Energy Products

Fig. 14.1 shows the forms of energy realizable from refuse and their inter-relationships. The biological routes of fermentation to ethanol and digestion to methane are not considered in detail any further, nor is direct combustion of raw or prepared refuse as this is discussed elsewhere in Chapters 12 and 13.

The energy products can be simply classified as 'primary' — resulting directly from one of the processing operations; or 'secondary' — resulting from a chemical conversion process (see Table 14.5). Both heat and methane are primary *and* secondary products.

It is not enough to consider only the energy content of the product. $1\,GJ(10^9\,J)$ of hot gas at 500 °C is less useful than 1 GJ light hydrocarbon fuel, but more useful than 1 GJ warm water at 40 °C. The quality of energy is also, therefore, important, and some of the characteristics used in assessing quality are summarized in Table 14.4. A single overall measure of quality cannot therefore be achieved. Some of the characteristics have been indicated for the above range of products in Table 14.5. In some respects, perhaps, a good overall measure of quality is current market price, for which actual data are provided. In a free trading situation the value of a commodity is set in the marketplace which will consider all qualities in an objective and commercial way.

Generally it can be seen that the more 'useful' products have a higher value, and particularly include those in liquid form.

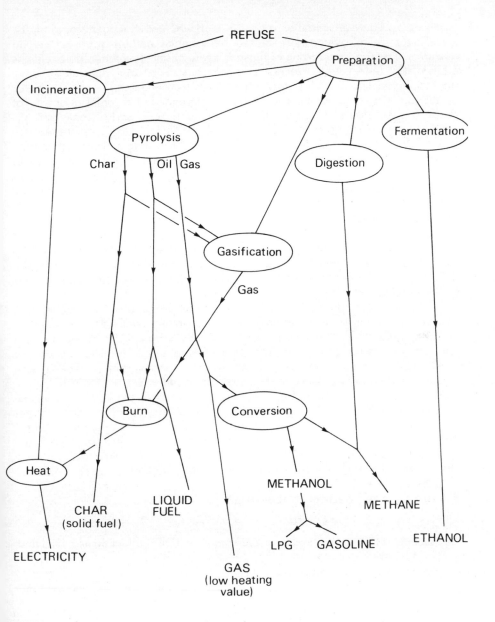

Fig. 14.1 Energy production routes from refuse.

THERMAL PROCESSES

Technology review

The thermal processes included are those where thermal degradation of the organic constituents occurs either in the total absence of air or oxygen — pyrolysis; or with only sufficient air or oxygen added to burn a small part of the organic materials thereby releasing sufficient heat to pyrolyse the remainder —

gasification[1]. There are variations of gasification when other reagents or catalysts, particularly steam (water), are added to enhance and/or suppress certain reactions. The most interesting of these is steam gasification when no oxygen is added and the overall process is analogous to steam reforming heavy hydrocarbons. This and other possibilities are discussed later.

Although very considerable effort has been expended on thermal processing of refuse (since 1968) with scores of processes being proposed[1, 4], only one has achieved commercial success — Landgard in Baltimore, USA — but there are no plans for further installation and the designers, Monsanto-Envirochem appear to have lost all interest. The produce is low-grade fuel gas for steam raising with no other resource recovery. The most widely publicized refuse gasification system was the Purox process developed by Union Carbide to a 200 tonne/day demonstration plant. With no commercial interest being expressed, this plant has now been dismantled. Union Carbide are understood to have plans for a second generation process perhaps orientated to the currently more popular biomass market than refuse. The air gasification systems that have been installed by Andco-Torrax are believed to be still non-operational. These and other relevant technologies have been adequately described in the companion volume to this book[1] and elsewhere[4-6].

In the short term, production of biomass is more likely to rely on utilization of wastes due to their lower (even negative) cost; greater availability; lack of new land requirement for growth; and lack of lead time for growth. The waste arising in greatest quantity is refuse, amounting in the UK to about 18 million tonnes per year from domestic sources which is handled by local government in centralized systems; and another possibly 6–9 million tonnes per year from industrial/commercial sources which is handled by private contractors. Agricultural wastes such as straw are very much less, at around 8 million tonne/year, and wood wastes from forestry a poor third. The large proportion of paper/card and putrescibles in refuse qualifies it for consideration as biomass, albeit with a high level of inerts and rather special properties. The current view is that refuse is merely a special form of biomass that deserves special attention on grounds of quantity and environment.

Significance of Thermal Processing

The UK biomass conversion studies referred to above[7, 2-5] examined:

> direct utilization to give heat/thermal energy or RDF production as a solid fuel,
> digestion to methane,
> fermentation, for example to ethanol,
> thermal processing to fuel gas, methanol, methane and synthetic gasoline.

> Feedstocks included refuse and wood.

As far as refuse, as a special form of biomass, is concerned, there are varying constraints for each option:

> *Incineration* by itself is a costly disposal method, and in the UK plants are currently being closed down due to high costs. Heat recovery is not widely practised in the UK, and from the limited experience available appears to be far from satisfactory. This view is restricted to UK practice for which justification on economic and political grounds can be provided. Elsewhere in Europe, incineration with heat recovery is successful and profitable.
> *RDF (refuse-derived fuel)* is currently the preferred product from central sorting processes, although in both loose (fluff or powder) or densified form (pellets or briquettes) there is neither a ready market nor suitable dedicated equip-

ment or plant readily available. Blending with coal is an obvious possibility dependent on price and solution of any consequent technical problems. The value of RDF can be compared to bulk coal on a heating value basis, which gives a current figure of £15–25/tonne RDF according to quantity and location. Equipment conversion or facility modification costs would reduce this value.

Digestion to methane occurs naturally in landfill and the methane rich gas can be recovered[8]. There are only limited examples of such exploitation in Europe, and the viability is unproven. Controlled digestion in an artificial environment such as large agitated tanks is potentially more attractive technically, but unlikely to prove viable on anything but very small scale applications. In all cases a substantial residue remains which for landfill is not a problem, but for a dedicated plant represents a disposal problem.

Fermentation also only processes part of the refuse. This feedstock creates peculiar microbiological control problems and possibly pretreatment requirements which, together, preclude refuse as likely substrate for a fermentation operation.

Thermal processing includes pyrolysis, gasification and liquefaction to give primary products of gas, sometimes liquid oil and sometimes solid char; or secondary products including methanol, methane or gasoline by chemical processing operations. A well designed process with appropriate technology would maximize conversion, minimize residues and minimize cost. The nature of the processes confers the benefit of economy of scale which means the bigger the process, the lower the cost of each unit produced. Secondary products can have enhanced physical and chemical properties and thus command a premium price, and the added value could justify the capital expenditure involved. Finally the thermal processing part is relatively insensitive to feedstock or quality, except that high moisture levels (above perhaps 30% water) should be avoided. In principle at least, thermal processing offers a very attractive alternative to recovering the energy value of refuse.

The thermal processing study[5] comprised four case studies covering a representative range of reactors and gas compositions. The results are summarized in Table 14.6 which gives energy efficiencies, weight yields (weight product per unit weight feed), and total production cost for both methanol and methane products. Included is further justification of the analogy between biomass (e.g. wood) and refuse as far as thermal processing is concerned. All the processes are of modest size and it is interesting to see how low the production cost is for the more efficient processes. This is discussed later.

A simplified flow sheet for an oxygen gasification based process is shown for illustration in Fig. 14.2[2]. This is the only study based on a refuse rather than wood (biomass) feed. Every step in this process has been proven at a commercial scale of operation, and all steps except the oxygen gasification, gas clean 1, and methanation are understood to be available commercially. The flowsheets for the other processes are very similar and differ only in detail according to the gas composition, and conversion steps necessary for efficient production.

Energy and Costs

The energy efficiencies of the process summarized in Table 14.6 are plotted against production cost; for methanol in Fig. 14.3 and for methane in Fig. 14.4. There is a surprisingly good correlation as shown by the solid lines for the 250

Table 14.6 Energy Efficiency and Production Costs for Methanol and Methane, 1980 basis[5]

	Methanol				Methane			
	Energy efficiency[d]	Weight yield	Production cost[b,e]		Energy efficiency[d]	Weight yield	Production cost[c,e]	
	(%)	(%)	£ per tonne	£ per GJ	(%)	(%)	£ per tonne	£ per GJ
Low-temperature pyrolysis[a,f]	35	29	253	11.1	—	—	—	—
High-temperature pyrolysis[a,f]	41	34	209	9.2	39	13	428	7.8
Oxygen gasification[g]	48	50	174	7.7	48	19	378	6.9
Steam gasification[a,h]	55	51	149	6.6	77	29	209	3.8
Current product price			130	5.7			140	2.5

a These processes were based on a biomass (wood) feed, while that for oxygen gasification was based on a sorted refuse feed. As the largest component of refuse is cellulose as paper and putrescibles, with high molecular weight polymers as plastics and textiles, this can reasonably be considered analogous to wood as cellulose with lignin (a high molecular weight organic). Wide experimental evidence confirms that the products from both feedstocks are very similar from similar thermal processing reactor systems.

b At a methanol production rate of 250 tonne/day.

c At a methane production rate of 250 tonne/day.

d All energy requirements are provided in-house.

e Capital is amortized at 10% over 10 years. Feedstock is costed at £20/dry tonne as either wood or prepared and densified refuse. All other production costs are properly accounted for, including labour, maintenance, overheads, etc. There is no provision for a return on the investment.

f Bench-scale laboratory investigations were used as the basis for these conceptual processes.

g The semi-commercial 'Purox' oxygen gasification process was the basis for this process. The demonstration plant has now been dismantled and at the time of writing there are plans for a second generation pressurized reactor. These figures thus represent the most likely 'state of the art' yields with current technology and sensible, but not optimal, process design.

h Pilot plant results from a novel pressurized reactor system were used for this process.

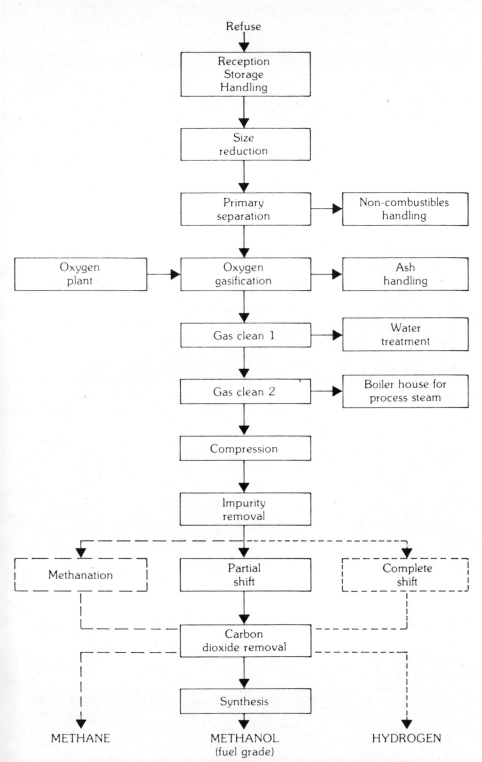

Fig. 14.2   Conceptual processes for converting waste to methanol and other chemicals[1].

167

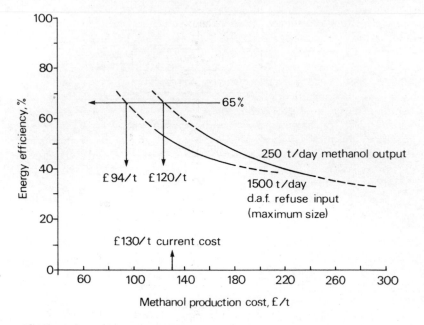

Fig. 14.3   Methanol: energy efficiency and production cost.

tonne/day outputs in both figures. Production costs have also been estimated for the maximum conceivable size of refuse based plant of 1500 DAF tonne/day or nearly 3000 tonne/day raw wet refuse[9]. These are the lower lines in both cases, and do not correlate with the upper lines due to different yields from the same input of refuse.

Considering methanol first, the maximum energy efficiency from the case studies summarized in Table 14.6 is 55%. From the data presented earlier in Table 14.3, it would seem unreasonable to expect optimization studies and/or

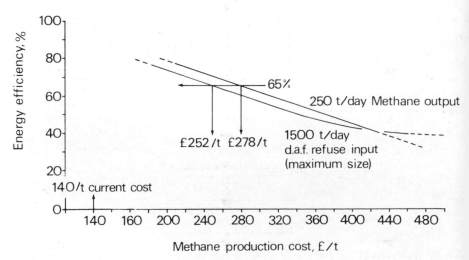

Fig. 14.4   Methane: energy efficiency and production cost.

168

technological development to give an energy efficiency greater than 65%. Extrapolation of the upper line of Fig. 14.3 for a 250 tonne/day methanol plant leads to an estimated minimum production cost of £120/tonne at this efficiency; or, from the lower line, a minimum production cost of £94/tonne at the maximum conceivable sized plant and maximum conceivable energy efficiency. Comparison with the current market price suggests that process optimization with respect to energy could prove attractive.

For methane the calculated maximum energy efficiency is 77% for steam gasification, although doubts have been expressed on the authenticity of the source data. By similar considerations as for methanol, it might be deduced that this estimate, although properly obtained, is unrealistically optimistic; and more reasonable maximum figures should be obtained from the 65% energy efficiency line as shown. (Explanations for the apparently optimistic energy yields are beyond the scope of this chapter. The case studies are based on results for steam gasification reported in the literature, which have been properly assimilated into a complete process[5].) The refuse fed oxygen gasification to methane system has a similar energy efficiency as the methanol system, and analogous improvements might be expected. By comparison of minimum methane production costs from refuse/biomass to current market price, methane therefore appears to be an unattractive prospect as a high grade fuel.

IMPROVEMENTS IN ENERGY EFFICIENCY

There are several aspects to energy losses in a process to convert refuse to methanol. There is the reactor system with pretreatment, post-treatment and products; the subsequent conversion operations to chemically adjust the product composition and synthesise methanol; and the energy recovery and exchange system for the whole process. Losses or inefficiencies may be accounted for as power and thermal losses, chemical/material losses, or chemical reaction requirements.

The range of products from a thermal processing reactor are summarized in Table 14.7. Temperature has a significant effect in the composition although there are many other process variables which affect the products including type of reactor, pressure, moisture content, particle size, and many other factors. Due to problems of heat transfer, pyrolysis (as opposed to gasification) tends to be a relatively low-temperature operation, with practical maximum temperatures of around 800 °C. There is thus a relatively high yield of methane which appears to peak at about 750 °C; considerable quantities of liquid of liquid hydrocarbons both miscible and immiscible with water; and a solid residue containing appreciable quantities of carbon as char. Table 14.8 shows relative proportions of products from both low (500 °C) and high (900 °C) temperature pyrolysis of wood at laboratory scale. It can be seen that a considerable part of the energy in the products is tied up in the liquid and solid residue.

Gasification with air, oxygen-enriched air or oxygen provides the heat for thermal degradation by burning part of the refuse, and thus tends to be a high-temperature operation with maximum temperatures approaching 1500 °C when pure oxygen is used. Under these conditions no solid carbon remains and any liquid hydrocarbons produced are usually recycled in some way for complete degradation to gas. The products from gasification are typically therefore a maximum quantity of gas and a minimum quantity of inert residue. All the energy in the products is concentrated in the gas phase. A representative analysis is shown in Table 14.8. Steam gasification is a special situation when operation at pressure encourages methane formation which is exothermic and under the conditions of this particular operation, autothermal operation is claimed (see 5).

If the end product for example is methanol, or any other specific chemical or product, any energy contained in the liquid and solid products must be utilized to give reasonable efficiency. For example, the organic liquids might be steam reformed or partially oxidized to give more synthesis gas. There is, however, currently no technology known to be able to handle oxygenated hydrocarbons such as these, although difficulties are not anticipated. (The efficiencies quoted earlier in Table 14.6 assumed that a suitable technology could be made available on demand.) Similarly the energy content of the char needs to be utilized which could be by gasification as with the liquids to give more synthesis gas for subsequent conversion. Alternatively the in-house energy requirements for heating, power or chemical reaction could be met by direct combustion and steam raising, or gasification with subsequent use of the fuel gas. All of these additional processing operations increase the cost and inefficiency of the process as reflected in the data of Table 14.6, where the pyrolysis processes are more costly than the gasification processes due to the additional steps needed to realize the energy content of the liquid and solid product streams.

Table 14.7   Products from Thermal Degradation of Refuse

Gas	Liquid	Solid
Carbon monoxide	Water	Char
Carbon dioxide	Dissolved organic compounds	Ash
Hydrogen	Immiscible organic compounds	Other impurities such as
Methane	including tars	glass
Higher hydrocarbon		
Nitrogen		
Sulphur compounds		
Chlorine compounds		

Table 14.8 aksi gives analysis of the gas produced as a primary products. In all cases some methane is produced which has the highest energy content of the constituents at 55 GJ/tonne. For maximum energy efficiency this methane must be properly utilized. The problem is well illustrated by considering production of methanol, which appears to be the most attractive high value product from waste as reported above. The options for using the methane are shown in Fig. 14.5 and include:

1. Reforming before methanol synthesis.
2. Reforming all the high methane level purge from the methaonl synthesis loop and recycling the synthesis gas.
3. Reforming the methane in the methanol synthesis recycle only.
4. Recycling the methanol loop purge to the reactor for suppression of methane formation. This depends on the extent of approach to thermodynamic equilibrium for effectiveness.
5. As (4) but with (3) also according to the thermodynamic constraint referred to in (4).
6. Methanate the purge to give an SNG by-product.
7. As (6) but with (3) also.

Table 14.8 Products from Thermal Processing Reactors – Feed on a Dry Basis

	Heating value GJ/tonne	Pyrolysis		Gasification	
		Low temperature	High temperature	Oxygen	Steam
Gas	20*	25% wt	33% wt	76% wt	98% wt
CO		34% vol	27% vol	41% vol	1% vol
H_2		4% vol	26% vol	24% vol	28% vol
CO_2		42% vol	26% vol	25% vol	45% vol
CH_4		16% vol	18% vol	5% vol	18% vol
Hydrocarbons		4% vol	3% vol	5% vol	8% vol
		100	100	100	100
Water	0	27% wt	29% wt	0	***
Organic liquids	40	15% wt	10% wt	(0)	0
Char and residue from wood	30	33% wt	28% wt	–	2% wt
Ash from refuse	0	–	–	24% wt	–
		100	100	100	100

*depends on composition.
**internally recycled.
***water is consumed in the reaction.

171

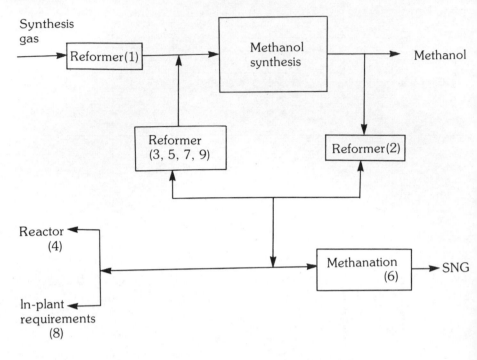

Fig. 14.5   Alternatives for handling methane in methanol synthesis.

Table 14.9   Energy Requirements for a Refuse Oxygen Gasification to Methanol Process

	GJ/tonne methanol
Reactor losses	(9.3)[a]
Oxygen plant	4.4
Fuel supply blower	0.4
Compressors	5.8
Steam reformer	3.1
Shift	0 [b]
CO_2 removal	0.8
Methanol synthesis	0 [b]
Distillation	1.5
Purge gas credit	− 0.5
	15.5
Contingency for minor uses, 10%	1.6
Total	
net	17.1
gross at 80% conversion efficiency	21.4

[a] The reactor energy losses and in-house requirements are accounted for in the mass balance over the Purox reactor — part of the refuse is oxidized to meet this requirement which does not therefore need to be provided externally.

[b] Both the shift reaction and methanol synthesis reaction are exothermic. Credits have not been included at this stage although the heat released could be useful when optimizing the process.

Table 14.10   Energy Balance for a Refuse Oxygen Gasification to Methanol Process

Input	Energy content GJ/tonne methanol	Output
Refuse feed 2 tonne (DAF)	47.3	
	(17.1)	(Net process requirements)
	24.4	Gross process requirements
	22.7	Methanol 1 tonne

8. Use the methane containing purge gas for in-house energy requirements for example in the reformer furnace for (1), (2) or (3); or in a boiler for steam raising.
9. As (8) but with (3) also.

This range of options has not yet been investigated, nor optimized. It does not even provide all the alternatives, but serves to indicate the extent of optimization needed.

A methane reformer is an expensive unit operation to build and has a considerable requirement for process energy. Thus maximizing energy efficiency will not necessarily give the same result as minimizing cost, and a trade-off needs to be evaluated. In all the case studies referred to in Table 14.6 option 1 was adopted where all methane and higher hydrocarbons are reformed prior to methanol synthesis.

Energy Balance and Improvement

The energy requirements of the oxygen gasification of refuse route to methanol are summarized in Table 14.9 for illustration, with the overall process energy balance given in Table 14.10. (Detailed mass, energy and economic balances have been published for the four case studies mentioned above[5].) This is an energy self-sufficient process with all energy requirements being provided by processing additional refuse, to give additional clean raw synthesis gas for use as fuel. To meet these energy requirements the refuse feed has to be increased by 50%, thereby reducing the energy efficiency from a 'theoretical' 72% to an 'actual' 48%.

How can this be improved? A well known strategy is to examine each requirement starting with the largest, and assess the potential for reduction.

Table 14.9 shows that the largest single usage is the 5.8 GJ/tonne in compressing synthesis gas from 1 bar in the thermal process reactor to the 50 bars required in the methanol convertor. If the reactors operated at 2 bars the compression energy requirement would reduce to 4.8 GJ/tonne, and at 4 bars would reduce to 3.7 GJ/tonne. A pressurized reactor thus has an energy and cost advantage in reducing compression requirements but at the expense of a more complex and expensive reactor which will give different products at higher pressures. Such cost-benefit relationships have not yet been studied, but could yield valuable improvements.

The oxygen plant is available as a well developed standard package plant, and there is unlikely to be much room for improvement. Downstream separation of nitrogen from an air gasification operation will suffer from unknown technology and high learning effects, and would not be expected to offer any advantage.

Reforming is the next largest user of energy, and the options available have already been discussed earlier in the context of methane which show that there is much scope for optimization.

Distillation of the final product methanol is required only if a water-free methanol is required for chemical purposes or as a fuel extender for blending with gasoline or diesel. For direct use as fuel, or conversion to gasoline, crude methanol is satisfactory. There are numerous minor energy requirements, some of which are detailed in Table 14.9. Others include pumping, instrumentation and lighting. Energy credits are available from both the shift and methanol synthesis reactors, which have not been included in these preliminary studies, although the purge gas credit is included which would be used as a fuel gas.

Finally there is a clear need to optimize the energy flows and energy recovery systems between all parts of the process. This can best be achieved by a well designed process simulation package which can match energy demands and energy surplus to give maximum energy efficiency. There is still a trade off between cost minimization and energy efficiency maximization which requires careful solution.

Projections of energy efficiency improvements up to 65% as discussed earlier (Fig. 14.3) and below, may not therefore be unreasonable.

The production costs of methanol and methane by oxygen gasification of refuse have been summarized in Table 14.6, and probable minimum attainable costs from an optimised process shown in Figs. 14.3 and 14.4 (all at 1980 prices). Methanol is clearly the most economically interesting product to consider further.

Sensitivity Studies

Economy of scale is an important economic consideration which has not yet been explored in this contribution. Fig. 14.6 shows the economy of scale for production costs of methanol at the base conversion efficiency of 48% and probable feedstock cost of £20/tonne (as densified RDF) as the solid line on the graph.

The dot/dash line below is the analogous plot for prepared RDF at £10/tonne to show the effect of reduced feedstock cost should this become available. A break-even point between production cost and current market price is only just achieved at the maximum plant size considered realistic of 1500 tonne/day DAF refuse.

The bottom two lines show the effect of achieving the 'ultimate' 65% energy efficiency (see Fig. 14.3) again with the same two feedstock costs. At these higher efficiencies, the maximum methanol output is increased, for the same DAF refuse input and the economy of scale can be further exploited to give a methanol production cost at maximum plant size and higher feed cost of about £80/tonne. With the market price at £110-130/tonne, this provides an acceptable margin for a commercial return.

ECONOMIC PROJECTIONS

The other significant economic factors that will affect the viability of refuse to methanol proposals is the projected and continued real increase in energy costs by about 4% per year. This is currently happening in the UK with natural gas, which is the feedstock for methanol made conventionally. As feedstock costs account for just over half the total production cost of methanol, the real increases in energy costs will give a conventional methanol cost of over £200/tonne in 1980 prices by the year 2000. Real increases in energy costs will also, of course, have an effect on methanol produced by thermal processing of refuse and other such material but at a much lower rate and the effect is shown for one situation, the year 2000, as the dotted line in Fig. 14.6. Thus the concept appears to become increasingly attractive with time.

The possibility of a commercially viable methanol from refuse process which offers an attractive financial return on investment increases therefore with time and with technological progress. Work is already in hand to both optimize the process, and experimentally and theoretically develop reactor systems. The versatility of thermal processing systems is an added improved attraction as a wide variety of materials could be processed individually and/or collectively, including agricultural wastes and coal fines. By the later 1980s such processes may have a demonstrable commercial attraction.

There are, however, factors beyond technical and economic which will encourage or deter developments of such ideas — these include attitude, awareness, politics and a variety of fiscal incentives. A greater interaction of private industry and the public sector will have a favourable effect on such factors in implementing new ways of utilizing refuse.

OTHER PROCESSES

Although this chapter has concentrated on refuse, a range of analogous thermal processes have been developed for more specific packaging wastes, notably plastics[10]. Fuel gas, oils and/or waxes may be recovered as fuels or chemicals by thermal degradation processes. Implementation, however, requires special circumstances such as quantity and availability which are not generally applicable. Recycling as plastic material is not necessarily an attractive prospect energetically[11] as the specifications for a recycled plastic product are significantly different than from primary products. There are also a number of interesting thermal processes for pyrolysing tyres and rubber waste to give a high grade fuel oil at up to 50% by weight of the tyres; together with a gas for in-house processing, and a solid char which is compatible with coal. Although not yet implemented, such a process has considerable potential and is already potentially commercially viable, and technically proven. The attractiveness lies in the very low cost of feed-stock — a negative cost in certain situations — and a major oil product that is fully compatible with similar products.

CONCLUSIONS

The technology and economics for thermal conversion of refuse to methanol and similar products are sufficiently interesting to justify active development. More encouragement is, however, needed by local and national government, and can at least be initiated by educationally bridging the technology gap between governmental administrators and scientists.

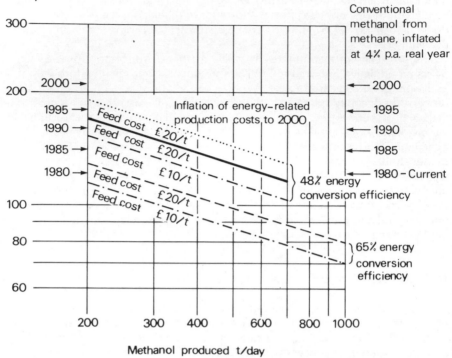

Fig. 14.6 Sensitivity analyses for methanol production costs — economy of scale, feedstock cost, technological development and energy cost inflation.

REFERENCES

1. BRIDGWATER, A.V. In: A.V. BRIDGWATER and K. LIDGREN (Eds.) *Household Waste Management in Europe: Economics and Techniques*, Van Nostrand Reinhold, 1981.
2. STAFFORD, D.A., HORTON, R. and HAWKES, D. In: *Energy from the Biomass*, The Watt Committee on Energy, June 1979.
3. EMERY, A.N. and KENT, C.A. In: *Energy from the Biomass*, The Watt Committee on Energy, June 1979.
4. ADER, G., BRIDGWATER, A.V. and HATT, B.W., *Conversion of Biomass to Fuels by Thermal Processes, Phase 1*, Report to ETSU, Department of Energy, 1978.
5. ADER, G., BRIDGWATER, A.V. and HATT, B.W., *Conversion of Biomass to Fuels by Thermal Processes — Optimisation Studies, Phases 2A, 2B, 2C*, Reports to ETSU, Department of Energy, April, July, September 1980.
6. BRIDGWATER, A.V., *Energy from Household Waste*, Swedish Recycling Foundation, May 1981, University of Lund.

7. Energy Technology Support Unit, UK, Department of Energy. Various publications.
8. TABASARAN, O., in Reference 1.
9. BRIDGWATER, A.V., HATT, B.W. and ADER, G.; Proceedings International Conference, *Energy from Biomass* Brighton, 1980, Applied Science Publishers, 1981.
10. BRIDGWATER, A.V. and MUMFORD, C.J., *Waste Recycling and Pollution Control Handbook*, George Godwin, 1979.
11. INGEN HOUSZ, J.F., in Reference 1.

Dr. Tony Bridgwater is Senior Lecturer in the Department of Chemical Engineering at the University of Aston in Birmingham. After working for several years with a major oil company, he joined the staff of the university and has developed interests in a wide range of business aspects of the chemical and process industries and also resource conservation, recycling and environmental protection. He is currently founder editor of *Process Economics International*, after also being responsible for launching *Engineering and Process Economics*. He is also a member of the editorial board of *Resource Recycling and Conservation*. He has published over 70 papers in the above areas and recently his interest has been focused on the recovery of valuable forms of energy from organic waste including biomass. His major publications include *Waste Recycling and Pollution Control Handbook*; *Chemical Waste and By-Product Recovery*, and *Household Waste Management in Europe — economics and techniques*.

15 The Role of Energy Considerations and Conclusions: answers to questions posed in the introductory chapter

K. Lidgren, A. V. Bridgwater and the contributors

At the conclusion of the seminar, attention focused on identifying areas of concern; fallacies; and problems relating to the energy content of packaging and waste. The discussion identified 15 particular points, which are listed as questions in the introductory chapter. Each of these is now 'answered' as a means of both solving some problems and putting them into perspective. None of them provides a complete answer by itself, but each should be considered with the relevant chapters of this book. This chapter collates the views of the participants, and in particular proposes policies for effective consideration of energy in packaging and waste.

1   Can a common method be derived for energy analyses and modelling?

The result of energy analysis of any system is a gross energy requirement of that system. This gross energy should be an expression in units of energy of the total energy resource that must be extracted from the earth in order to support that system. This apparently simple concept is beset with many difficulties since the numerical value for gross energy requirement depends crucially upon the choice of system; it depends for example upon the mix of fuels employed, the technology used, the country in which the operations take place and the precise collection of operations included within the system. Thus statements such as 'the energy required to produce a kilogram of aluminium is 300 MJ' are quite meaningless until the underlying assumptions and definitions are specified precisely. The notion that some universal value can be quoted for the energy required to produce a specific commodity is quite wrong.

It would no doubt be convenient if some single standard could be adopted for energy analysis, but the uses to which energy analysis can be put are so diverse that the imposition of such a standard would impose a constraint on the subject that would greatly decrease the flexibility and value of analyses.

The price that has to be paid for this flexibility is that simplistic interpretations of analyses must be resisted and it must be realized that the same type of complexities that exist in economic modelling also exist in energy modelling. The one plea that should be made repeatedly is that the assumptions underlying any analysis must be lucidly explained and these assumptions must form an essential and integral part of the result.

2 In energy analysis, what figures should be employed: a mean, a maximum, best technology currently available, or a range?

It is important, firstly, to identify or define the purpose of the analysis — this will help to select the most suitable figures for the analysis. For example, the objective might be to compare different existing processes which carry out the same function using historic data. A simple analysis might employ mean data, and more sophisticated analysis might include maximum values to assess extreme situations, and a range of values to assess sensitivity.

The result of an energy analysis depends on several assumptions, including choice of process, level of technical development and degree of obsolescence. There is always a tendency for more recent processes or machines to be more efficient. This creates the problem of which data to use in energy analysis:

(i)   extreme values, such as maximum or minimum specific energy consumption;
(ii) mean values, such as arithmetic, geometric, mean square or weighted average;
(iii) best available technology, which can refer to either
    (a) most economical technology with minimum cost, or
    (b) most efficient technology with regard to lowest energy consumption;
(iv) best possible technology which considers probable developments in the future on a specific time scale, and again may refer to either
    (a) most economical technology; or
    (b) most efficient technology.

The choice of value or values is largely determined by the scope of the analysis: it may be a historical analysis, a status report or a future or trend analysis with consequent uncertainties and a broader range of possible values. It is worth pointing out that specific energy consumption does not necessarily diminish with time, as there are other changing influences, such as technological resource extraction demands illustrated by the changing specific energy demands for copper extraction with ore grade in Fig. 15.1, and increasingly stringent environmental protection legislation.

3 Should historic energy investments be written off, and only new energy investments in machinery and equipment be considered?

When governments are faced with an energy decision (or for that matter any decision) the best choice depends on the prevailing socio-economic and technological conditions. Those conditions, which are called the state-of-the-world (or just states), include all the relevant variables, and describe the world as it is now. The present state-of-the-world is dependent on states which existed in the past, and the choices made in the past.

The basis of this question is whether, in making today's choices, historic choices relating to the value of energy should be explicitly accounted in either an energy or economic sense: i.e. should the past be explicitly taken into account in present decisions. An example will best illustrate the answer.

Assume that at some time in the past a decision was made to construct an energy facility, because analysis demonstrated that it had net benefits. The criteria used for evaluation could be either economic or energetic, and therefore it makes no difference in which units benefits are measured. Today the facility is partially

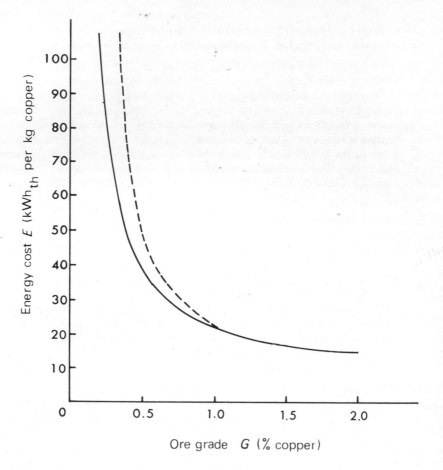

Fig. 15.1 Energy cost per kg of copper as a function of ore grade. The solid curve is based on optimistic assumptions, the dashed curve on current technology. Reproduced from Chapman

completed, and further analysis has revealed there are now net costs to complete the project. This is quite possible since decisions are made under uncertainty, and the passage of time may reveal new information. The question is therefore whether a project which has a net cost should be continued because money or energy was invested in the past, all of which will be lost if the project is stopped.

Clearly the answer is that the past should be ignored in the present decision. Nothing that can be done will cover the cost expended on the project to date, and continuing the project will lose more. The best the decision-maker can do under the circumstances is to stop the project, since that has the least net cost. The past is irrelevant, except as it explains the present state-of-the-world.

4 Should the energetic value of waste be conserved by downgrading it as little as possible?

Arguments for conserving the energetic value of waste rely on the presumption that energetic value is a reasonable measure of a wastes potential usefulness.

Wastes with high energetic value generally offer possibilities as an energy source, for recycling or for by-product utilization. If this presumption is accurate, a policy of conserving energetic value has at least two important environmental advantages:

(i) It is essentially the same as conserving virgin resources, through the greater use of secondary material.
(ii) It would seem initially to reduce demands on the environment in two ways. First, less virgin material extraction means less environmental disruption. Second, the use of waste implies that it is not disposed of to the environment (with the potential damage), but instead remains in the production and consumption system.

These, briefly stated, are the two virtues in preserving energetic value and they rest on the assumption that energy content is a reasonable measure of future usefulness. Even if this is a valid assumption, it is not sufficient grounds for public decision making. If public policy is to encourage the preservation of energetic value, it must also be demonstrated that public policies designed to preserve energetic value would in general perform better than other means to correct market imperfections.

This is clearly a complex question which empirical analysis should resolve. Two points are worth noting, however, about public policies to preserve energetic value in waste and its two presumed virtues. With respect to the second claimed advantage, it is not always the case that by-product use or re-use is environmentally favourable. Secondary materials generally require productive transformations before they are directly used. These activities are polluting, and sometimes more so than the use of virgin materials. Recycling paper, for example, generates more residuals than the direct use of wood pulp.

The contention that preserving energetic value is tantamount to conserving virgin materials, and that doing so is desirable, is also not clear. First, the transformation required in secondary material preparation may have different inputs than primary materials. If true, virgin resource exploitation may only be shifted from one resource to another rather than reduced in aggregate. Secondly it is sometimes believed desirable to conserve resources because of the finiteness of those that are nonrenewable. In such cases, exhaustion can have serious, if not dire, consequences.

The argument that resources must be preserved is not new. History is replete with prognosticators of impending doom for civilisation's habitat. In the past, movement to a new habitat was a solution, or technological change has saved civilisation from the predicted cataclysms. Technological change has the effect of expanding the set of resources available in two ways. First, it makes new types of materials useable; in the case of energy, for example, it has historically expanded the types of energy sources, first from wood to coal, and then later to oil and uranium. Secondly, technological change has the effect of making more of a given material available. In the case of coal, technological change, which includes new exploration and recovery methods, makes more coal economically available for production.

While technological change has always made pessimistic predictions incorrect in the past, it may not always do so in the future. It is therefore necessary to be clear about what resource depletion would look like. First, it would not be a sudden running out of resources. The price system, while it may undervalue conservation, can be expected at some point to signal government and other economic agents of the impending exhaustion of resources through higher extraction prices. Adaption would begin, although perhaps not soon enough, but there would not be a sudden extinction of resources.

Secondly, it is necessary to avoid speaking of 'resources' in a general sense. Not all resources are equally scarce. Current use rates of many materials do not suggest any near term problem. In many cases, potential technological change offers adequate substitution potential in the long term. Energy is an excellent example. If oil is nearing depletion, coal resources are adequate for the next 200 years. In the longer term the fusion reactor and solar power offer the potential for adequate energy supplies.

If resources are increasing in scarcity at different rates, and technological change offers the possibility of attenuating the scarcity of some, is a public policy of conserving the energetic value of all waste an effective one? It is such a generalized approach to a material-specific problem that it seems unlikely. The environmental regulatory experience of the 1970s suggests that rigid, generalized regulatory practices are very inefficient. The second generation of regulatory forms now being instituted are more flexible and case-specific, and therefore encourage efficiency. *It must be remembered that efficiency saves resources, including virgin materials.*

In summary, the presumption must be that preserving energetic value is not a desirable goal. With the market system's historical record, the burden of proof is on the proponents of energetic value. They must supply the empirical analysis which can ultimately resolve the question.

5 Should direct and/or indirect energy inputs be minimized? Is it necessary to distinguish between the various forms and grades of energy?

Energy analyses provide the opportunity to examine the consequences of any action regarding energy balances. Usual practice is to analyse energy inputs and outputs up to a well defined boundary, and this should preferably coincide with the limits of normal commercial activity. The so-called 'primary' energy inputs — oil, coal, gas, etc. — may be analysed from the point where human activity starts, and the energy level of all the inputs must be clearly defined: a single unique expression for all energies and materials does not exist. Indirect energy should be analysed by the usual categories of quality, such as heat at a specified temperature, heating values (higher or lower) of fuels, mechanical or electrical energy, etc. It is essential to differentiate between different forms and qualities of energy — hot water, for example, cannot be directly equated to electricity or fuel oil. Some expressions, such as 'secondary', 'useful' or 'final' energy, are generally poorly defined or explained, if at all, and should be avoided.

Minimizing energy inputs in any form generally leads to conclusions which are in conflict with economic considerations, since energy reduction or conservation usually requires a financial investment which is not necessarily justified by the value of energy saved. A somewhat simplistic view is that any economically acceptable energy conservation is already practiced, and further measures would have an adverse economic effect on the product. Normal economic criteria cannot be abandonned at the expense of energy reduction; therefore, although changes in energy prices can be considered, decisions must be based on conventional economic criteria.

182

6 Should utilization of the energy content of packaging and waste be maximized, and/or its dissipation minimized?

One of the initial spurs to the development of energy analysis as a discipline in its own right was the environmental fear that increased industrialization would lead to an increase in the heat release to the atmosphere. Since this can only be lost from the earth by radiation into outer space, and since radiation rate depends upon the temperature of the radiating body, excessive heat release, it was believed, would lead to an increase in the mean temperature of the earth's surface with a concomitant set of problems associated with disturbing significantly the planetary ecological balance. Apart from a few extremists, few people really considered the problem was very serious in the short term, but projections into the future led to some alarming possibilities. In view of the very uncertain nature of the changes that might occur it seems sensible to minimize the rate of release of energy into the atmosphere.

Following this argument, there are essentially two ways in which dissipation of energy can be minimized. One is to use energy by reducing or holding steady the rate of production of goods using existing technology. The other is to improve the efficiency of use of fuels so that there can be growth in the production of goods without significantly increasing the total energy release.

There are also sound economic and commercial reasons for using energy more efficiently, and since the 1973 oil shortages most industries have been seeking ways of improving their performance. Such moves are to be welcomed because not only do they assist in solving the environmental problem but they also aid conservation of the limited fossil fuel resources available to an industrialized society.

In general, therefore, for environmental, economic and conservation reasons, the aim should be to promote both the minimization of dissipation and the maximization of utilization. Energy analysis plays a role in this exercise in two ways; by providing a quantitative description of existing practices against which future developments can be measured, and by providing an analysis technique which can be used to predict ways in which production systems (particularly extended production systems) could be modified to reduce total energy consumption.

7 Should low energy-consuming materials be substituted for high energy-consuming materials?

It is necessary to consider not only all direct and indirect requirements in evaluating materials, but also the functional requirement of the product. The net energy requirement must include all direct energy inputs in the raw material itself and the gross process energy requirement. The question of whether to include indirect and/or historic energy must be left to the analyst, as long as this is clearly defined and comparisons are made on identical bases. Set against the energy inputs are energy outputs and credits, which should be considered in the same way as inputs, and account should be taken of the usefulness, value and conversion efficiency of these credits in establishing net energy requirement.

Of perhaps greater significance is the amount of material required to fulfil a given duty or function, and hence the energy requirement per function is more important than that per unit weight of material. For example, a packaging application may require three times as much material with half the net energy requirement as the alternative. In energy terms this is less attractive.

The marketplace, however, is the ultimate judge of acceptability and preference, in which energy requirement is related to its cost, which in turn is reflected in the total product cost.

8   Can energy be saved in the packaging sector? What are the consequences?

Investigations have shown that conversion of virgin materials to packaging raw materials accounts for up to 90% of the total energy usage in production and distribution of a package. This means that the process industry accounts for the major part of the energy usage within the packaging sector without actually being part of it. Paper and plastics, for example, have many other applications besides packaging — consequently, the energy problems of the process industry cannot primarily be considered a packaging problem. What the packaging industry can do, however, is to use the material that functionally and economically satisfies the demands made on each package. By that, the price mechanism of the market economy should contribute to a successive transition to less energy-consuming packaging alternatives.

If the control of packaging consumption resulting from increased energy prices is not considered sufficient, government can resort to other steering instruments. It is unlikely, however, that any such measures will result in a reduction of total energy usage by society.

It should be noted that packaging, by protecting products, reducing loss, facilitating transport and handling, evening out seasonal variations, contributes to a considerable reduction in the energy used in the production and distribution of goods. Energy optimization solely in respect of the packages themselves, without consideration of the consequences for other sectors in the production and distribution system, may consequently lead to an overall increased energy usage.

It should also be noted that economic, hygienic, administrative, practical, technical and marketing aspects greatly restrict the possibilities for drastic changes in packaging specification and selection in most areas. In addition, a change just from one packaging alternative to another will not directly affect the millions of decisions taken daily on the basis of, among other things, energy prices, and which in practice direct the energy usage in society.

Since single-use packages have assumed a position as symbols for the so-called 'energy waste, paper cup mentality', measures which are perceived as being intended to reduce 'waste' can nevertheless be politically viable and may have a positive psychological effect, e.g. on the tendency of people to cooperate in other forms of savings activities. It is delusory to believe that an enforced change in the selection of packages (within the few areas where a change is at all possible) can by itself result in any perceptible change in the total energy usage of society.

9   Should public decisions be made using the criteria of minimizing and/or conserving energetic value?

Human beings seek to accomplish a number of goals through governments. Economic growth, distributional equity, and national security are only a few of the legitimate objectives of public policy. Energy production and use contribute to the attainment of these objectives. For example, a country which imports most of its energy has a risky energy supply and will therefore have more limited freedom of operation in international relations.

Energy is not, however, the only factor which determines the security of a nation, nor is it the only one which contributes to the other objectives. Economic

184

growth rates depend, for example, upon all the factors of production, such as labour, capital and land availability. Energy is not even the most significant factor in attaining most of those objectives.

To limit analysis to the energy component is therefore too narrow a focus, because it is not the only objective governments have, nor is it the only determinant of the level of other objectives.

10 Should there be concern with conserving energy; recovering energy; conserving mineral resources; recovering/recycling mineral resources; or various combinations of these alternatives?

Questions concerning energy and mineral conservation and recovery have conflicting objectives. The best way to optimize any system is by economic analysis on the basis that all inputs and outputs are properly priced by the marketplace. There has been no better criterion since Hammurabi. In general, conservation is significantly more effective than any kind of recovery or recycling as, for example, process energy is reduced both directly and indirectly, and there are no conversion losses or utilization problems. In particular, it should be noted that only a small fraction of the energy initially employed can ever be recovered by any kind of recycling activity.

In proposing that, in principle, conservation is more effective than recycling, the investment in energy and materials required to effect conservation must not be ignored. The viability of such investment needs careful examination on energetic, material and particularly economic grounds. Comparison of the merit of energy versus mineral conservation at recycling requires evaluation in the same way as system optimization — that is, on an economic basis presupposing that, as above, all goods are priced in a manner that reflects their scarcity and value.

11 Is there too much preoccupation with energy — is it exerting too great an influence on our lives?

If it is assumed that production and consumption is undertaken for the purpose of meeting human needs and desires, then allocating resources so as to minimize the energetic value of impacts is one appropriate allocation rule to the extent that man's multifaceted wants are satisfied. Therefore, it is reasonable to ask if it is the best allocation rule, and if it is sufficiently comprehensive that it can be the sole criterion for rationing inputs among activities?

As an allocation rule it has a number of liabilities (see Chapter 11): for example, it does not admit of a means for weighting different goods and services through time. People have preferences for the timing of their purchases: sooner, in general, being preferred to later. To treat productive activities as devoid of this time dimension is to misallocate intertemporally.

Additionally energy use is only one of the aspects of production and consumption that are important. Other resources are also scarce, and perhaps even more scarce than energy. To treat it as the sole criterion for allocation is therefore to overemphasize its importance. Since its scarcity is reflected in other indicators of the economic system function or dysfunction, such as prices, it would also seem to be an inferior criterion by which to measure performance. Prices weight, in homogeneous units, different inputs and reflect relative scarcity. If the energy content of inputs declines, prices will *ceterus paribus* rise. Price also reflects other important characteristics of inputs, and is therefore deserving of attention in public

185

policy making. If it functions imperfectly on occasion, it would still usefully serve as at least one indicator, since energetic value is also a somewhat defective indicator of total system performance.

12 What is the best way to use the energy value of household waste up to 1990?

To answer this question the waste generation pattern needs to be evaluated. Based on recent developments, an increase in waste generation is not expected, but changes in waste composition are possible. There is a tendency towards extended use of pre-prepared (convenience) foods, which will move much food preparation waste from household waste to industrial waste. On the other hand this will mean more packaging materials. Newspaper volume may also decrease in the long term due to increasing access to television databases, although this development will probably not have gone far by 1990. The extent of paper recycling programmes, however, seems to be increasing in most European countries. The effects are indicated in Table 15.1. The average specific waste generation (kg per capita and year) will probably decrease, the calorific value increase, and the total energy potential decrease.

Table 15.1

| Probable component change | Effects on | | |
	Household waste stream	Calorific value	Total energy potential
Less food waste	−	+	−
More packaging materials	+	+	+
Less newspaper	−	−	−

+ positive/increasing.
− negative/decreasing.

One important objective for the future is to minimize waste generation. Much waste is the product of over-sized packaging materials; fashion products; complex products unsuitable for recycling of materials; and the result of a 'throw-away' society. The best instrument for minimization of 'inevitable waste' is recycling. Material quality can thus be conserved, raw materials can be saved, the energy content is reduced and energy savings made compared to production from virgin materials. Both source and central mechanical sorting of materials for recycling are expected to be further developed and more widely used in the future, particularly for production of refuse-derived fuels (RDF).

The other treatment option is beneficiation, either biochemically or thermally. Biochemical degradation yields new land (many years after completion of a landfill), compost, or combustible gas and a compost-like product (from anaerobic degradation). Thermal processing yields heat (incineration) or combustible gas and/or oil (gasification or pyrolysis). One option is to purify and dry the waste to give a storable product (RDF) that is better suited for burning in conventional boilers. RDF production can also involve a certain degree of materials recycling.

Landfilling and composting involve no energy recovery or conservation. The compost is a useful product in areas with a shortage of soil, and the choice of treatment option should be based on careful evaluation of local conditions. Anaerobic digestion, which yields both an energy-rich gas and a soil conditioner, may prove a very valuable method of recycling

If there is no need for soil, thermal treatment with energy recovery is an obvious choice. The most efficient way is incineration with transfer of heat to a suitable transfer medium, but it requires immediate use as industrial process heat or for district heating. Gasification and pyrolysis also give a high energy yield, and have the advantage that the products are storable and easily transported. The advantages of RDF are mentioned above, and the energy yield from incineration of this product is also high. Electricity production gives a much lower yield if it is not combined with utilization of surplus heat.

Direct incineration with heat recovery is a well established method which will continue to be extensively used in the future. Viable systems for quite small waste arisings have also appeared on the market in recent years. This means that the old idea of centralized operation may change, with every community having its own incinerator providing heat for local needs.

Gasification and pyrolysis have so far not been demonstrated to be readily applicable to household waste, but it is anticipated that the problems will be overcome in the near future and that this method will become a more common way of upgrading the energy content of waste.

Perhaps the most significant problem to be solved is that of identifying and/or developing markets for recovered products — both energetic and material. It is in this area that most encouragement should be directed as technology is rarely a limiting factor.

13 How important is energy cost in different packaging systems?

The cost of a product is made up of many components, of which energy in its various forms makes a contribution, and this has been adequately described elsewhere in this book. The process industries, which produce most packaging materials, usually have a sophisticated cost analysis capability, and trends over the last 15 years or so have indicated that the process energy contribution to the total product cost has roughly doubled from typically 10-15% to typically 20-30% in cost terms, while the most significant cost for most processes remains the raw material. This generalization conceals extremes such as air separation processes where the feedstock is — still! — free. More fundamental analysis of the entire production system from natural resource to end product shows that cost can be related to:

(i)   the arbitrary value of a natural resource,
(ii) labour costs,
(iii) 'profits',

and, of the natural resources, those that are energy based are more significant than those that are mineral based. That current international financial problems are largely blamed on oil pricing problems tends to confirm the relative importance of energy costs.

Individual materials can be analysed for energy, mineral and labour costs for fundamental analysis from resource to end product; or in a wide variety of simple and sophisticated ways for specified boundary limits. Different forms of energy input and output need to be priced according to current or other appropriate rates; and forecast real changes in prices can be readily taken into account or be the subject of sensitivity analyses. It has already been explained that money represents the only acceptable homogeneous unit for inter-relating different forms and qualities of energy. Energy cost, therefore, will continue to dominate evaluation and choice in energetic terms, particularly if this energy cost represents a significant proportion of total product cost. Regional, temporal and political variations will produce different answers to the same problem, according to place, time and intervention; and there will never be a single universal solution to any packaging problem.

14 What is the role of the consumer in the management of packaging systems?

Large quantities of packaging materials, such as glass, paper, plastics and metal, are passed to the consumer together with the commodity packaged. For reasons which include costs and rationalization, the filling industry and distribution trade attempt to transfer the problems of packaging waste and material recovery to the consumer or the community by pushing one-way packages. The additional cost of these packages and their disposal must be borne by the consumer. Thus, conventionally, the ecologically aware consumer has to assume responsibility for recycling those material flows which comprise a considerable energy input. The consumer is therefore involved in packaging systems in two ways. First, he acts as the final stage in the distribution chain and second, he is the first stage in any recovery/recycling process.

In many packaging systems, distribution is a significant contributor to the total system energy requirement. In general, the most energy efficient transport systems are those involving bulk loads. However, as the goods progress through the distribution chain, the possibilities for efficient bulk packaging and transport become less and the final distribution from retailer to point of use can very seldom employ any form of bulk pack. As a result, the energy per unit delivered in this final stage is very high.

The recovery and recycling of packaging materials depends crucially on the actions of the consumer. If all packaging waste is simply disposed of by the consumer along with the rest of domestic refuse, his energy consumption is low but recovery of the components from this solid waste stream usually requires significantly higher energy expenditure than would be the case if the consumer had acted as an initial sorting operation. If the consumer acts as the initial sorting mechanism, then sacks or other receptacles must be provided to allow storage of the separated waste components and the provision of these receptacles effectively increases the consumer energy while possibly reducing the energy of subsequent processing stages.

The significance of the consumer acting as the first step in a recycling/recovery system is that his costs to the system are minimal, although the total energy requirement is unlikely to be minimized. The consumer can, for example:

(i) recycle whole containers for re-use — in this respect greater harmonization of shapes and sizes would help considerably;
(ii) extend centralized collection points for pre-sorted packaging, such as glass, metals, plastics;
(iii) pre-sort waste in the home for separate collection;
(iv) have minimal involvement and rely on central sorting plants to recover those energy or material values that are ecologically and/or economically viable. This passive involvement in recovery is the least conducive to efficient operation and optimum action, and is also among the more costly.

188

Although attempts have been made to assess economics and material recovery efficiencies with unconvincing results, in terms of overall net energy requirements quantitative ranking of these alternatives requires accurate calculation of the energy used by consumers in performing operations specifically related to packaging systems, which is extremely difficult. It is for this reason that consumer energy is omitted from most packaging systems. However, the fact that the calculations are difficult is hardly a good reason for omitting this component and this represents one area in which considerable work still needs to be done.

15 Concluding comments: What intervention should there be in controlling energy usage and recovery?

Manufacture, distribution and disposal of containers are all processes in which resources in the form of materials and energy are consumed. Containers are also products which end up as waste after a very short lifetime.

A number of investigations on the resource requirements of different containers have therefore been carried out. Common to all the investigations carried out up to now is the expression of total energy consumption as a certain measurement. However, the models, used to calculate this total energy input (gross energy) are not always the same, and therefore the results may sometimes be difficult or impossible to compare.

This is by no means a new problem: it arose several years after the second world war when the first so-called energy balances were calculated. Since then there has been widespread debate on the most suitable model for the conversion of different kinds of energy to one common measuring unit. It is obvious that electrical power and fuel cannot be added directly, but there are differences of opinion as to how the gross energy in the production of electricity should be calculated: for example, how should electrical production based on water and nuclear power be evaluated? Depending on the model used, different values are obtained for the gross energy requirement.

The energy figures presented in the various investigations should be viewed against the background of this calculation problem. Data with many significant figures can create an impression of scientific exactitude, but as the bases of the calculations are sometimes uncertain, an estimate of the order of magnitude can be of greater value than presentation of exact figures.

In most industrialized countries with a high level of packaging, the energy consumption for this packaging from raw material up to and including waste management is about 2% of the total national energy consumption. Since, for various reasons, a return to a 'container-free' society seems utopian, it must be appreciated that realistic energy savings within the packaging sector, enforced through political decisions, can be only considered as marginal.

Are energy calculations of no interest then? Of course they are, but the interest in energy calculations should lie with the companies in the packaging sector rather than, as today, being a feature of the political debate concerning packaging. The reason for this is simple: if the political standpoint in a country is that the domestic energy consumption should be reduced, the natural action seems to be to ration energy via a price increase. This will result in energy being saved where it is most easily saved, and this will also apply to the packaging sector.

Energy is a productive factor in the same sense as, for example work and capital. It is therefore natural that companies want to appreciate the significance of this factor of production as it is a normal production cost, of comparable importance to salaries and interest, for example. Furthermore, this particular production cost seems to be the one most susceptible to change, which emphasises still more the importance of determining its significance by means of energy calculations.

As containers normally have a very short lifetime, there is also good reason to consider energy consumption after the package has been used for the purpose for which it was originally produced. The current trend in waste handling is towards solutions which utilize the internal energy of packaging waste, and the dominant waste management method currently seems to be some form of thermal processing.

An extension of the energy calculations to include waste treatment usually results in a reduction in total energy consumption if energy is recovered from the waste either directly or indirectly.

In conclusion, it seems reasonable that those companies which have an interest in distributing goods should control the consumption of energy for alternative containers via energy analyses. It also seems reasonable that society should ensure that the 'internal' energy of the waste, in the form of packaging, is re-used through material and/or energy recovery.

Index

195